SOVEREIGN CITY

GLOBALITIES
Series editor: Jeremy Black

GLOBALITIES is a series which reinterprets world history in a
concise yet thoughtful way, looking at major issues over large
time-spans and political spaces; such issues can be political,
ecological, scientific, technological or intellectual. Rather than
adopting a narrow chronological or geographical approach,
books in the series are conceptual in focus yet present an array of
historical data to justify their arguments. They often involve a
multi-disciplinary approach, juxtaposing different subject-areas
such as economics and religion or literature and politics.

In the same series

Why Wars Happen
Jeremy Black

A History of Language
Steven Roger Fischer

The Nemesis of Power
Harald Kleinschmidt

*Geopolitics and Globalization
in the Twentieth Century*
Brian W. Blouet

Monarchies 1000–2000
W. M. Spellman

A History of Writing
Steven Roger Fischer

*The Global Financial System
1750–2000*
Larry Allen

Mining in World History
Martin Lynch

*Landscape and History
c. 1500–2000*
Ian D. Whyte

*China to Chinatown
Chinese Food in the West*
J.A.G. Roberts

A History of Reading
Steven Roger Fischer

Cinemas of the World
James Chapman

Navies in Modern World History
Lawrence Sondhaus

Sovereign City

The City-State through History

GEOFFREY PARKER

REAKTION BOOKS

Published by Reaktion Books Ltd
79 Farringdon Road, London EC1M 3JU, UK

www.reaktionbooks.co.uk

First published 2004

Printed and bound in Great Britain by
MPG Books Ltd, Bodmin, Cornwall

British Library Cataloguing in Publication Data
Parker, Geoffrey
    Sovereign city : the city-state ancient and modern. -
    (Globalities)
    1. City-states - History
    I. Title
    321'.06

ISBN 1 86189 219 5

Contents

Nation, Empire and City: A Geopolitical Typology of States

At first glance the world political map looks much like a kind of multicoloured jigsaw made up of pieces of many shapes and sizes that appear to fit together in quite a random manner. These varied pieces represent the sovereign states into which the political world is divided, and they range in size from enormous pieces of jigsaw, representing huge states such as Russia and China, to tiny pieces representing island states such as Singapore and Malta. While this cartographic pattern may appear at first sight to have little meaning, it actually indicates the continued existence of a number of different types of state that came into being at various times and which owe their existence to quite different sets of circumstances. While each state is individual in its own particular way, it is possible to group them into a number of categories, the three most evident of these being the nation-state, the empire – or imperial state – and the city-state. A fourth category can also be discerned that consists of groupings of states within the three other categories.

The most common type of state in the present-day world is the nation-state and the multicoloured world political map is basically a representation of this fact. It is so much the commonest geopolitical form that states are now more often referred to as being 'nations'. Thus we have the 'Arab nations', the 'African nations', the 'European nations' and, above them all, the 'United Nations'. However, if we rolled back the political map we would find that in the past the multicoloured jigsaw produced a completely different picture and that the other major categories of states were present to a far greater extent than they are today. If we rolled back the map a thousand years to the beginning of the second millennium we would discover that the empire was the more usual geopolitical form. If we then rolled it back just over another thousand years we would find that, in certain parts of the world at least, the city-state was widespread. In reality, at least for most of the time, each of the geopolitical categories has been present and one usually finds something of a mixture of different types of state. Nevertheless, at any particular time, there is usually what one may term a normative type among the states in existence. This normative type also tends to constitute an ideal to which most of the states aspire. For a variety of reasons, political, economic and cultural, this is considered to be the most desirable type of state and there is a strong tendency for most of them to attempt to emulate it. Being of the normative type also gives a state a certain legitimacy that may otherwise be denied to it. This is to be seen in the fact that today most states are happy to be called 'nations' rather than just 'states', but this often signifies an aspiration rather than a reality. Even political entities that hardly resemble nations still use the term to describe themselves and this signifies that they have an aspiration to be regarded as nations. At any given time there is also likely to be a queue of non-sovereign 'nations' waiting in the wings to become fully fledged members of the sovereign state club. A recent example of this followed the fall of the quasi-imperial Soviet Union in 1991. A host of new states then appeared on the scene that soon rejoiced in being called 'nations'. Most of these had never existed before as sovereign political entities or if they had it was only during short periods in their history. But the memory was strong, the aspiration was powerful and they have triumphantly emerged into the light of the twenty-first century as sovereign states.

The principal feature of that particular geopolitical category we call the nation-state is the existence, or the aspiration towards, a high level of homogeneity within its boundaries. This homogeneity may take the forms of language, culture and history, or indeed all three of them, and together they encapsulate the term 'nation'.[1] Since the Latin *natio* signifies birth or common origin, this also implies an ethnic basis to this type of state. The people of one nation thus come to see themselves as being fundamentally different from those who are members of another nation. The French political geographer Vidal de la

Blache regarded the existence and nature of the 'we' as being essentially defined by the presence of the 'other'.[2]

While the nation component is based on the nature of the people, the state component is based on the nature of the territory which they inhabit. This is made up of a mixture of physical and human geography that together produces a particular landscape deemed to be characteristic of the homeland. In this way the homeland becomes a kind of physical expression of the nation. One early political geographer, Sir William Petty, compared it to a human body, the 'heart' of which is the capital city.[3] Around this is the body of the state within which the vital functions are concentrated. Later political geographers pictured the state as having a core–periphery structure with the most important functions being concentrated in the core region around the capital and the periphery containing and supplying a variety of physical resources essential to the state's physical well being. There are industrial and agricultural areas supplying the needs of the people and the whole is bound together by a communication system. The frontiers both separate the state from other states and afford it protection from outside attack.[4]

Thus ideally these nation-states are seen as being self-sustaining entities possessing their own independent internal structures. They are physically insulated from one another and all contacts with their neighbours are carefully monitored and controlled. The attainment of this ideal model has been the aspiration of most states during the past century. Even when so many of them clearly lack many or most of the characteristics of the nation-state in accordance with the accepted criteria, they have still aspired to become more like those that clearly possess these characteristics. This has been so to such an extent that it came to be believed in certain circles during the twentieth century that nation-states were in some sense 'natural' phenomena having a kind of Darwinian right to exist.[5] However, analysis shows them to be largely artificial phenomena, the origins of which have lain in warfare and dynastic aspirations and the subsequent attempts of state governments to impose their own uniformity on pre-existing diversity. For instance, national languages have usually emerged out of a variety of regional dialects and have normally been based on the particular dialect to be found in the core area. The reality is that the nation is something that has been created by the state for its own purposes in order to blow life into what is otherwise only too often an uninspiring piece of territory. In this way, the nation has become the object of an ideology – nationalism – that was and still is capable of generating enormous passion, often accompanied by equal amounts of hostility towards other nations.

The imperial state is a very different type of geopolitical phenomenon. It comes into existence as a result of territorial expansion on a large scale by a particular nation or group of people. Such expansion is usually triggered by rulers desiring to increase their power and influence and who accomplish this by playing on the dissatisfactions of their peoples, encouraging them to see others as potential prey. By means of successful expansion, they gain control over territories and peoples very different from their own and they then use the physical force at their disposal to impose structures designed for the maintenance of their power. Empires are thus essentially about the dominance of one particular group of people over others and this dominance is then consolidated into political structures that centre on the territory of the dominating people. This evolves into a core–periphery structure similar to that of the nation-state but on a much larger scale.

The most famous empire, and the one that has given its name to the whole phenomenon, was that of Rome. Just over 2,000 years ago the Roman *Imperium* expanded across Europe and the Mediterranean to become the largest state that had existed up to that time in the region. This empire had originated in the expansion of one city that gradually extended its influence eastwards into Asia and northwards into maritime and continental Europe. At around the same period the Han Empire in China and the Mauryan Empire in India were both phenomena of a very similar type. While the successor states to the Han Empire brought unity to China for much of the next two millennia, India has been ruled only intermittently by imperial states that have rarely been able to secure control over the whole of the subcontinent. Traditionally the Russian Empire considered itself as being the true heir to Rome, and following the Revolution of 1917 the Empire fell and was replaced by the

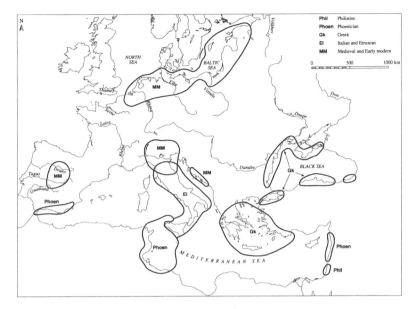

1 Groupings of city-states in Europe and the Mediterranean.

Soviet Union. This state itself possessed many of the geopolitical characteristics of an empire and did not fit easily into a world
in which the principal political aspiration was the creation of
nation-states.[6] Following its fall in the early 1990s its component parts were set free to become nation-states in their own
right. The largest successor state, the Russian Federation, possesses most of the characteristics of a nation, albeit on a gigantic
scale. However, the Federation, although called Russian, contains within it a number of non-Russian peoples, some of whom
themselves aspire to the achievement of a completely independent status. This fact reveals that this federation, although
nominally national, still retains many of the trappings of an
empire.

The third major category of state, and the one with which
this book is principally concerned, is the city-state. This consists of those cities that are also themselves states and which are
thus either completely independent or have secured a high
measure of freedom in the transaction of their affairs. While in
the past there have been periods when the city-state has been
the norm in many parts of the world, today in the age of the

nation-state, only a handful of them are left and they no longer in any sense constitute a norm in any part of the world. They form a kind of residue of small particles on the political map. The few survivors are all that is now left to give some indication of the very different geopolitical conditions in which they once flourished. In Europe, which only a few centuries ago was home to literally hundreds of city-states, Monte Carlo, Andorra, Liechtenstein and San Marino are just political oddities, the existence of which may be attributed more to accident than design. They have owed their continued existence to historical and dynastic factors and to the rivalries of the larger states that surround them. Others only slightly less eccentrically tiny, such as Luxembourg and Albania, also owe their independence more to the rivalries of the great powers in recent times than to any sustained will to freedom on their own part.

In contrast to the situation in Europe, in other parts of the world the city-state has experienced a minor revival in the post-imperial age. Notable examples of such states are Singapore and Hong Kong, both of which have played significant roles in the evolution of modern South-East Asia. These two island cities demonstrate the differences that may exist in the status of the city-state. These range from those that are by any criteria completely sovereign states to those that possess a large measure of autonomy within larger states. While their imperial origins were similar, Singapore is now completely sovereign while Hong Kong, while it has a high measure of autonomy in its internal affairs, has never achieved that complete independence that constitutes true sovereignty.

The political status of any particular city may also change over a period of time and the extent of its independence may increase or decrease in accordance with new circumstances. Thus the north German cities of Hamburg, Bremen and Lübeck were able gradually to secure a large measure of independence from the Holy Roman Emperors to such an extent that by the fourteenth century Lübeck in particular could be considered to have become virtually a sovereign state. When the Second German Empire came into being in the late nineteenth century, these three cities still retained considerable residual autonomy and were granted the status of free cities within the Empire. However, during the early twentieth century the independence of the three cities was whittled down, until by the 1930s hardly more than the memory of their former independence remained. At the other end of Europe, Venice had been a completely sovereign state since its foundation and it remained so for more than 1,000 years. Its independence was finally brought to an end by Napoleon in the late eighteenth century and the once proud city-state was absorbed into the biggest empire Europe had known since ancient times.

The term sovereignty as used in this book must thus be considered as being a variable attribute. It is often difficult to pin it down with any degree of precision, but the difference between a city that is and always has been firmly a part of a nation-state or empire and one that has had an independent existence as a city-state is very clear. A large British city such as Birmingham, for all its industrial and commercial importance, has never been in anything but the former category and its civic pride is bound up with its essentially municipal status within the United Kingdom. On the other hand Milan, Birmingham's twin city in Italy, was a sovereign state for a long period of time and still prides itself on the retention of many reminders of its former independent existence. Likewise Frankfurt, its twin city in Germany, was for centuries an imperial free city and as such possessed a high degree of autonomy in its local affairs. While the idea of a sovereign Birmingham would sound fantastic to most of its citizens, and would certainly not enter seriously into the thoughts of even the most ambitious of the city fathers, in Milan there are many who seek greater freedom from the Italian state in the context of a post-nation-state Europe.

While these three principal categories of state can clearly be identified on the political map, a fourth category can also be discerned that in a way transcends them all. This is produced by the grouping together of a number of states that may then in certain circumstances itself take on the features of a state. Groupings of this sort may be established both to regulate relationships among the states themselves and to regulate relationships with other states. The purpose of the grouping may thus be to solve inter-state problems or to protect the group from external danger. It may have a wider remit and be intended to serve both these purposes. The groupings set up by the ancient Greek city-states were in the latter category and dealt both with internal and external problems. They proved to be of limited value but were more successful at protecting the Greeks from external dangers than at regulating inter-state relationships. They certainly did not lead to the establishment of new 'states' in any accepted sense of the term. The Greek city-states cherished their independence far too much to allow it to be eroded in this way.

At later times, inter-state groupings of this sort have been highly variable in their impact. They have ranged from alliances established for specific purposes and to combat particular dangers to groupings that have had a wider remit and have become more permanent. In the modern world the more comprehensive groupings of this sort have become known as federations or confederations. Despite the limited role implied in the Latin *foedus*, meaning league, from the outset such groupings have been considered as being states. The historic tendency of such federal states has been for the central government to acquire ever more power and in so doing to limit the sovereignty and the freedom of action of its component parts. The first modern federation of this type was the United States of America, which came into existence in the climate of late eighteenth-century idealism and rationalism. During the next century it survived an attempt by a group of its component states to break it up and to establish a looser 'confederation' in its place. In this the individual states would have retained their sovereignty and the powers of the federal government would have been held severely in check. In the wake of the failure of this attempt at fundamental change, the federal government was gradually able to impose limits on the independence of the component states. This originally loose grouping had itself become sufficiently powerful for a new state to emerge out of it. In line with the current convention, the American federal state, and others organized along similar lines such as Australia and Canada, are also called 'nations', although they do not fit easily into this category in the typology of states.

As has been observed, while all four of the categories of states outlined here have been in existence in one form or another for most of the time since recognizable states first came into being, the incidence and importance of each of them have varied considerably through history. Each category will therefore be considered as being a component part of the whole, both geographically and historically. While this book will, of course, focus on only one of these categories – the city-state – the wider context in which it exists will always be borne in mind in order to understand the reasons why at certain times it has dominated the geopolitical scene but declined into insignificance at others.

The origins of the city-state are to be found around the shores of the eastern Mediterranean in ancient times and from there it spread westwards across the Mediterranean and eastwards into the Black Sea and adjacent parts of the Middle East. The most significant area into which it expanded outside the Mediterranean world was into northern Europe, where it had a second flourishing in the later Middle Ages and in early modern times (see illus. 1).

The city state has been always far less characteristic of other parts of the world and was virtually absent from the political arrangements of the great civilizations of India and China. While a version of the city-state was brought eastwards as far as the Indus valley by Alexander the Great, there was no concept at all of the city-state in Chinese political thought. It is generally known that China did have associations of merchants, but these never acquired anything like the importance that they came to have in the west, where they became major components of the city-states and often evolved into city governments. In China the city was always essentially a node in the administrative network of empire, and the idea of the city as being in any sense 'free' was quite meaningless.[7]

In this book the development of the city-state will be traced chronologically from ancient times to the contemporary world. The ancient Mediterranean, in which it achieved a role so important that it became central to all political ideas and ideals, will first be examined. This will be followed by an examination of the rise of the empires which brought this world to an end and of the subsequent waning of their power, particularly in western Europe. This in turn produced a situation in which the second flourishing of the city-state then took place in Italy, the

Low Countries and the Baltic. This period was itself brought to an end both by the emergence of new imperial states and by the rise of the modern nation-state in western and northern Europe. While by the twentieth century the city-state had all but disappeared in Europe, with the fall of the European empires the phenomenon emerged for the first time in other parts of the world, notably in South-East Asia and the Middle East. This globalization of the city-state will be examined in the context of political change in the post-Cold War world and the painful birth of a 'new world order' associated with this. Finally, the possible future role of the city-state will be examined in the context of the questioning of established geopolitical categories and the changing international scene in the early years of the twenty-first century.

The Birth of the City-State

The political fluidity and ethnic complexity of the eastern Mediterranean region had been considerably increased by the dramatic fall of the Minoan Empire in the middle of the second millennium BC. Migrant peoples from the north were drawn into the political and economic vacuum created by the demise of the great thalassocracy that for long had controlled the seas and islands between the coasts of Egypt and Greece. During this period the eastern Mediterranean world was dominated by feuding tribal states vying with one another for pre-eminence. Such pre-eminence was most easily achieved over the great land areas stretching eastwards from the Mediterranean to the Persian Gulf and it was here that the first imperial states had been established.

Among the migrants who moved into the eastern Mediterranean were the Philistines, a bronze age people who had come southwards from the region of the Danube. They and other similar groups were known to the Egyptians as 'the peoples of the sea' and they were seen as being invaders who had to be resisted. They eventually settled around the eastern seaboard of the Mediterranean, roughly along the strip stretching between modern Tel Aviv and Gaza. After a time they became city-dwellers and they were the first people who are known to have founded recognizable city-states as their basic form of political organization. Of course, the Philistines were moving into a region in which cities had already been in existence for millennia and there were many cities in the immediate vicinity on which they could model their own. The Jordan valley, in which some of the very earliest cities, such as Jericho, were located, lies a mere 50 to 80 kilometres to the east of the

Mediterranean coast at this point. The city had been the single most identifiable feature of the ancient civilizations of Mesopotamia and Egypt. In Lewis Mumford's phrase, civilization is 'the culture of cities' and most of the great advances that had taken place in earlier millennia had been associated with this fact.[1] However, these earlier cities were commonly within large territorial states such as Egypt and Babylonia, and there is little evidence of their having had any really independent political existence during those times.[2]

The most important settlements of the Philistines included Gaza, Gath, Ashkelon and Ashdod, which were all located either on or very near to the coast. They appear to have been a relatively advanced people with a knowledge of metal working and an ability to engage in manufacture and trade, and they soon entered into trading relationships with the surrounding peoples. Their immediate neighbours in the interior were the Canaanites, a Semitic people of pastoral nomadic origin, and relations with them were generally far from good. Disputes and conflicts took place that appear to have been mostly related to trade. By the end of the second millennium the Canaanites had been displaced by the Israelites, who were also originally pastoral nomads but who had maintained close contacts with the great civilizations of both Mesopotamia and Egypt. The conflict that then took place between these two very different peoples is documented in the Bible and elsewhere. The Philistine cities appear to have established a form of federation that enabled them to act together militarily against the common enemy. In the Bible they are invariably referred to collectively as 'the Philistines' and their army as 'the host'. While the Israelites under King Saul were at first defeated by them, David, the new king who replaced Saul after the latter's death in battle, was more successful against them. We read in the Bible quite simply that 'David smote the Philistines, and subdued them'.[3] Thus by the early years of the first millennium BC the independent existence of these first city-states was brought to an end and they were incorporated into the empire over which David, and subsequently his son Solomon, ruled. This empire proved to be transitory, and after its fall the Philistines for a time regained their independence. However, in the ninth century BC they were conquered by the Assyrians and after this never again regained their independent status.

At around this time, another people had also established themselves on the eastern seaboard of the Mediterranean immediately to the north of the Philistines. These were the Phoenicians, and they had come from the east rather than the north and appear to have had a common ancestry with the Semitic Canaanites. However, on reaching the shores of the Mediterranean BC they had become city-dwellers in much the same way as the Philistines had done, and by the end of the first millennium BC they had also established independent city-states. These were located along the coast stretching from northern Israel to Syria and the most important of them were in what is today the Lebanon. Their major cities were Acco, Achzib,Tyre, Sidon and Byblos, and like the Philistines they also entered into some kind of a loose confederation. However, unlike the Philistines they were powerful enough to be able to resist the Israelites under David and Solomon and to maintain an independent existence. It was around the beginning of the first millennium that the Phoenicians became the great traders of the ancient world and they were the first people of whom it could be said that maritime trade was the mainstay of their existence. They gained economic control over the greater part of the eastern Mediterranean and subsequently extended their trading operations westwards beyond the Sicilian Narrows. They were thus a unifying force within the Mediterranean and it is due to their activities that for the first time the inland sea began to take on the shape of a recognizable human region. Their trade routes followed the coasts and islands and the most significant of these, the so-called Phoenician route, stretched from Tyre in the east via Egypt along the north African coast to the Straits of Gibraltar. From there the Phoenicians sailed out into the Atlantic Ocean and began trading in commodities obtained from the western seaboard of Europe. The most lucrative of the commodities in which they traded were metals such as copper, iron, silver and tin, for which there was a huge market in the lands around the eastern Mediterranean. Their searches for these and other commodities took them ever further afield, and as their shipbuilding and navigational skills improved, they also became the great explorers of the ancient world. These Phoenicians were also responsible for some of the greatest advances in science and technology. Besides shipbuilding, navigation and associated activities, they developed metal working using bronze. They produced parchment and developed a new system of writing based on the alphabet. There is evidence of the manufacture of glass, linen, jewellery and the purple dye that gave them the name *Phoenikes*, the red people, by which they were known to the Greeks. They entered into very lucrative economic relations with the Israelites under both David and Solomon, and there was a close alliance between Hiram of Tyre and both monarchs. The Phoenicians contributed both raw materials and technological skills to great projects such as the building of the Temple in Jerusalem. 'Timber of cedar and timber of fir' were supplied for this purpose and Hiram of Tyre arranged that 'my servants shall bring them down from the Lebanon unto the sea: and I will convey them by sea in floats unto the place thou shalt appoint me, and I will cause them to be discharged there, and thou shalt receive them.'[4] During the first half of the first millennium BC the Phoenicians became the principal driving force in the economic and technological advance of the Mediterranean and the city-state was the political form within which they flourished.

The arrival of the city-state on the world scene took place at a time and in a place in which a particular set of geopolitical conditions operated. The Mediterranean is an inland sea, which was ideal for the simple maritime technology of the time to be developed and improved upon. It was also an area in which wealth and poverty were close bedfellows and the urge to economic improvement arose out of necessity. This was because while any particular part of the Mediterranean region would have possessed only relatively limited resources, when taken as a whole the situation was very different. By bringing these resources together and making them more readily available, maritime trade was able to convert the relative poverty of individual areas into the considerable wealth of the whole. Maritime trade thus unified the lands around the Mediterranean and created a whole that was far greater and more impressive than merely the sum of its parts. The independent cities around its coasts were the agents for this transformation and it was in their urban environment that the various elements associated with commercial success were brought together successfully. These included shipbuilding, navigational skills and manufacture, all underpinned by impressive scientific advances. As Mumford observed, since the beginnings of civilization, the city had provided the ideal environment for such innovation to take place.[5] However, excessive central control in the larger territorial states had set limits on this process and in many cases had prevented it from taking place at all. The Phoenician experience demonstrated for the first time that the economy operated most successfully, and with the greatest innovation, when the city was an independent entity with a minimum of outside interference.

The success of these first true city-states was thus a consequence of their effectiveness as geopolitical units in an environment in which maritime trade had become the principal basis of economic life. In these circumstances the territorial state had proved to be far less effective and even acted as an impediment to successful economic and scientific advance. There were many reasons for this difference, including the particular forms of government adopted, but most fundamentally territorial states were inherently limited by their territoriality while city-states were at the same time both very local and very far-reaching phenomena. On the one hand they were local enough to be responsive to the immediate conditions within which they found themselves while on the other they had a wider perspective on the world deriving from the trading operations that were inherent in their existence. Their mariners were at home in all the places where they traded and they made contact with many different peoples and were exposed to a variety of influences and knowledge emanating from many different places. Unlike the territorial states, their boundaries did not set limits to their perspective on the world. This minimalist approach to territoriality and territorial control meant that resources could be concentrated most effectively on the business of wealth creation. These first city-states were thus the invention of people who had discovered that maritime trade could transform poverty into wealth and who needed a political system that could enable this to be conducted most effectively

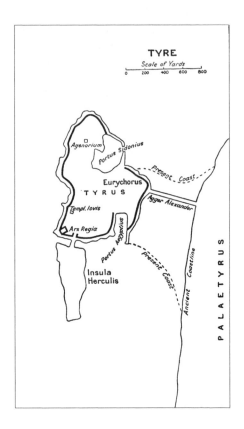

2 Tyre: mother city of
the Phoenician world.

and with a minimum of interference. They were well aware that
the maximization of their material well-being could be brought
about only by the most effective deployment and use of the
resources available to them. This in turn necessitated the city-
states being strong enough to maintain their freedom and
independence from the aggressive states of the hinterland,
which sought to incorporate them into their own territories and
then to use their considerable wealth for the purpose of further
territorial aggrandisement.

The Phoenician cities in particular were highly successful in
maintaining their independence for a long period of time and
this success owed much to the physical geography of the strip of
coast on which they were located. Unlike the coast to the south
inhabited by the Philistines, the particular features of their
location made it especially difficult for land-based empires to

conquer them. Tyre was located on an island connected by a causeway to the mainland (see illus. 2), and Sidon was on the coast well protected from the land. Likewise Acco was on a peninsula to which entry from a landwards direction presented difficulties. In addition to this the whole Phoenician coast from Mount Carmel northwards is flanked by a huge double range of mountains reaching over 2,000 metres in height, and this made any attack on these cities from the interior a difficult and hazardous operation. It was thus geography that was the original cause of their freedom and geography that then helped them to retain it, despite their being located in an area of the world that was in dangerously close proximity to the centres of powerful and aggressive states such as the Assyrian Empire.

The use of the sea both as a natural highway of commerce and as a protection from the incursions of land power was thus the key to the success of these first city-states. Through maritime trade they were able to create considerable wealth in areas that had only limited natural resources and through maritime exploration they were able to extend the range of their trading operations and so increase the size of the area within which they operated. 'They gathered wares from all the world', wrote Ludwig, 'the silver of Tarshish, the gold of Thasos, the incense of Arabia and ivory from India'.[6] They established an economic order and in so doing they created the human region that became the principal field of their operations.[7] The geographically diverse and territorially fragmented nature of this region meant that it did not itself become a state but remained a loose grouping of smaller states that did not impinge upon the independence of its members. While they remained fully sovereign they devised systems of shared sovereignty for such purposes as trade and defence. Through their aggregation of wealth, they were able to increase the resources available both to sustain their maritime power and to ensure their security. They were, in Ludwig's opinion, 'the first amphibians', and, protected from outside dangers, they were able to create a system that enhanced rather than diminished their independence. In this way they were able for long to remain outside the spheres of influence of those territorial powers that sought to impose their own kind of order on the world by the use of force. The main feature of the geographical distribution of these Phoenician city-states was that they had originally formed a cluster in a particular region and then expanded out from this to establish colonial settlements. Within the original cluster was a mother city that came to have an ascendancy over all the others. It was the most wealthy of the cities, and from this wealth came power. However, this was not then translated into a political or military ascendance, and each city-state retained its independence modified only by the obligations arising from membership of the loose overall grouping. Each of the Phoenician city-states was, in Braudel's phrase, 'an autonomous world' in its own right.[8] Sited on easily defended headlands and islands, they turned their backs on their mountainous hinterland and communicated with one another, and with the rest of the world, by sea.[9] They then sought to recreate what Braudel referred to as being their 'ideal urban geography' in the colonial settlements dotted on islands and peninsulas across the Mediterranean from North Africa to Spain. The existence of a major axis of communication was important for connecting the whole group together and for facilitating their trading operations. While colonies were founded and the cities in this way expanded over a larger area, the original cluster became a core region that was at the heart of the economic, cultural and defence activities of the whole maritime region.

By the middle of the first millennium BC the known world of western mankind centred on the eastern Mediterranean and the adjacent Middle East. This was divided into two sub-regions, a maritime and a continental one, each of which was characterized by its own particular type of state. In the maritime sub-region it was the city-state, the whole existence of which was bound up with its maritime location. In the continental sub-region it was the territorial state, the existence of which was equally bound up with its continental location. To territorial states wealth and power were achieved through the acquisition of more land, while to city-states these attributes were the products of trade. Each of these two types of state was ill at ease in the element of the other and their political structures were designed specifically to cope with the conditions of their own element. The principal core region of the city-states on the eastern shores of the Mediterranean lay close to the junction of these two disparate areas and this proved to be both their strength and their weakness. Its strength was that it enabled the city-states to trade profitably with the territorial states of the interior and to supply them with the raw materials, manufactured goods and technology that they lacked. Its weakness was that they were vulnerable to the unwanted attentions of aggressive states bent on territorial expansion. While the city-states were for a time able to fend off the attentions of the territorial states, the rise of ever more powerful states in the Middle East, coupled with persistent divisions within the maritime world itself, was to be their undoing. The centuries following the establishment of the first city-states saw the rise of the Assyrian Empire and in the ninth century BC this brought about a fundamental change in the Mediterranean world. Expanding rapidly from their homeland in northern Mesopotamia, the Assyrians reduced Babylon to dependency and advanced westwards to the sea. The whole of the eastern Mediterranean littoral, home of the first city-states, rapidly fell into their hands. In 878 BC the Phoenician city-states lost their independence and became subjects of the king of Assyria. This conquest of the core region of the Phoenician world resulted in the complete disruption of the commercial system that had been built up over the preceding centuries.

Phoenician maritime activity had long extended into the western Mediterranean and colonies had been established there. One of these was Kirjath Hadeschath, the 'new town', which is known to us as Carthage. By tradition this city was established in 840 BC in the wake of the Assyrian conquest of Tyre, although there is evidence that there was a settlement in the area earlier than this. The Phoenician world then relocated westwards and Carthage became its new centre. Situated close to the junction between the western and the eastern Mediterranean seas, and where the distance between Africa and Sicily is a mere 100 kilometres, it proved to be ideal for the transport of metals from the western Mediterranean and northern Europe and for trade southwards across the Sahara and around the coasts of Africa. Safe from the attentions of the land empire that was making the eastern Mediterranean so danger-

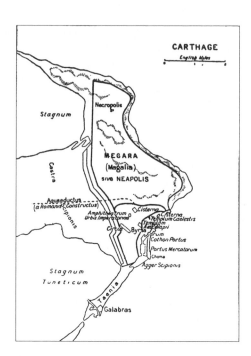

CARTHAGE

Stagnum

Necropolis

MEGARA
(Magalia)
sive NEAPOLIS

Castra

Scipionis

Aquaeductus
(a Romanis Constructus)

Amphitheatrum
Urbis Imperatorum

Circus

Byrsa

Cisterna
Cisterna
Templum Caelestis
Templum
Aesculapii
Forum
Cothon Portus
Portus Mercatorum
Choma
Agger Scipionis

Stagnum
Tuneticum

Taenia

Galabras

3 Carthage: new
centre of the
Phoenician world.

ous a place for the vulnerable city-states, Carthage was soon at the centre of a revived Phoenician maritime trading system that represented a new lease of life for Phoenicia.[10] The Phoenician route from the eastern to the western Mediterranean remained but its pivot had shifted well to the west. The Carthaginians clearly inherited the dynamism of their Phoenician forebears and this is seen in the continuation of exploration further than ever before.

The site of Carthage was in many ways similar to that of Tyre (see illus. 3). It was built on a rocky peninsula linked to the mainland only by sandbars and swamps. It was thus safe from the dangers posed by the native peoples of the North African hinterland and, as with Tyre, was able at first to concentrate most of its attention on the sea. Like its predecessors in the eastern Mediterranean, this Phoenician colony adopted the political form of an independent city-state. Like the Phoenician cities to the east it had been at first a monarchy, but this changed and a form of oligarchic government was introduced. This centred on the leading families, which had the biggest say in affairs of state. Despite the retention of the monarchs, their powers were limited and there was a popular assembly that was given some say in government.[11]

Over a period of time Carthage took increasing control over the territory that surrounded it and this acted both as a buffer against attack from the land and as an agricultural area for supplying the immediate requirements of the population. As a result of these things, together with its trading operations with Africa, a certain symbiosis with its surrounding territory took place that was very different from the completely maritime orientation of the Phoenician cities to the east. A certain limited territoriality crept into the Carthaginian state and this made it more of a regional power in North Africa than the original Phoenician cities had ever been in the eastern Mediterranean.

The Phoenicians continued to be the dominant economic force in the western Mediterranean and Carthage remained the leading city until the third century BC when this position was challenged and eventually brought catastrophically to an end (see chapter Five).[12] Well before this, further developments had taken place in the eastern Mediterranean that involved the flowering of the greatest city-state culture in the ancient world, that of the Greeks. Despite their vulnerability to attack from the east, and the continuous problems to which this gave rise, the great achievement of the Greeks was being able to combine the maintenance of their freedom from foreign domination with the establishment of freer societies within the city-states themselves. It was with these people that the city-state of antiquity reached its apogee.

THREE

The Ancient Greek *Polis*

'It seems incredible', wrote Thomas Callander, 'that in what seems a moment in time, in a tiny corner of Europe, occupied by less than five million landsmen and islanders endowed with scanty natural resources, there should have been created a culture, a commerce, a social order and a polity . . . renowned beyond all others as the most original and brilliant'.[1] It was these Greeks who were to set their seal on the city-state and give it a conceptual coherence.

Like many of the other peoples who settled around the shores of the Mediterranean, the Greeks had moved southwards from eastern Europe in a series of waves during the second millennium BC. These included the Achaean, the Dorian and the Ionian waves, and these particular people settled around the Aegean Sea in the northern part of what had been the Minoan sphere of influence. This became the land of the Greeks, *Hellas*, which the Romans called *Graecia*. The Achaean Greeks, whose most important city was Mycenae in the northern Peloponnesus, were strongly influenced by Minoan civilization. The Dorian Greeks had also moved down into the Peloponnesus, and from there migration took place across the Aegean to the western coasts of Anatolia, and it was there that the first recognizably Hellenic civilization came into being. One of the salient features of this Ionian civilization was the city-state, and among the more important of these were Miletus, Ephesus and Halicarnassus (see illus. 4).

Although their geographical origins were very different, the Greeks moved into virtually the same physical environment as that already occupied by the Phoenicians, and their response to it was a similar one. As with most of the lands that have a

Mediterranean climate and geomorphology, there was limited agricultural potential and natural wealth. 'Hellas and poverty have always been foster-sisters', observed Herodotus,[2] and, like the Phoenicians, the Greeks countered this by turning to maritime trade. By this means, they were soon able to avail themselves of the diverse products of a far larger area. Settled as they were around the north-eastern fringes of the Mediterranean sea, the Greeks were sufficiently removed from those major centres of imperialist activity that had made the eastern seaboard, the home of the Philistines and Phoenicians, so vulnerable to attack from the interior. However, like the latter people, from early on in their history their political system was based on the city-state.

While the islands and peninsulas around the coasts of the Aegean afforded good protection for these fledgling Greek city-states, the location of the Ionian cities also gave them ready access to the peoples of Anatolia. As a result of the contacts between the two, the civilizations of coast and interior became increasingly intertwined. Most important in this respect were the Lydians of western Asia Minor, who developed a close symbiotic relationship with the Ionian Greek cities to the west of them. The Lydian capital, Sardis, was located on the Hermus river, a mere 50 kilometres from Miletus, and contacts between the two proved productive and fruitful. The situation here was a far more positive one than that between the coast and interior in the eastern Mediterranean, where conflict had been more the norm. The Lydians were an advanced people, and through them the Ionian cities acquired a knowledge of the skills of metalworking, pottery and painting. Most significantly, they acquired the knowledge and use of coinage, and this was to become of central importance in the expansion of their commerce. The symbiotic relationship between the two is evidenced by the last Lydian king, Croesus, who attempted to gain control over the Ionian cities. Strongly influenced by Hellenic civilization, Croesus used his legendary wealth in order to endow the Greek shrines, in particular that at Delphi.

At first the Greeks had been excluded from the eastern Mediterranean by the Phoenicians, and as a consequence they had been forced to move northwards through the Hellespontus

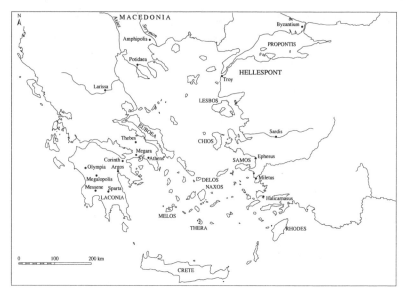

4 Cities of the ancient Aegean.

(Dardanelles) into the Black Sea. There they found an area that was in many ways physically similar to the Mediterranean and with which they could trade. Important trade routes were opened up via Cheronessos (Crimea), Colchis (Georgia) and through the Caucasus Mountains into Mesopotamia. Despite tales of abduction and revenge in the *Iliad*, commercial rivalry was the reality underlying Homer's epic poem. The Trojan War reveals the conflict between the peoples of the west and the east of the Aegean and the crucial importance to the early Greeks of control of the Hellespontus in order to secure their communications with the Black Sea. Following the establishment of control over the Straits area, Miletus, Phocaea and other Ionian cities went on to found colonies around the Black Sea, which became part of the Greek commercial sphere and an extension of Hellas to the north. The development of this routeway enabled the Greeks to trade with the east without being subjected to the dangers to which they would have otherwise have been exposed further south.

The defeat of the Lydians by the Persians in 547 BC resulted in a major shift in the epicentre of the ancient Greek world.

Both the Lydians and the Greeks of Asia Minor were annexed to the Persian Empire, and a longitudinal divide opened up through the Aegean between the free cities of the Greek peninsula and the conquered cities of Ionia. While after their conquest by the Assyrians some three centuries earlier the Phoenicians had been obliged to move 1,000 kilometres to the west in order to rebuild their civilization on the coasts of North Africa, in the case of the Greeks only a relatively minor displacement was necessary across the Aegean, which at its narrowest point is only 200 kilometres wide. The inhabitants of the Greek peninsula itself retained their independence and the principal centre of Hellenic civilization moved westwards. The cities there thrived as centres of commerce and industry and were able to maintain their system of independent city-states. The support given to their subjugated kinsfolk in Ionia by these independent Greeks was the basic cause of the Persian decision to embark on the conquest of Greece itself. This proved to be unsuccessful, and the massive defeat of the Persians by the Greeks, which culminated in the sea battle of Salamis in 480 BC, lifted the threat from Persia. The 'wooden walls', of which the Goddess Athene spoke when consulted by the Athenians on their best strategy, were their ships, and they proved best able to defend themselves in their own element. The Greek victory ensured the continued independence of the city-states, secure on their islands and peninsulas and defended by these 'wooden walls'.

By this time the Greeks had also successfully challenged the commercial dominance of the Phoenicians and, since the centre of Phoenician activities had been forced westwards, the Greeks moved into the eastern Mediterranean and established colonies as far afield as the coasts of Egypt, where they founded Naucratis, and Cyrenaica, where they founded the five cities of the Pentapolis. Above all it was westwards into southern Italy and Sicily that the Greeks moved, and there they established some of their most famous colonies, including Syracuse, Megara, Croton, Sybaris and Tarentum. The whole of this area was later known to the Romans as 'Magna Graecia', and it was to flourish for long as one of the most important centres of Hellenic civilization.

The Hellenic civilization that Callander described as being so 'original and brilliant' was expressed in the arts, architecture and philosophy, and was underpinned by the maritime trading system and defended by powerful naval forces. Politically it was organized on the basis of the *polis*, the city-state. There were a large number of city-states in the Hellenic world and they had nearly as many different forms of government. Their role changed over time and likewise their forms of government changed also. However, in one form or another the *polis* survived, and the Greeks of antiquity had never any real doubt that it was the best form of government available and indeed the only form of government that they ever seriously contemplated. By the eighth century BC the Greeks had adopted that political form that, as has been seen, had already become widespread throughout the Mediterranean. Over time they went on to improve on it so that it became one of the most enduring features of their civilization. This *polis* took a variety of different forms and evolved in different ways, but it is the Athenian version that has come to be the best known.

The Greek *polis* never did mean just the city, that is to say the urban area, alone. From the outset it signified the city together with its surrounding territory. This originally came into being through the amalgamation of the smaller rural communities by a process known as *synoikismos*. Thucydides describes this in regard to Athens as follows:

> In the days of Cecrops and the first kings . . . Athens was divided into communes, having their own town-halls and magistrates. Except in case of alarm the whole people did not assemble in council under the king, but administered their own affairs, and advised together in their several townships . . . But when Theseus came to the throne, he, being a powerful as well as a wise ruler, among other improvements in the administration of the country . . . united all the inhabitants of Attica in the present city. They continued to live in their own lands, but he compelled them to resort to Athens as their metropolis . . . A great city thus arose which was handed down by Theseus to his descendants, and from his day to this the Athenians have regularly celebrated the national festival of the *Synoikia*, or union of the communes, in honour of the Goddess Athene.[3]

5 The Acropolis in Athens.

The effect of all this was to create a sense of unity and purpose among the inhabitants. The original meaning of the word *polis* was stronghold, and its origins lay in defence. Around the stronghold the *acropolis* or high town was built, and with the pacification of the surrounding countryside this began to extend outwards from the defensive hill. At the base of the *acropolis* a larger town rose up based on commerce and industry, and eventually the principal centre of government was moved into this. Thus at an early stage the *acropolis* also came to be associated with the religious rights of the *polis*. It was regarded as being a holy place on which the temples were built, and most important among these was the temple of the patron god or goddess of the city (see illus. 5).

Thus the *polis* referred both to the state and its territory, and the average size of this was roughly that of an English county. By the fifth century BC Attica, the territory of the *polis* of Athens, had an area of 2,500 square kilometres, which was about the size of the county of Kent (see illus. 7). Boeotia, the *polis* of Thebes, which lay just to the north of Attica, was about the same size. Argolis, the *polis* of Corinth in the northern Peloponnesus, was about a third larger than Attica, while the small *polis* of Megaris on the isthmus itself was less than a quarter of its size. Most of the island states of the Cyclades were smaller still, some being no more than 20 to 30 square kilometres in area. The urban part of the *polis* was the *asty* and the surrounding territory the *chora;*

together they formed an integrated urban–rural system in which the city was the centre of commerce and industry and the surrounding countryside produced agricultural goods and raw materials. From early times the Greeks had been able to import grain from the Black Sea area, and this left the agricultural land around the city for the intensive production of such high value cash crops as the vine and the olive. Together with fruits and vegetables and animal herding for meat and milk, the *chora* was usually able to produce a large proportion of the basic require-ments of the *asty*. The surplus of what was produced was then exported, and this both stimulated such industries as the making of amphorae, in which to carry wine and olive oil, and the build-ing of ships in order to transport such products. It produced an income that enabled those products and raw materials which Attica did not possess to be imported, above all the grain on which the growing city came increasingly to depend.

The *polis* was a sovereign entity with complete control over its own affairs, both internal and external. After the initial process of *synoikismos* was accomplished, and the *asty* and *chora* were functioning as an integrated unit, the resulting entity was generally considered to be the optimum form of government. The *polis*, said Aristotle, exists for the good life.[4] In other types of state the people existed for the well-being of the state, but in Greece the state existed for the well-being of its people. There appears to have been little doubt in the minds of its citizens that it was the right size to discharge its political and economic func-tions in the most efficient manner. The *polis* was, said Aristotle, 'natural' while other geopolitical entities, and he had in mind particularly empires, were thus bound to be 'unnatural' cre-ations. Most importantly, from the viewpoint of the discharge of the functions of government, the *polis* was regarded as being small enough for its citizens to be able to participate in its affairs. This made them feel a loyalty to their own city-state, which was less likely to be the case in larger states.

In the case of Athens, over time political evolution had taken place, the aim of which had been to involve more of the citizens in the affairs of the state and increase the identification of each citizen with the state in which he lived. These *polites* made up only a relatively small proportion of the total population and originally formed a kind of urban aristocracy. Over time their numbers increased as lower orders of society were given the right to citizenship. However, citizenship was always confined to males over a certain age and normally restricted to those who had actually been born in the city and who possessed a certain minimum property qualification.

In the beginning the *polis* had been governed by a monarch, the *basileus*. While it had at first been absolute, the power of the monarch had generally been reduced over time until it became largely nominal. The monarchy was finally abolished in Athens in 683 BC. This was then replaced with government by the *aristocratia*, the most important families consisting mainly of landowners. The holders of the supreme power, the archons, were chosen from this class and the titular head of state was the *archon basileus*. The advisory council was the *Areopagus*, named after the hill on which its sessions took place, and also composed of members of the aristocratic class. With the rise in the importance of the merchants, this class was also eventually brought into government. Solon (640–560 BC), who had been appointed archon in 594 BC, went ahead with a number of important reforms, including the establishment of the *ecclesia*, a new assembly, the members of which were chosen by the citizen body as a whole. The smaller *boule* council was set up for the day to day running of the city. The principal objective that Solon set himself was the achievement of *eunomia*, balance in the state among the various classes of society, and his successor Cleisthenes went on to increase the overall level of participation by enlarging the number of *polites* in the state. The apogee of the whole process came with Pericles (495–429 BC), whose 'democratic revolution' of 461 BC put the elected *ecclesia* at the very heart of government and limited the importance of the *boule*. At the same time the aristocratic *areopagus* was reduced to a purely ceremonial role. In *The Politics*, Aristotle discussed the question of where the sovereign power in the *polis* should reside and came to the conclusion that the best place for it was with the people. 'The majority ought to be sovereign . . . For it is possible that the many, no one of whom taken singly is a good man, may yet taken all together be better than the few, not individually but collectively.'⁵

The *polis* had been initially protected by the stronghold around which the process of *synoikismos* had taken place, and territorial expansion of the area under its control had usually followed. The size of this was initially determined by the natural region, such as a valley or plain, in which the *polis* was located, and its boundaries were natural barriers such as mountains, rivers or coasts. Attica consisted of a rocky peninsula protected on its landward side by the Cithaeron-Parnes ranges reaching heights of 1,400 metres, while Boeotia to the north centred on the valley of the river Asopus, which was also bounded by high mountains. Argolis was defined mainly by its long coastline, which together with the narrow isthmus of Corinth made up some three-quarters of its boundaries. These states were thus mostly well-defined geographical units that had to be defended, and defence was the job of the armed forces. The army was based on the *hoplites*, who were drawn from the citizen body and whose heavy armour was intended as a kind of mobile defensive wall. The navy provided defence from attack by sea and protected the extensive maritime trading operations that were the lifeblood of the *polis*.

The greatest flourishing of the Athenian *polis* took place during the period following the defeat of the Persians, when Pericles rose to become the dominant political figure in the city. Although Delphi with its Temple of Apollo was referred to as being the *omphalos* of the world, in so many ways Periclean Athens became its real centre. Besides its intellectual and artistic achievements, material prosperity and maritime ascendancy, this was the time when Athens became most democratic and the citizen body participated to the greatest extent in its government. It was the time when the arts and philosophy flourished and when the great rebuilding of the city took place following its destruction during the Persian Wars. Between 447 and 432 BC this culminated in the building of the Parthenon on the highest point of the Acropolis adorned with statues and friezes of the gods. Around it were other sacred buildings, including the Erechtheion, the Propylaea and the Temple of Athena Nike (see opposite). 'The architecture of fifth-century Athens', wrote Heurtley, 'reached a splendour unknown in Europe up till then and perhaps unsurpassed since; and in this glorious

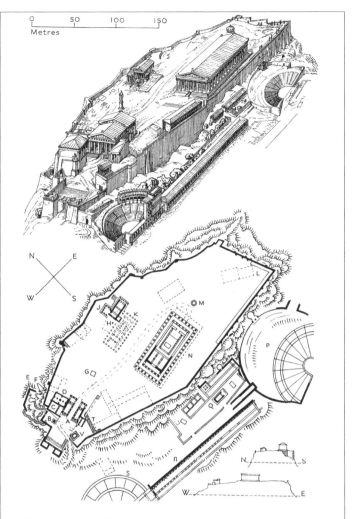

Based on drawings from (1) H. Luckenbach, *Kunst und Geschichte,* pp. 41–2 (Munich and Berlin, 1920); (2) Sir Banister Fletcher, *History of Architecture,* p. 77 (London, 1896, 10th ed. 1938).

A	Propylaea	L	Platform for votive statues
B	Pedestal of Agrippa	M	Roman temple
C	Pinacotheca	N	Parthenon
D	Roman cistern	P	Theatre of Dionysus
E	Clepsydra	Q	Aesculapium
F	Caves of Apollo and Pan	R	Stoa of Eumenes
G	Statue of Athena Promachus	S	Odeum of Herodes Atticus
H	Sacred Olive tree	T	Mycenaean wall
J	Erechtheum	V	Temple of Athena of Victory
K	Old Temple of Athens		

6 Reconstruction and plan of the Acropolis in Athens.

setting the writers and thinkers of the city produced works that have become the inspiration of later times'.[6] To Pericles, who was deeply involved in their construction, the great buildings of Athens 'cheer the heart and delight the eye day by day'. He summed up his view of the role of his city in the famous Funeral Oration for those who had just perished in the Peloponnesian War. 'Our city as a whole is an education to Hellas', he asserted, 'and . . . her members yield to none . . . for independence of spirit, many-sidedness of attainment, and complete self-reliance in limbs and brain'.[7] This may be seen as being the apogee of the *polis* as existing, in the words of Aristotle, to promote 'the good life'.

There was also an alternative kind of *polis* in the Hellenic world and this was exemplified by Sparta, the city with which Periclean Athens was plunged into the Peloponnesian War in the final decades of the fifth century BC. Sparta had originally had many of the same features as Athens and the other city-states. Like Athens, it had been formed by *synoikismos*, the bringing together of a number of villages in the Eurotas valley of the Peloponnesus around a stronghold much like the Acropolis in Athens. It became an independent city-state that was proud of its Dorian heritage and its mythical descent from Heracles, thought to be based on a legendary Mycenean chieftain in the service of the king of Argos. It spread out over the fertile plain of Laconia, which was well protected by high mountains to west and east. Like Athens, it had been initially ruled by monarchs, but in the early eighth century BC a constitutional settlement, the Great Rhetra, had drastically curtailed the powers of the monarchy, widened the basis of government and brought in the aristocracy and the lower classes. A citizen body came into being that possessed both rights and responsibilities, most important among the latter being military service for the defence of the city.

This is where the resemblance between Athens and Sparta comes to an end. While the size of the Spartan *polis* of Laconia was only slightly larger than that of Argolis, it steadily increased in size. The biggest expansion took place with the conquest of the neighbouring *polis* of Messenia in 735 BC and eventually the expansion of its sphere of influence to cover the whole of the Peloponnesus. Thus by the fifth century BC the Spartan city-state had grown to the size of an English region such as the West Midlands or a small European nation-state like the Netherlands, rather than that of an average English county as Attica was. The Messenians were effectively enslaved by the Spartans. They became the *helots* and their function was to perform all menial tasks, leaving the Spartans free to concern themselves principally with defence and politics. The citizen body of Sparta became and remained a kind of aristocracy ruling over a large territory and population.

The Great Rhetra decreed a separation of powers in the government of the state among the *apella*, the *gerousia* and the monarchy. While the *apella* was elected by the citizen body, the *gerousia* consisted of the aristocracy and at the head of the state were two kings. The real locus of power lay with the *gerousia* and so Sparta became and remained an oligarchy. While Athens engaged in numerous experiments in government covering the whole gamut from monarchy to democracy, after the Great Rhetra the Spartan constitution did not change further and it remained an oligarchy for the rest of its existence as an independent *polis*. This same unchanging quality was reflected in Spartan society as a whole. It was strict and controlled and all citizens owed absolute allegiance to the state. The degree of freedom accorded to even the small citizen body was limited and the great majority of the people possessed little freedom at all. A central feature was the conscription of all young males into the army, where they then spent a long period of their lives. This made for a militarized and militaristic society into which a great deal of aggressiveness was built. Unlike almost all other Greek cities Sparta had no walls. Its army was its defence and its territorial expansion over the whole of the Peloponessus, which is virtually an island except for the narrow isthmus at Corinth, ensured its security. The large land area of this peninsula was also of central importance for the supply of its foodstuffs and natural resources. As a result of this, Sparta engaged in trade to a far lesser extent than did most of the other city-states. Surrounded by its large and easily defended territory, it became ever more economically self-sufficient. This together with its inland location increased its isolation, and it participated to an ever smaller extent in the wider life of the Hellenic world.

Athens and Sparta represented two alternative models for the *polis* in the ancient Greek world and each of them reflected closely the geographical conditions of its existence. Athens was a maritime state. Although the Athenian *asty* was itself actually located slightly in the interior, being some 15 kilometres from the Piraeus, it was closely linked to the sea via its outport. From the beginning trade had been its lifeblood and this was protected both by the huge fleet in the Aegean and by the Great Walls. The construction of these was begun during the administration of Cimon and linked Athens to the Piraeus, so ensuring that the city could not be cut off. Through the Piraeus flowed the goods and traders of the world and this opened Athens to influences from a wide area. Its keynote was its freedom and diversity and the wide participation of the citizen body in its government. Sparta, on the other hand, was a land state. Located well in the interior of Laconia, some 30 kilometres from the nearest port, it became inward-looking and sought both its economic well-being and its defence through its dominating position in the Peloponnesus. This control was ensured by its large and efficient army, which was also the instrument for the maintenance of the state and the subjugation of the peoples who lived under Spartan rule. It was, wrote Dickinson, as though the Spartans were 'camped' in the midst of a hostile population and a state that was based on such a situation had always to remain on a military footing.[8]

The geographical differences between Athens and Sparta also underlay the profound political differences between the two. Although both have been accorded the overall name of *polis*, and they were part of a world of city-states, the two were really very different political creations. Aristotle challenged whether the word *polis* should be universally employed to describe city-states and considered that the existence of a *politeia*, a constitution – and a democratic one at that – was the most important criterion for its existence.[9] In many ways the city-states of Athens and Sparta can be regarded as being prototypes for two very different sorts of state based respectively on sea power and land power. The two were present in microcosm

7 The city-states of southern Greece and the Peloponnesus.

in the Greek peninsula and, like other such different states in later history, they proved to be incompatible and came into conflict with one another. Eventually, each attempted to impose its own model of political life on the whole of the Greek world, but both models entailed the attainment of a dominant position over the other states. Their lack of success in this enterprise was the main reason for the failure of the *polis* to be the model for states in subsequent history.

The most fundamental problem faced by the Greek city-states was that of how to live together in peace. From the earliest times there had been rivalries and conflicts and an unwillingness to accept any overall leadership. This is very clearly demonstrated in the independent attitudes of the Greeks in the Trojan Wars as recounted in Homer's *Iliad*. They were reluctant to accept the authority of Agamemnon, the king of

Mycenae, who had been placed in overall command of the expedition against Troy. This attitude was exemplified by Achilles, son of King Peleus of Thessalia, who fought the Trojans bravely but 'sulks in his tent' and refuses to fight any more after being subjected to what he considered to be an insult by Agamemnon. It took the death of his friend Patroclus for him to agree to a resumption of the war. The ancient Greek world had a social, cultural and economic dimension but was very far from having a political one, and each city-state guarded its independence jealously. Personal loyalties and feelings of kinship motivated common action among these people to a far greater extent than formal organizational structures ever could.

For most of the time the Hellenic city-states existed in a condition that approximated to one of 'no war – no peace' and conflicts among them over boundaries, trade and dynastic questions were regular occurrences. However, Greeks from the various city-states regularly met together on their travels throughout the Hellenic world and beyond. Besides this, Greeks were constantly meeting in the great Panhellenic shrines to the gods, which were both places of pilgrimage and of social interaction. The most important of these was Delphi, which Semple saw as being 'the Mediterranean clearing house for geographical information owing to its numerous visitors'.[10] It must also have been a centre for news and gossip and a place where opinions were exchanged and the state of the world discussed. The substitution of peaceful pursuits for war underlay the institution of another Panhellenic festival, the Olympic Games, which by tradition began in 776 BC. Taking place every four years at Olympia in the city-state of Elis (see illus. 7), this was intended to substitute peaceful competition for war in the relations among the cities. Similar games then took place elsewhere in the Hellenic world, most important among them being the Pythian Games in Delphi itself.

The lack of political unity became a major problem only when the Greeks were faced by a common enemy, and the state that proved to be the most dangerous threat to their independence was the Persian Empire. During the Persian Wars, which began in 490 BC, ad hoc armies and navies had to be assembled for the defence of Hellas and temporary commands had been instituted. Following the end of the Persian Wars, as a result of the dangers to which their disunity had exposed them, and the closeness they came to defeat, the Athenians embarked on the creation of a permanent defensive alliance among the city-states of the Aegean. This Delian League, which came into existence in 477 BC, had its headquarters on the Aegean island of Delos, the birthplace of Apollo, where the treasury of the League was also located. Amongst its most enthusiastic members were the cities of Ionia, only recently liberated after a long period of subjection to Persia. Their vulnerable location had made them all too well aware of the need for a common defence against external threats and they avidly grasped the offer of Athenian protection. The most important contribution of Athens, by far the largest and richest member, was their powerful fleet. The Athenians encouraged the smaller states to contribute money in lieu of men, thus leaving them to manage the wider defence effort themselves. A notable absentee from this arrangement was Sparta, which refused to join and which was prepared to go it alone and place complete reliance on its powerful army for its own defence. It saw little need to enter into overall arrangements of any kind with the rest of the Greek world. Partly because of a sense of insecurity engendered both by the attitude of the Spartans and by the continuing Persian threat, Athens gradually assumed a dominating position over the League. The nature of the League then changed as Athenian control became tighter and Athens began to show distinctly imperialistic tendencies. This whole process was accelerated by the war with Sparta precipitated by Athenian interference in that state's affairs following a helot revolt in 465 BC. As a result of this the treasury of the League was moved from Delos to Athens. This was done on the pretext of greater security, but it was clear that Athens was actually embarked on pursuing a path towards imperialism. It was adding political hegemony to its preponderant economic and naval position in the Aegean. Sparta increasingly saw this as being a threat to its own security and confrontation and war between the two ensued.

This Peloponnesian War that began in 432 BC between the Aegean maritime confederacy led by Athens and a Peloponnesian confederacy led by Sparta was in geopolitical terms a war between sea power and land power. Within the Greek world it was a microcosm of the land power–sea power confrontation that had taken place between the Persians and Greeks at the beginning of the century. While in the Persian Wars Greek sea power had prevailed, in this civil war it was land power that eventually defeated sea power. The land power Sparta learned lessons from its initial failures and took to the sea, in this way defeating the Athenians in their own element as well as on land. The 'wooden walls' failed to protect Athens and in 404 BC the city was forced to surrender. In this way the Athenian ascendancy over the Greek world was finally brought to an end.

The victorious Spartans demanded the surrender of the Athenian fleet, the demolition of the Long Walls linking Athens and the Piraeus, and the giving up of most of the Athenian colonies. Yet Sparta had also been gravely weakened by the war and was not able to sustain its newly acquired ascendancy over the Greek world. During the next half-century Thebes, and again Athens, challenged Spartan power, and in 371 BC the peace of Callias between Athens and Sparta signalled what was in effect a kind of permanent truce. The Spartans recognized Athenian naval pre-eminence while at the same time the Athenians recognized Spartan pre-eminence on land. Within the geopolitical microcosm that was Greece, both the land–sea conflict and the conflict of imperialism versus the autonomy of the *polis* had been played out. After the war ended both remained unresolved and the solution of the central problem of the relationships among the city-states had to await resolution by outside intervention.

The Hellenic city-states, so successful at maintaining their independence, thus singularly failed to devise ways of living together in a peaceful way. The great shrines, such as Delphi, with their proffered advice on the best course of action, together with their vibrant social and cultural life, and the Panhellenic Games at Olympia and elsewhere certainly con-tributed to giving *Hellas* a strong sense of common identity but the conversion of this into any kind of Hellenic state was firmly resisted. The Persians had attempted but totally failed in their attempts to bring the Greek city-states into their world empire. The Athenians had then tried to group together the city-states under their leadership but had been opposed from within by a powerful rival state having very different ideas about the nature of the Hellenic world.

It is difficult to make generalizations about the overall nature of the *polis* that the ancient Greeks created and cherished. Its most clear-cut geographical feature was its small size. Small was certainly beautiful to the Greeks; everything had to be on a human scale, and this applied as much to the *polis* as to everything else. The *polis* was the unit in which their civilization was contained and problems in its structure and function had repercussions on everything else. 'The present kingdom of Greece', observed Dickinson, 'is among the smallest of European states; but to the Greeks it would have appeared too large to be a state at all'.[11] This was particularly important because participation in the affairs of the state by the whole citizen body was deemed to be essential. It was an Athenian assumption that the citizens should be able to assemble together to take decisions on the hills of the Pnyx or the Areopagus or in the more ample space of the Agora below. The *agora*, the collecting place, was where the whole of the citizen body was expected to assemble to debate the issues of state. As democracy took hold, all full *politeis* were expected to participate and those who did not do so were dubbed *idiotes*, people who preferred private pleasure to public service. Such people were always regarded as being beneath contempt.

Although the size of the citizen body that ran a particular *polis* varied from the very small and exclusive to the very large and inclusive, in all cases monarchy had been brought to an end, or rendered powerless, and the basis of government had been widened. The method of government that replaced the absolute monarch varied both among and within the city-states. Within many there was for long periods an almost permanent condition of political flux and even of incipient civil war. Those who wielded power were constantly being challenged by those who did not. Although not existing in a formalized way, this meant that there was in reality both a government and an opposition. In the more democratic states, the positions of the two could be changed by constitutional means, but in the most authoritarian it produced much unrest and civil war.

Yet, despite the great differences among them, the *polis* represented an immense advance for humankind on almost everything that had gone before. Dickinson observed that 'in the best days of the best states', the *polis* was an example of government for the benefit of the people and humanity was liberated in a manner that was and remained quite alien to the empires of the east.[12] The trouble was that there were also many bad days, and many of these had to do with the vexed question of the relationships among the cities themselves. The ultimate failure of the classical *polis* can be attributed more than anything else to the lack of progress in creating an organization that, while itself not being a state as we would understand it, could be a vehicle for the harmonization of the relations among the sovereign cities.

The next attempt to create something of this sort was to take place in the following century under the leadership of a state on the periphery of the Hellenic world. In so doing, however, the *polis* as philosophers such as Plato and Aristotle conceived of it came to an end and was replaced by a state of a very different type.

FOUR

The Hellenistic Foundations

Macedonia, the state that brought the Hellenic world to an end and replaced it with the Hellenistic world, was not Greek at all. Its centre was the mountainous country lying immediately to the north of the Greek peninsula, but it had long been closely associated with the Greek city-states to the south. This had led to a desire on the part of the Macedonian aristocracy to become more fully a part of the Hellenic world. They had been subjected to considerable Hellenic influence and their sons often had Greek tutors and spent time in Athens and other Greek cities. The Macedonian capital, Pella, in the valley of the Axius, was only 40 kilometres from the Mediterranean, and its relationship to the Greek cities of the Chalcidice peninsula was not unlike that of the Lydian capital, Sardis, in relation to the cities of Ionia. However, unlike the Lydians, who had an advanced civilization of their own, the Macedonians had little that was of value to the Greeks. What they did possess was military power and they had used this to create a territorial state of considerable size stretching from the Balkan mountains to the coasts of the Aegean. Following the end of the Peloponnesian War, and the chronic weakening of the city-states of the peninsula, Macedonia moved from the periphery to the centre of Greek affairs. Philip II of Macedon (359–336 BC) saw the role of his country as being to put an end to the destructive divisions that had done so much damage to the Greek world and in particular to end the rivalry that persisted among the leading city-states of Athens, Sparta and Thebes. He believed that Macedonia had the duty and the power to do this and during his reign the country became closely involved in Greek affairs.

Athens itself was very divided on the question of Macedonian involvement. There were many in the city who saw this half-Greek state as being a new threat to the independence of the Greeks, while others welcomed Macedonian participation as a way of bringing the civil wars to an end and imposing some kind of order on the fractious city-states of Hellas. Those holding the former view were led by Demosthenes, who considered Philip to be a barbarian and a menace to the democratic liberties of his city. In the *Philippics*, the impassioned speeches of denunciation that the orator made on this subject, he warned of the dangers to the whole of the Greek world posed by the territorial ambitions of the Macedonian king. In contrast to this, Isocrates in his *Philippus* orations welcomed Philip's leadership as a counterweight to the long-standing threat from Persia. In the event those who followed Demosthenes won the day and a combined army of Athenians and Thebans took the field against the Macedonians. At the Battle of Chaeronea in 338 BC the Macedonian army routed the Greeks and the country lay at the feet of the conqueror. Philip summoned and presided over a Panhellenic congress at Corinth that was attended by representatives of most of the Greek city-states with the notable, but not surprising, exception of Sparta. The congress established the League of Corinth and the autonomy of the city-states under the overall protection of Macedonia was guaranteed. A framework for the conduct of future inter-city relations was then formulated, and a governing council, the *synhedrion*, was established to deal with disputes. Macedonia seemed to be on the verge of accomplishing what the Athenians, and then the Spartans and the Thebans, had notably failed to do during the preceding century. However, in the midst of all this, in 336 BC Philip was assassinated and replaced on the throne of Macedonia by his young son, Alexander III. Fuller expressed the opinion that 'the battle of Chaeronaea was decisive; on its fateful field . . . was sounded the death-knell of the independent polis'.[1] However, this may be a premature judgement on the fate of the *polis* which does not take into account the complexity of the events that followed Philip's death.

Educated by Greek tutors including Aristotle, Alexander was thoroughly versed in Greek culture and approved of the policy embarked upon by his father. Among other things, Aristotle would certainly have instructed Alexander on the importance of the *polis* and its central role in Greek civilization.[2] He saw his mission as being the continuation of the process of bringing order to the turbulent Greek world so that the great civilization would be freed from strife. However, Alexander's idea of unification became apparent when Thebes, by tradition the oldest of the Greek city-states, revolted against the Macedonian hegemony. The city was defeated and the revolt was suppressed with great harshness, culminating in the complete destruction of the city. Other city-states, jealous of the pre-eminent position of Thebes, had encouraged this act of brutality and so in effect connived in the curtailment of their own autonomy.[3] After the obligatory consultation with the Oracle at Delphi, Alexander then decided that the priority for the new order was to deal once and for all with the historic enemy Persia, and particularly to liberate the Ionian cities on the eastern side of the Aegean. In 335 BC Alexander and his Macedonians crossed the Hellespontus and rapidly defeated the huge Persian army at the battle of Granicus. After a series of lightning campaigns, within four years the huge Persian Empire had fallen and its last king, Darius IV, was dead. In 331 BC Alexander ascended the Persian throne as *Shah an Shah*, the Great King. One of his first acts after crossing into Asia had been to free the Ionian cities and to guarantee their independence. This guarantee was subsequently extended to the cities of the Greek peninsula itself. However, the destruction of Thebes gave a foretaste of the limits to the independence of the *polis* in the new Macedonian world order.

As *Shah an Shah* Alexander now had wider considerations than the unity of the lands around the Aegean. The precipitate collapse of the Persian Empire had totally changed the world scene. Within a decade the peripheral state that had subjugated Greece had been converted into the conqueror of the world. This conquest had been accomplished by Alexander in the name of Greek civilization, the basic institution of which was the *polis*. The *polis* then became a central feature of the Hellenization process instigated by the conqueror. As he advanced ever deeper into Asia it was the *polis* that became the centre of the new Greek life that sprung up in remote and far-flung places. It was intended as the visible sign of the triumph of Greek civilization and it became the long-term legacy of Alexander's transitory presence. Scattered across west and central Asia and on into northern India, the cities that Alexander founded represented the imposition of the Hellenistic order on massive human and physical diversity. As with the Hellenic world before it, the *polis* became the most important feature of the human geography of this Hellenistic world.

The cities founded by Alexander were for the most part completely new, although some of them were built on or near to the sites of earlier ones. They were mostly located in lands that had rarely if ever before been penetrated by the Greeks and which had no tradition of Hellenic civilization, let alone any concept of independent city-states. The tradition there had been that of tribal groupings and empires, and the cities that existed, such as the Persian capitals of Susa, Passargadae and Persepolis, were essentially political creations. The cities of Ionia had a long history but, despite their close association with Lydia and their absorption into the Persian Empire, they had always been far more a part of the Greek world to the west than the Asiatic world to the east.

It was after the final conquest of the Persian Empire in 331 BC that Alexander founded the first of his Hellenistic cities in Asia, and as he moved ever deeper into the continent the rate at which he founded them increased. He founded these cities much as other conquerors built castles or defensive fortifications. The most common name given to these foundations was Alexandria, although many other names were also used. One of the earliest of these Alexandrias was founded at Gulashkerd to the east of Persepolis in southern Persia soon after the fall of the Empire. As Alexander moved on into Central Asia he then established Alexandria Eschata (Khojent) to the east of Samarkand and Alexandria Oxiana (Kilif) on the Oxus river. In Afghanistan, across which Alexander's army marched on the way to the Khyber Pass and India, altogether five Alexandrias were founded. These include what are now Herat, Kandahar, Ghazni and Jellalabad. A fifth, Alexandria Kavkazia, was located just to the north of modern Kabul and close to another such city,

Nicaea. Five Alexandrias were also established in India, one of them, Alexandria Portus, being on the site of modern Karachi. Altogether about 70 new Greek cities were established in the east and about 40 of them appear to have incorporated the name of the conqueror himself. Alexander returned westwards to Babylon, which he had decided to make the capital of his empire. He died in 323 BC at the early age of 33 while engaged in the planning of this final new foundation on the banks of the Euphrates.

However, the most famous Alexandria of all, and the very first of the Hellenistic foundations, was not in Asia at all. It was in Egypt and it was founded in 332 BC during the brief visit that Alexander paid to Africa before he dealt the final blow to the Persians. Situated at Rhacotis between the freshwater Lake Mareotis and the Mediterranean, its exact site was said to have been chosen by Alexander himself in response to many omens. A planned city, it grew rapidly and soon had a large population, most of whom were emigrants from Greece. However, it soon became multi-national, having particularly large colonies of Jews and Egyptians. After the death of Alexander, and the breakup of his empire, Egypt fell to one of his leading generals, Ptolemy. Ptolemy himself then established a dynasty that lasted for more than 200 years.

Although Alexandria was geographically a part of their domains, and the Ptolemies had a residence there, Alexandria Aegyptus was sufficiently powerful to be able to secure and retain a large measure of independence. More importantly, it rapidly became the largest and most successful of all Alexander's foundations. It seems unlikely that Alexander ever envisaged so paramount a role for this city. It was founded to demonstrate the renewed Greek presence on the southern shores of the Mediterranean and the unity of the Mediterranean world under Greek leadership. However, its central location in relation to Alexander's new world order soon gave it considerable importance in the maritime trade between east and west. Within a century of Alexander's death, its size and wealth had made it a principal centre of convergence of people, products and ideas from all over the world. There was a certain inevitability in the way in which this city moved into the position of being the acknowledged centre of the new Hellenistic world. It was not planned for such a role, as had been Babylon or Persepolis before it, but a combination of geographical circumstances dictated its destiny.

The wealth that was generated by the trade of Alexandria was then used for the enlargement and beautification of the city. Around its large harbour impressive palaces and public buildings sprung up. The great lighthouse, the Pharos, built on an island overlooking the harbour, was a beacon for mariners and became one of the wonders of the ancient world. A network of canals transformed the port into a hub for international shipping. The most important of these were the canal that linked Mareotis to the Nile and another that joined the Red Sea to the Nile. As a result 'the transport of the world travelled through Mareotis', commented Sly,[4] and Ludwig asserted in wider vein that 'it was this harbour which made Alexandria the intellectual capital of the world for the last three centuries before Christ'.[5] One of the most important buildings in the whole of the Hellenistic world was the Mouseion, the house of the muses. A cross between a museum, a library and a university, much of the knowledge of the world came to be stored there and new ideas about the nature of the world and the universe were born within its walls. During the Hellenistic period Alexandria took over from Athens to become the new 'education of Hellas'. A place that had not existed at all in the middle of the fourth century BC had risen on the swamps and sandbars of the Nile delta to become a century later the most important city in the whole of the Hellenistic world. 'Alexandria is the world' was said to have been written on one of the manuscripts in the Mouseion. In this amazing building complex, great advances look place in many fields, most notably in mathematics, astronomy and geography. The geographer Ptolemy typified that assembly and organization of the knowledge of the world that took place in this city. Thus it was Alexandria rather than Babylon that became the real capital of the new Hellenized world that emerged out of the entangled ruins of classical Greece and Persia.

The Hellenistic foundations were thus the geographical manifestation of the new world that had been brought into being by the conquests of Alexander. While the empire soon crumbled after his death, they remained scattered over a vast territory lying between the eastern shores of the Mediterranean, the Oxus-Jaxartes basin in Central Asia and the Indus valley in northern India. The principal axis of this Hellenistic world lay along the historic fault line between the Greek and Persian spheres. What had been a confrontational frontier was transformed into the centre of the new civilization. Although this civilization was fundamentally Greek, it arose out of a symbiosis between the Greek and the Persian, the West and the East. This axis stretched from the Propontis around the eastern Aegean and Mediterranean coasts to Egypt. Here the most successful and enduring of the Hellenistic cities were established, most of them by the *Diadochoi*, the immediate successors of Alexander. These cities included Nicaea, Prusa, Alexandria Troas (Troy), Philadelphia, Attalia, Antiochia, Laodicea and, above all, Alexandria Aegyptus. This axis fused together the formerly antagonistic Hellenic and Persian worlds for the first time in a positive and creative manner, and the flourishing cities along it became the principal centres of a new Hellenized and urbanized world.

To what extent can these Hellenistic foundations be considered to be city-states in the classical sense of the term? Did the defeat at Chaeronea really sound the death knell of the *polis*? The ostensible objective of Alexander's invasion of the Persian Empire a few years later had been the liberation of those Ionian cities that had again fallen into Persian hands, and one of his first acts as liberator had been to grant them constitutions and to guarantee their independence. The Alexandrian foundations were then established on the principles of the *polis* and they were given constitutions based on that of Athens. Thus the first Alexandria was granted a democratic constitution consisting of an *ecclesia*, *boule* and *dikazontas* (magistracy). The city was divided into *demes* and tribes and it included a surrounding territory with which it had a close and symbiotic relationship in the manner of the Greek *polis*. Alexandria was thus in many ways a new Athens lying nearly 1,000 kilometres to the south on the other side of the Mediterranean. Although maintaining close contacts with the east, it was as Mediterranean a city as its Hellenic predecessors had been. Jones expressed the opinion that it was a true *polis* 'in the fullest sense of the word' and it was 'an autonomous community centred in a town but ruling a rural district'.⁶ Schneider sums it all up as follows:

> In Alexandria the Greeks had created their last and greatest city-state. Egypt was merely a backdrop for the magnificent metropolis, where only dirty villages existed, with the exception of the crumbling old capital of Memphis. Alexandria was located at the crossroads of three continents; it was the melting pot of the most advanced cultures of antiquity; the mother city of European sciences was on African soil.⁷

If indeed Alexandria 'was the world' then its model of the *polis* must also have been the model for the other cities of the Hellenistic age. While the other foundations on the great Hellenistic axis around the Mediterranean were, although smaller, similar in their political structures to Alexandria, those further to the east in the old Persian Empire never attained the same significance and the existence of many of them appears to have been relatively transitory. The foundations in Afghanistan and India remained small and insignificant by comparison with those in the west, although like the great Egyptian city, they were all initially given constitutions and populated by Greek settlers. There the Greek way of life with its temples, libraries, theatres and gymnasia was carried on in lands remote from Greece and inhabited by people who had almost nothing in common with the Greeks.⁸ Most importantly, they did not incorporate territories, and were thus very much divorced from the surrounding countryside. They existed in lands that had been only briefly ruled by Alexander himself and then by his successors, the Seleucids. These Hellenistic foundations in the remote regions of Asia remained for a time beacons of Greek civilization in hostile territory. While their temples and public buildings were Greek, for the most part they did not attain the status of city-states in the full sense of the term. In such remote places, the term *polis* would have meant something very different from what it meant to Aristotle. It varied between those foundations that were able to maintain a considerable measure of independence over a relatively long period of time to those that from the outset had little or no independence.

In the second century BC the arrival of the Parthians put an end to the Hellenistic period in the east and with this the Hellenistic foundations there disappeared into obscurity. Little is known of what happened to them and their subsequent history is speculative. Many eventually re-emerged as new Islamic foundations such as Herat and Kandahar and with these a new Islamic urban geography came into existence in western Asia.[9] By the beginning of the Christian era, the Hellenistic world had contracted westwards and the historic fault line between west and east began to reappear once more. However, the foundations lying along the Hellenistic axis continued to prosper and Antioch, Ephesus and Nicomedia remained large and important centres of industry and commerce. Alexandria itself retained its role as the major centre of the Hellenistic world into the second century AD, by which time the Hellenistic world order had given place to a new one.

For 300 years after Alexander the eastern Mediterranean and the western part of what we now call the Middle East remained in the Greek economic and cultural sphere. The principal drive towards this Hellenization came from the cities founded by Alexander and the *Diadochoi*. Using the term in its widest sense, these foundations were certainly city-states, but while the strongest of them were able to retain a high measure of independence from the surrounding territorial powers there were almost always limitations on this. That sovereignty that had been the proudest possession of their Hellenic predecessors was only rarely to be found in them. While the *Diadochoi* at their best kept the peace and left the cities alone, this was not always the case and many of them were absorbed into the imperial states that surrounded them. Yet they remained for long the principal economic centres and, in the remotest regions, the centres of civilization. They varied from the pivotal importance of the first Alexandria in Egypt to the relative insignificance of those many forgotten Alexandrias in Afghanistan and northern India. However, on whatever the scale and however remote, in a small way they contributed to the advance of humanity and provided the basis for future development.

During the early Hellenistic period, the two most important geopolitical forms of the ancient world, the city-state and the imperial state, achieved a kind of *modus vivendi*. The symbiosis that then took place between them produced geopolitical forms which were in many ways different from either and which gave some promise of being able to combine freedom with order in a way that the classical Greeks had clearly found to be the most intractable of their problems. However, the great leap forward that took place in the knowledge and understanding of the world during the Hellenistic period did not change political thinking sufficiently for this to endure. Huge advances took place in the fields of astronomy, mathematics and the earth sciences in particular, but the *polis*, which had evolved so impressively in Athens and other cities of classical Greece, and had been conceptualized by Plato and Aristotle, languished and declined. In Greece itself the cities remained, proudly cherishing the vestiges of their rights and freedoms and still held together in the Hellenic League overseen by Macedonia. In the end, here too it would be imperialism that triumphed, and when it did so the *polis* would be not its partner but its victim.

FIVE

No Mean City: Rome from *Urbs* to *Imperium*

The western Mediterranean had not succumbed to conquest by the Macedonians or to any other attempts to secure control over it. Since early times, the city-states of the eastern Mediterranean had established colonies in the west and most of these had gone on to become city-states in their own right. The most important among the early colonists from the east were the old rivals, the Greeks and the Phoenicians. While the former sailed around the northern coasts of the Mediterranean to Italy and then on to southern France and Spain, the latter kept mainly to the shores of North Africa and reached Spain from the south. The hostility that had long existed between Greeks and Phoenicians in the eastern Mediterranean was then replicated in the western Mediterranean.

The centre of the changes that took place in the western Mediterranean was the Italian peninsula. While this possessed many physical similarities to Greece, in human terms it was very different and, as a result of immigration from both north and south, a far greater diversity of peoples and cultures had become established there. By the fifth century BC the southern part of Italy together with Sicily had been colonized by the Greeks. Important among the cities of this 'Magna Graecia' were Sybaris, Tarentum, Croton, Paestum and Cumae, and while most of these became independent city-states, they were quite as much a part of the Hellenic world as were those of Ionia or the Greek peninsula itself. Trade and culture flourished together and these city-states looked eastwards to Greece rather than northwards to the relatively backward and alien Italian peninsula of which they were geographically a part. The Greeks had also established colonies along the eastern coast of

Sicily, in particular Syracuse, Megara, Naxos and Messina. On the western side of the island a number of Phoenician cities had also been established. These were a mere 200 kilometres from Carthage and within the latter's commercial sphere.

In contrast to this, the opposite end of the peninsula, centring on the valley of the Po, was occupied by Celts who had migrated southwards across the Alps from the upper and middle Danube regions. They were a farming people who lived mainly in villages and had few settlements of any size. Although reaching the shores of the Mediterranean, they did not become part of that Mediterranean culture that centred on city-states, trade and Mediterranean agriculture, which concentrated on the production of the vine and the olive. They remained essentially a north European culture which happened to be located south of the Alps. For them an ample supply of good farmland for crops and animals was of the greatest importance and this had been the main reason for their southwards migration.

In the centre of the peninsula, between the geographical and cultural extremes of north and south, were two other peoples, the Etruscans and the Italii. The Etruscans were on the northern side adjacent to the Celts and the Italii were further south and adjacent to the Greeks. The Etruscans were a Mediterranean people more akin to the Greeks, while the Italii were a north European people who had much in common with the Celts. The origins of the Etruscans remain obscure and have been traced to many parts of Europe. According to Herodotus, they were Lydians who migrated from their homeland at around the time of the Trojan War. There now appears to be a general consensus that their origins were in the eastern Mediterranean and from there they had moved west and established colonies on and around the coasts of Italy to the west of the Apennines. They practised a Mediterranean type of agriculture and engaged in commerce both with other Mediterranean peoples and across the Alps to northern Europe. They established cities, the first of which according to legend was Tarquinii on the river Marta. From the outset, the cities took the form of independent city-states organized into a loose confederation.[1] These cities were built around strongholds on high land that was chosen carefully and was well located for purposes of defence. Most of them were constructed well away from the coasts, and Arretium and Cortona (Curtun) were deep in the interior of the peninsula, some 200 kilometres from the coast. Other important Etruscan cities were Volterra, Clusium, Veii and Perusia, and they formed a distinct cluster enclosed by the rivers Arno and Tiber. In their form of government they were monarchies ruled over by priest-kings who were also the military leaders and the supreme source of authority in the city-state.[2]

From the viewpoint of future political developments, the last of the four groups of people, the Italii, were the most important. Like the Celts, they were an agricultural people engaged in arable and pastoral farming and they had migrated over the Alps from northern Europe. As they moved along the mountainous spine of Italy they sought to occupy and settle the richer lands in river basins such as the Volturno, the Gargliano and the Tiber. They were not principally an urban or trading people and they engaged in only limited trade with their immediate neighbours. They were organized into tribes which occupied areas of land roughly defined by geography. The Latini were the tribe who lived on the western side of the peninsula between Liris and the Tiber. In the Tiber valley these people came into contact with the Etruscans expanding southwards. Thus it was along the Tiber that the Mediterranean city-dwellers came into contact with the hill farmers. The cities of Veii and Caere lay just to the north of the Tiber, which formed a buffer zone against the Italii. In material terms the Etruscans were altogether the more advanced people and they were soon able to secure a position of dominance in the Tiber basin.

It is in this geographically transitional area where two very different cultures came into contact that the origins of Rome are to be found. There is much mythology associated with the beginnings of the city. The traditional date for its foundation was 753 BC, but it seems improbable that this has any more authenticity than does the story of Romulus and Remus. According to the legend, these twins, the sons of Rhea Silvia, were the victims of a dynastic dispute. They were suckled by a wolf and eventually returned to found the city of Rome – of which Romulus became the first king – on the Palatine hill just to the east of the Tiber. However, it seems much more likely that Rome was in fact an Etruscan foundation located in the middle of territory that was farmed by Latin tribes. By the middle of the sixth century BC the city was ruled by the Tarquins, a dynasty of Etruscan kings who had established themselves in the valley of the Tiber. In 510 BC the last of these kings, Tarquinius Superbus, was expelled and the *res publica* came into being. There were to be no more kings and the new government was established along oligarchic lines. Rome had gravitated from the Etruscan sphere into that of the Italii, and a series of wars with the Etruscans was a regular feature of the city's early years of independence. In 493 BC Rome entered into a defensive alliance with the other Latin tribes, and with their support her position gradually strengthened. Her hold over the others became tighter and rebellions by the other tribes against Roman authority were harshly put down. This particularly applied to the warlike Samnites to the south who were not finally defeated until 290 BC. This was followed by the final defeat of the Etruscans in 283 BC, which signalled the beginning of the dominance of Rome over the whole of the central region of Italy. The Romans were now the neighbours of the Greeks in the south and of the Celts in the north. Following the defeat in 275 BC of Pyrrhus, king of Epirus and a would-be Alexander of the west, the whole of the Italian peninsula, including the mainland parts of Magna Graecia, was brought into the Latin League under Roman control. Finally in 264 BC this league was replaced by the Roman state of Italia, which consisted of the whole of the peninsula from the Straits of Messina to the river Rubicon on the southern edge of the basin of the Po.

It was at this point that the Rubicon, an insignificant little river flowing eastwards into the Adriatic, entered history as the northern boundary between the new Italia and the Celtic lands. The Gallia Cisalpina remained part of that northern Celtic world that had more in common with Gallia Transalpina than with the Italian peninsula in which it was geographically located. A territorial state of the size of Italia was something that to the Greeks was far too large to be a state at all. It was on quite a different scale from Attica or even Laconia. While the latter was roughly the size of a modern English region, the new Italia was the size of a modern European nation-state. Such a state could not possibly be considered to be a *polis* in the sense in which the Greeks understood the term. Was Rome, then, ever a true *polis* in the Greek or even in the wider Mediterranean sense?

Rome had actually come into existence at around the same time as the Greek city-states came to maturity. By the fifth century BC, the time of the classic Hellenic *polis*, it had already thrown off Etruscan domination and become an independent state. In this respect it was a city-state quite as independent as was Athens at the time of the Persian Wars. Like Athens, it had removed its kings and established a form of government more in keeping with a city-state. The Senate, the pivotal institution of Roman government, was an oligarchy that drew its membership mainly from the landed aristocracy. The executive was placed in the hands of two consuls who were drawn from the same class. The lower class, the *plebs*, were at first excluded from government but, following civil unrest, concessions were made and the Tribunate of the *plebs* was established in 494 BC. Then in 451 BC a unified legal system for all citizens of Rome, of whatever class, was instituted. In 449 BC a popular assembly, the *concilia plebis*, was established, with a subsidiary decision-making role alongside the Senate. The consulship was opened to the *plebs* in 366 BC and this class was subsequently given the right to own land and property and to be recruited into the army. As Rome rapidly gained ascendancy over the rest of the Latini, the city-state of Rome came to include the whole of Latium. This was a not dissimilar situation to that of the Greek *polis*. Although Latium was considerably larger than Attica, it was not that different in size from Laconia. Rome and Latium were the *asty* and the *chora* that together formed a political, economic and social unit. Thus in the fifth and fourth centuries BC Rome was to all intents and purposes a *polis* as the term was generally understood throughout the Mediterranean world.

This was how Rome had developed in the early centuries of its existence, but it was its subsequent behaviour that increasingly distanced it from the Greek model. This particularly entailed the creation of what was, by the standards of the ancient Mediterranean, a state of enormous dimensions. It was just as though Athens had unified the whole of the Greek

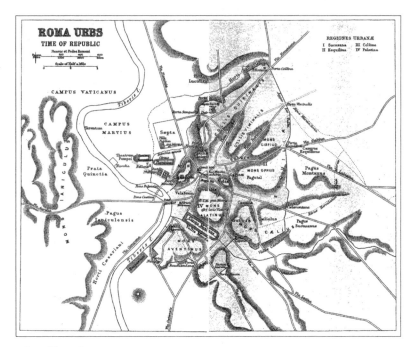

8 Republican Rome.

peninsula around itself, something that it did not come anywhere near to doing, nor would the Greeks have considered this to be at all desirable. The putative Athenian Empire had been a thalassocracy that sought to bind together a group of maritime city-states. Rome, on the other hand, introduced the territorial concept, and territoriality on this scale did not enter into Greek thinking at all. There was clearly a single-mindedness together with an aggressive approach in Rome that fostered such developments. An examination of the geopolitical conditions in which Rome came into being sheds some light on the way in which it subsequently became a very different state from the *polis* of the Greeks.

As has been observed, Rome came into being in that indeterminate frontier region lying between the Etruscans and the Italii. Early Rome was therefore a marchland state and the geopolitical evidence shows that it is in such places that militarism and territorial aggression are most likely to flourish.[3]

This arises from the dangers and uncertainties to which economic and political life is exposed on the periphery of the wider culture areas. The fact that the Italii were essentially a farming people engendered their concern for the importance of territory and their aggressive attitude towards urban peoples. In attempting to gain the support of the other Italii against the common enemy, the heavy-handed methods of the Romans then produced rebellion amongst them. The Romans were confronted by a powerful and economically advanced enemy to the north and equally dangerous enemies in the mountains to the south. The origins of Rome were thus associated closely with the constant need for defence against them both. A singular development then took place. Rome, which had originated within the lands of an agrarian people, itself became larger and more powerful than any of the cities in that Mediterranean city culture that lay to the north of it. The symbiosis of the Etruscan and the Latin cultures appears to have produced a large and impressive city imbued with a strong sense of the value of territory as an adjunct to power.

The initial objective of Rome had been to secure and maintain its independence from the dangers by which it was surrounded, but in so doing it created a large territorial state that gradually eliminated the independence of the other peoples who lived within it. Again this is characteristic of the behaviour of powerful frontier states, but it is the growth of one huge city from which the whole process was generated that is the unique geopolitical contribution of Rome.

From very early on, Rome had been far larger and more powerful than any other town in Latium. It was thus in a unique position to assume the leadership of the Latini and eventually of the Italii as a whole. The Roman oligarchy consisted of landowners whose whole life and culture were bound up with their land rather than the city. It was from the land that they drew their wealth and they generally preferred to spend their time on their extensive rural estates rather than in the cramped and noisy city. They were certainly Romans, but to them Rome was as much a rural as an urban phenomenon. The philosophers of ancient Rome also trumpeted the rural virtues as being the best, while the city with its commerce and its *plebs* was looked down upon as being a kind of necessary evil. To them the city of Rome had initially been little more than a convenient centre for the transaction of political, economic and social business. From the outset Rome had been ruled by country people, and it was the rural philosophy that prevailed among them and which they brought with them to town.

Cato 'the Censor', who was a byword for austerity and puritanism, was the foremost protagonist of the rural virtues. In *De re rustica* he expressed this trenchantly when he observed that 'When our forefathers would praise a worthy man, they praised him as a good husbandman . . . and they believed that praise could go no further.' He then went on to assert that 'Husbandmen make the strongest men, and the bravest soldiers'.[4] Cato had in mind those 'farmer-warriors' whom he saw as being the real basis of both the physical and the moral power of Rome. He was clearly a great admirer of Cincinnatus, a farmer who had lived in the fifth century BC. A former distinguished soldier, Cincinnatus had been 'called from the plough' to help save Rome from the Aequi. He was elected dictator, emerged victorious in battle and, having done his duty, resigned and returned to his small farm. This story demonstrates how from the outset Rome had been imbued with a strong sense of duty based on a fusion of the agricultural and the military traditions. It can be no coincidence that according to legend Rhea Silvia, the mother of Romulus, was the daughter of Mars, the god of war, who was also particularly associated with all things agricultural.

Although in many respects it conformed to the classical idea of the *polis*, the Latin *urbs* was far from having the same connotation as the Greek *polis*. While the term *polis* referred to the whole entity of the city and all its facets, the *urbs* usually referred only to the city as a physical entity. While thus the *polis* was always a city-state, the *urbs* may or may not have been one. While Hellas was imbued with the concept of the city-state as one of their highest achievements and most treasured possessions, this was not the case with Rome. The affection and respect that the Greeks held for the *polis* the Romans reserved for the *re rustica*.

The reality was that Rome did not fit easily into the Greek or any other model. It was a unique geopolitical phenomenon, a fact that both its early behaviour and its subsequent transformation confirm. It represented a fusion of the urban and the rural which gave birth to a city that was in many ways more like a country and a country that was bound up with the fortunes of one city. While the more usual pattern in imperialism was for the country to take over the city as part of its territorial conquest, here the opposite took place and one city, imbibed with rural ideas, itself absorbed the countryside. This was the basis for the great transformation of Rome from *urbs* to *imperium*.

The transformation itself was not actually completed until after another series of wars had extended the control that the Romans exercised over Italia into control over the whole of the western Mediterranean. These were the Punic Wars with the Phoenician city-state of Carthage, and they lasted from 264 to 146 BC. When the first one broke out Rome was still governed as a city-state, the *chora* of which had expanded inordinately to the size of a modern country. When the last of them came to an end Rome was mistress of the western Mediterranean, and within a matter of a few decades had moved into a position of dominance in the east.

The new Roman state of Italia that had been created in 264 BC looked out onto a sea that was dominated by Carthage, some 600 kilometres to the south. Carthage had assumed the position of being the leading city in the Phoenician world after those of the Levant had been absorbed into the Persian Empire. Being heir to a long tradition of Phoenician city-states going back a thousand years, in most fundamental ways Carthage was a more typical Mediterranean city-state than was Rome. First, like the other Phoenician cities, it was a maritime state and the principal basis of its power was its navy. Second, its lifeblood was commerce and this commercial activity had taken its mariners across the Mediterranean and beyond. It certainly possessed most of the important qualities of a *polis*. These included a constitution, and oligarchic government and control over a hinterland that could supply it with its immediate needs. Although the city was nominally a monarchy, real executive power was in the hands of the two *suffetes*, magistrates who were elected annually. There was an aristocratic assembly, which was responsible for legislation, and a popular assembly, which had a largely advisory role.

Even the Greeks recognized the qualities of this form of government, and Aristotle expressed the surprising opinion that 'in many respects it is superior to all others'.[5] There were also a number of Phoenician cities along the adjacent coasts, important among which were Hippo Regius, Hippo Diarrhytus, Utica and Hadrumetum. All of them had the political structures of city-states, but Carthage was recognized as being the mother city that exercised control over important matters such as trading arrangements and foreign relations. Carthage had usually exercised this position of hegemony with tact and there had been little real attempt to transform it into a large and centralized state after the manner of Rome.

Thus while the new Roman Italia was basically a land state established and sustained by military power, Carthage was a sea state established and sustained by trade and protected by its navy. Rome rapidly reached the conclusion that maritime power and trade were essential prerequisites to the increase of its wealth and the further consolidation of its power. As a consequence of this the next stage in its development entailed its entering more fully into the maritime affairs of the Mediterranean. Given that Rome looked out onto a sea which was in effect a Carthaginian lake, this policy decision by the Roman oligarchy made conflict with Carthage inevitable.

As a result of this, a strange replay of the old Greek–Phoenician conflict then took place in the western Mediterranean with the increasingly Hellenized Romans confronting the heirs to the Phoenician trading empire. A hundred years of war ensued between the sea state and the land state. Eventually it was the land state that triumphed and, like Sparta before it, it did so by becoming amphibious. The initial spectacular triumph of Hannibal in Italy during the Second Punic War was converted into defeat when his army was cut off from Carthage by the Roman fleet. The Romans were then able to launch an attack by sea on Carthage itself, and, when it came, the defeat of the city was absolute. By the end of the Second Punic War in 201 BC the western Mediterranean had been transformed from a Carthaginian into a Roman lake. Stripped of its naval and commercial hegemony, Carthage was reduced to being a city-state perched uncomfortably on the edge of the expanding Roman sphere. Even after this drastic reduction in the power of its rival, the war party in Rome, led by Cato, insisted that the gravely weakened Carthage still presented a danger. Cato's admonition to action, 'Delenda est Carthago', became the slogan of the war party, and in the end this was converted into official Roman policy. In 146 BC Carthage was again attacked and this time finally defeated. The city was completely razed to the ground, and subsequently a new Roman city was constructed where it had once been. Rome, blooded by success, immediately struck eastwards in pursuit of other real or imagined threats and within a matter of decades had occupied the rest of the Mediterranean. The imperial republic had come into being.

The Punic Wars completely changed Rome from being essentially the unifier of Italia to being the unifier of the whole of the Mediterranean. The *Mare internum* of the ancient world became the *Mare nostrum* of the Romans, an extended homeland in which Rome increasingly acted with an authority born of confidence. There were two factors that lay behind this total transformation. First, the belief that the only way to achieve real security was not just the defeat but the complete elimination of the enemy. This was the message of Cato, who also felt that the purity of Rome could best be secured by the elimination of an enemy that he deemed to be impure. In the justification for what was done, Rome pointed to the primitive barbarity of the Carthaginian religion and the child sacrifice that it entailed.[6] From the beginning the frontier state of Rome had faced a succession of external dangers and the conclusion was reached that danger had to be confronted with overwhelming force. Like Sparta before it, or Prussia in modern times, Rome's frontiers had become her armies and this fact underlay the increasing militarization of the state. Second, there was the realization that trade was a more effective producer of wealth than was agriculture and that to be really successful Rome had therefore to enter fully into the Mediterranean commercial world. Until then its oligarchy had broadly subscribed to the belief that land was power. This came to be replaced by a new belief that trade was power. However, when Rome did become fully a part of the Mediterranean world it did so after the conclusion of a successful series of wars against a maritime power that had sought to exclude all rivals. Rome therefore came as conqueror rather than as participant, and this fostered the belief that economic security was also dependent on the achievement of domination and the elimination of all competition. Born in the plains of Latium, the urban part of the Roman system had nurtured trade and the rural part had nurtured militarism. The two came together on a massive scale after the conclusion of the Punic Wars to achieve domination over *Mare nostrum* and then the world.

A second and more powerful symbiosis had also taken place that heralded the death of the *polis* and the birth of the new *imperium*. In this it was the rural element that gained the upper hand politically and, through this, it was territory and territoriality that prevailed. The philosophy of the rural virtues became the basis for the philosophy of imperialism. The *re rustica* virtues of strength, bravery, good management and concern for the interests of others were harnessed to the desire to dominate and the ability to bring this about. In the achievement of this the hybrid qualities that the city had inherited from its earlier history come to the fore: the military state had taken to the sea and the agricultural state had taken to commerce. Above all the territoriality that was inherent in the ownership of land was transformed into the territoriality of the ownership of a whole continent. The lands around the Mediterranean, and subsequently also northern Europe, became a great estate to be used and exploited for the benefit of Rome. For the oligarchy that ruled Rome, the *urbs Romana* had been transformed from a city-state into a base of operations and the centre of the control mechanism for the achievement and retention of world power. Initially the *imperium* had been the authority granted by the Senate to the *magistrati*, the high officials of the Roman state, for the performance of certain specific tasks in its name. Having done so, these *magistrati* were then summoned to report back to the Senate in Rome in order to receive fresh orders or to have their authority renewed. However, in the areas now conquered and administered by Rome, the *imperium* became virtually unlimited for those who held it. *Imperium* had become both the idea and the reality of life. It was only in Italia itself that the *imperium* was restricted and civil government and law, the *jus civile*, prevailed.

The legal transformation of Rome from city-state to empire was activated by the situation in those conquered territories, the *provinciae*, in which a virtually unimpeded *imperium* came to prevail. While in practice a transformation had taken place in the aftermath of the Punic Wars, the legal transformation was not accomplished until a century later. Meanwhile the *res publica* steadily moved into an imperial mode and this was brought about by events that took place not only outside Italy but outside the Mediterranean world itself. In the year 120 BC Provincia, the first Roman province in Gaul, had been established as a Roman toehold on the edge of the barbarian Gallia Transalpina. Provincia then became the principal base of operations for the Roman conquest of the lands to the north. This conquest centred on Gaul, which was a rich and populous Celtic land, and its possession added greatly to the human and physical resources that Rome had at its disposal. It also added considerably to the territory ruled in an authoritarian manner by *imperium* and thus to the importance of the holder of this particular *imperium*, the commanding general, Julius Caesar. As in the early history of Rome, the frontiers again came to play a crucial part in the nature and development of the state.

The Senate had for long been increasingly perturbed by the steady erosion of its power and in particular by the way in which the holders of the *imperium*, which the Senate had itself bestowed, had come to possess virtually unlimited powers over the conquered territories. The whole question of the government of the vast possessions that Rome had acquired was a vexed one, and oligarchy and authoritarianism were finely balanced in the power struggles that racked the city. In the year 50 BC Julius Caesar, by then the conqueror of Gaul, was recalled to Rome. The Senate had made a rule that no general was allowed to cross the Rubicon river into Italy proper at the head of his army. When recalled he was expected to do so not as a general leading an army but as the servant of the Senate. As such he was obliged to enter Rome alone. However, in the year 49 BC Caesar defied the Senate's ruling with epoch-making consequences. He led his army southwards and crossed the Rubicon with a full military accompaniment. By doing this he threw down a deliberate challenge not only to the authority of the Senate but to the Republic itself. The result of this was a civil war in which Caesar emerged triumphant. Authoritarian government was established and the power of the Senate was much diminished. The authoritarian forces engendered by the *imperium* had challenged and defeated the oligarchic and democratic forces of the Republic. The latter, however, were not extinguished and five years later a group of Senators led by the fiercely republican Marcus Brutus assassinated Caesar in the house where the Senate was meeting, and Rome was once more plunged into a prolonged civil war. During this time Caesar's heir Octavian rose to power and in the year 27 BC styled himself Augustus Caesar. The Senate then accorded him the title of *princeps* together with an unlimited *imperium* over the whole of the Roman world. This was the *imperium maius* and its holder was styled *imperator*. By the beginning of the Christian era, Rome, authoritarian, militaristic and bloated with its vast conquests, had finally abandoned the last vestiges of the city-state that it once had been.

The world into which Rome emerged triumphant had become untidy with a mixture of different types of states, large and small. However, basically it was still a world in which versions of the city-state were the pre-eminent political forms. The eastern Mediterranean into which the Romans had moved following the defeat of Carthage remained the centre of this city culture and was above all the area in which the Greeks still retained their pre-eminence. When the Roman Empire came into existence the great cities lying along the Hellenistic axis from Egypt to the Aegean were still the most important centres of wealth and civilization, and this was the world over which Rome sought to establish its control.

Just after Rome had secured her position of dominance, the Hellenistic axis, and indeed the whole of the eastern Mediterranean, underwent a fundamental cultural upheaval that was to have widespread political and economic repercussions. This was the arrival on the scene of Christianity as both a religious and political force. Jesus Christ had been born in the Kingdom of Herod, which during the reign of the Emperor

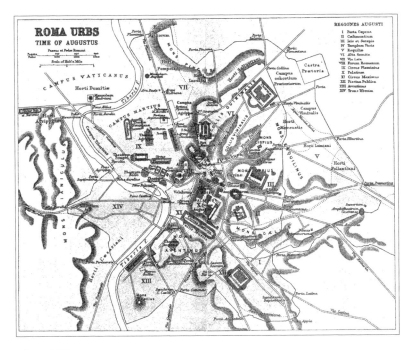

9 Imperial Rome.

Augustus became the Roman province of Judaea. Within a quarter of a century of the death of the first emperor, the Christian message was being widely disseminated by St Paul, a Judaeo-Greek from Tarsus. The extent of Paul's missionary journeys are an indication of the nature of the world of his day and of the most important cities within it. His activities, as revealed in the Epistles and the Acts, took him particularly to Antioch, Tarsus, Miletus, Ephesus, Thessaloniki, Corinth and Athens.[7] These cities were all located either on the Hellenistic axis or around the Aegean Sea. It is significant that most of them were Hellenistic foundations or re-foundations, and clearly it was this Greek world that mattered most to Paul and which he addressed in the Epistles. While Paul could boast of his Roman citizenship, the world with which he was most familiar was that of the Greeks, and this was also the strongest external influence on the Roman Empire. Paul's final Epistle was to the Romans and it was on the centre of the empire that the early Christian missionaries inevitably converged. The eventual conversion of Rome shifted the cultural epicentre of the ancient world westwards and a new axis came into being. Thus Empire and Christianity rose in tandem out of the ruins of Hellenistic civilization and Christianity eventually took over from Empire. After the fall of the Roman Empire, Rome became the centre of the Christian world, the ultimate destination of the missionary activities of Peter and Paul and the 'Rock' on which the Church was built. The papal messages prefaced by the announcement 'de urbis ad orbis' demonstrate the continued role of the great city no longer as imperial capital but as one of the great centres of the Christian world.

From the outset, the Romans had been highly influenced by the Greeks with whom they had first come into contact in Magna Graecia. Here it was that the Romans first encountered the great civilization of the Mediterranean and, more specifically, the city-state in the Greek sense of the term. From then on the Romans took every opportunity to embrace all things Greek. Greek art, architecture, philosophy, religion and many aspects of government were taken on board and became part of what was to become a shared Hellenic inheritance. Even after Greece was, in Gibbon's phrase, 'reduced to a province' of the Roman Empire, the Romans persisted in their great respect for the cultural and intellectual power of the conquered.[8] In Horace's words, 'Graecia capta ferum victorem cepit et artes intulit agresti Latio' ('Greece, taken captive, captured her savage conqueror, and carried her arts into clownish Latium').[9] The arts brought by the Greeks certainly included the art of government, and a Roman version of the *polis* became almost as central to their political concepts as it had been to the Greeks themselves.

As with the Macedonians before them, one of the purposes that the Romans had in moving into Greece was the restoration of the great civilization to its former glory and, as with Alexander, this included the city-states. Wherever city institutions were still in existence in the Hellenistic world the official Roman policy was to revive them. After the arrival of the Romans, local officials and councils continued with their tasks and local magistrates continued to administer their laws. The first empire had been, after all, a republican empire ruled by the city fathers of Rome in the name of its people. The *imperium* was bestowed by the Senate, or more precisely the 'Senatus Populusque Romanus', and this collective identity remained notionally at least the ultimate authority. After the Punic Wars, with Rome now mistress of the Mediterranean, there had been a widespread belief that this system could and should continue. After all, in the eye of the law, the holders of the *imperium* were simply magistrates of the city-state of Rome and it was Rome that dispensed the *imperium* and not the other way around. Cicero, the Roman Demosthenes, believed firmly in the concept of the city-state and in the adaptation of the old institutions to Rome's new role. He had been educated in Athens and had introduced Greek philosophical ideas to the Romans. He was as firmly convinced as Aristotle of the virtue of the Greek *polis*, and he used the term *civitas* rather than *urbs* to convey its meaning. He believed that it was the best vehicle for virtuous government in the wider interest and the achievement of *concordia* among all classes of society.[10] According to Ciceronian thinking, the destiny of the Roman *civitas* was to be the leader of a world of *civitates*.

In accordance with this idea, to which Augustus in principle also subscribed, Rome began to found its own cities in the newly conquered lands, and this involved the Ciceronian idea of the *civitas*. The first of these cities lay immediately to the north of the Rubicon in Gallia Cisalpina, which was the first of the conquered territories into which Rome introduced the Mediterranean city culture. Following the Social War from 91 to 88 BC, Rome extended citizenship to all who lived in Italia up to the line of the river Po. The first new Roman foundations began to appear there during the second century BC and they included Bonoma, Mutina, Parma, Placentia and Eporedia. In these new additions to Italia, together with adjacent Provincia and Spain, what Fowler termed 'miniature Romes' grew up equipped with the accoutrements of Roman civilization, including baths, theatres and civic buildings.[11] However, these were all constructed to a pattern and had a quality of uniformity about them that was far from the diversity of the Greek *polis*. After Rome had conquered territories on the other side of the

Alps, much the same took place there. Everywhere in these newly acquired territories cities were founded that became the centres of Roman civilization in much the same way as Alexander and the *Diadochoi* had founded their cities in the east. However, in this new Roman world the foundations also became centres of imperial power to a far greater extent than had taken place in the Hellenistic world after Alexander. Narbo Martius (Narbonne), Lugdunum (Lyons), Burdigala (Bordeaux), Durocortorum (Reims) and Colonia Agrippina (Cologne) became the provincial capitals of the newly conquered lands in Gaul, and in the three provinces of Iberia, Tarraco (Tarragona), Hispalis (Seville) and Emerita-Augusta (Merida) fulfilled similar functions. Clearly such places could not be considered as being in any real sense city-states. The *urbs*, while identified with Latin refinement and civilization, was far from possessing anything like the political connotations of the *polis*. The *civitas*, the urban community, took on the meaning of municipality. The citizenship of which St Paul was so proud was bestowed by the Roman Empire and not by the cities that he visited. The really significant units into which the Roman Empire was divided were not the cities but those *provinciae* within which they were located. These retained the connotation of conquered territories and thus it was conquest and not freedom that lay at the heart of the Roman imperial administration. The cherished liberties of the Greek cities in the east were in no way reflected in the new Roman foundations in the west. The principal role of these foundations was as centres of trade, industry, social life and local government within the empire. Their municipal administration was a far more humble and limited one than the government of a sovereign state. Just as the tools of empire had been forged out of the conquest of the west, so the model for the new urban geography of the Empire was also created in the west and the *polis* in the Greek sense never became a part of this.

Meanwhile, whatever independence the cities of the east continued to possess was subject to the overall authority of Rome. A few of them maintained their status as the allies of Rome and their limited freedom was guaranteed by individual treaties. But these were few and far between and the great majority were firmly under Roman control. 'The real life of the *polis* was now everywhere extinct or rapidly passing away', observed Fowler of the situation by the first century BC, 'The bodily appearance was there, but the spirit had departed.'[12] Slowly but steadily it was being crushed out under the massive weight of the *imperium*. Roman law and government also replaced the old local laws and finally in the third century AD the Emperor Caracalla introduced a single legal system throughout the Empire. By then the once proud cities of the east had themselves also been demoted to being the municipal towns of an empire, and the Hellenistic axis of cities was replaced by a radial system of communications centring on Rome. By then all roads indeed led to Rome. Despite the hopes of republicans like Cicero, in the end *polis* and *imperium* could not really coexist.

In this way, observed Fowler, 'one city-state had sucked the blood out of all the rest, and had herself lost her ancient statehood in the gigantic effort'.[13] At some point in the political process initiated by Rome the world in which the independent city-states had played so central a role had given place to a world in which Rome ruled alone. Although the *Senatus Populusque Romanus* continued to be notionally the collective ultimate authority, it had become but a shadow of its former self. With the bestowing of the *imperium maius* on Augustus power had shifted definitively and permanently elsewhere. It was now vested in a single individual and from then on the real centre of power was not even in Rome but wherever the emperor happened to reside at any particular time. From the second century AD the emperors became increasingly peripatetic and the centre of power moved in accordance with the location of the particular issues with which they were faced. Even the city of Rome itself had become increasingly marginalized, any importance that it had left being largely at the whim of the emperor. Some emperors rarely visited the capital at all, and in the fourth century the Emperor Constantine, who converted the Empire to Christianity, abandoned the city completely and built his new 'Christian capital' on the shores of the Bosporus.

Half a century later the Emperor Theodosius, faced with increasing problems on the frontiers, divided the Empire into two parts. The capital of the western part was not Rome but

Mediolanum (Milan) beyond the Rubicon in the former Gallia Cisalpina. The eastern capital and – officially at least – the over-all capital of the Empire, was the new city of Constantinople. From the outset this had been intended to be an imperial city and, despite being built on the old Greek city of Byzantium, there was never any connotation of *polis* attached to it. As its final collapse approached, the Roman Empire – philhellene to the last – had finally transformed itself into a Greek state. In so doing, it took on most of the external trappings of Greek civilization but few of its essentials. The *polis*, regarded by Aristotle and Plato as being one of its most essential features, was more completely absent than ever before. Yet paradoxically Constantinople, the site of which was said to have been chosen by Constantine in response to the commands of Heaven, was built on the site of a city that had itself in earlier times been a *polis*. This was to be Rome's final transformation. The city-state that had destroyed all the others was itself destroyed by the forces that it had unleashed. Gibbon expressed the opinion that 'the decline of Rome was the natural and inevitable effect of immoderate greatness . . . the stupendous fabric yielded to the pressure of its own weight',[14] while Schneider observed that 'In the long run the mayor of Rome was overtaxed if he was expected to rule the world, even though he bore the title of emperor.'[15]

It was perhaps the end of the Roman Republic that marked the real end of the city-states of antiquity. Their most character-istic feature had been that they were in all things intensely local. In the widest sense they were all part of *Hellas*, but their govern-ment, their laws, their arts, their ideas and their gods sprang from the soil on which they were built and were never imposed upon them from above. They were constructed on a human scale and they were about humanity and its needs in a way in which an empire could never be. The world of the *polis* was a diverse one and it produced an environment that was congenial to new thinking and to the birth of new ideas. In it mankind moved forward over a wide range of activities. This spirit was encapsulated in the Greek *philosophia*, the love of knowledge. In contrast to this, Rome eventually imposed its will over virtually all things and in so doing created a uniform and centralized world in which local freedom was sacrificed to the attainment and retention of power. In respect of the city-state, at least, it was the spirit of 'clownish Latium' that triumphed over 'the education of Hellas'.

It was some time before city-states again made their appearance on the political map of Europe, and their re-emergence began in that same peninsula in which a thousand years earlier one city-state had embarked upon the destruction of all the others. By that time the Roman Empire was gone and Rome itself was already in an advanced state of decay. At a later time Gibbon sat musing on the fall of Rome in the ruins of the Capitol and reflected that the great building had been 'so named as being the head of the world; where the consuls and senators formerly resided for the government of the city and the globe'.[16] He bemoaned those 'vicissitudes of fortune . . . which bury empires and cities in a common grave'.[17] While it was true that the Roman Empire was by then long in its grave, many of those cities that Rome had itself buried had risen again as independent states in the post-Roman world.

Serenissima: Venice and the City-States of the Adriatic

It was to be 500 years after the assumption of the *imperium maius* by Augustus Caesar in 27 BC before a really independent city-state again made its appearance in the Mediterranean. This was Venice, which arose among the unpromising swamps, islands and sandbanks at the head of the Adriatic Sea. While according to Jan Morris, Venice 'was born out of the fall of Rome',[1] Henri Pirenne saw it in a slightly different way as being 'a survival from the Roman world'.[2] By the time of its foundation the Roman Empire in the west had little more than a nominal existence, and in AD 476, within a few decades of its foundation, the last emperor, Romulus Augustulus, had been deposed and sent into exile in Naples. He had taken refuge at Ravenna on the Adriatic coast, and the last imperial capital was therefore only some 100 kilometres to the south of Venice. The last legitimate holder of the *imperium* had finally sought refuge beyond the Rubicon on the inhospitable coasts of the former Gallia Cisalpina.

Various dates have been associated with the actual foundation of Venice, but according to the Venetian tradition it was AD 421 when the first arrivals came from Patavium (Padua) some 20 kilometres inland. This traditional date is viewed by Norwich as being 'more plausible than authentic'.[3] Schneider focuses on the year AD 452 and attributes its foundation to the Hun invasion of the previous year when the first inhabitants had 'fled from the onrushing equestrian hordes of Attila'.[4] Whatever may be the truth about the exact date, the first Venetii were certainly from the cities of northern Italy which had become increasingly vulnerable to the onslaught of the barbarian hordes since the arrival of the marauding Goths just after

AD 400. It seems likely that most of the first inhabitants were from Aquileia close to modern Trieste, which was one of the first places to be attacked by the Goths. Its people then took refuge on the islands around the northern coasts of the Adriatic where they felt relatively safe from further attack. The whole of this stretch of coast is bounded by sandbanks called *lidi*, spits, lagoons and islands formed by deposited material from the deltas of rivers, especially from the Padus (Po) itself, which reaches the sea about 50 kilometres to the south. Venice came into being in what Ruskin termed 'a crowded cluster of islands' in the middle of 'a shallow lakelet [in] a great belt of sediment'.[5] Life was hard: there was no fresh water and even the most basic agriculture was virtually impossible. The only abundance was from the sea and there was plenty of fish and salt. Cassiodorus is said to have referred to these early lagoon-dwellers as being all salt-workers and sea-carriers.[6] Out of necessity, the first Venetians looked to the sea to provide for their needs and they were not to be disappointed.

While the site of the new settlement was relatively safe from the barbarian hordes that were ravaging most of northern Italy, its location in relation to the surrounding lands made its safety far more questionable. It was only a relatively short distance west of the Theodosian Line that since AD 395 had divided the Roman Empire into two halves and was in the indeterminate area which was for long contested between them. Considering himself to be the true heir to the Empire, the Byzantine emperor Justinian (527–65) embarked upon the reconquest of the west and brought the whole of the Italian peninsula back into the Empire. Thus while the initial objective of the Venetians had been to secure protection from the barbarians, the main danger to their independence actually came from the Byzantines. A Byzantine governor was installed on the Rialto, the largest of the islands, and the emperor demanded recognition of Byzantine sovereignty. According to the heroic Venetian tradition, the reply to this was 'No emperor and no prince can touch us here. We have raised this city ourselves from the lagoons'.[7] Soon after this the Venetians proclaimed a republic and announced that 'Venice is subject only to God'. In 726 comes the first record of a head of state, the Doge. St Mark the

Evangelist was chosen to be the patron saint, his relics being brought from Alexandria and interred in the church of San Marco in 829. Meanwhile, the first bishop of Venice had been installed on nearby Jessolo island.

By the end of the first millennium, Venice had become the largest and most prosperous city in Europe after Byzantium itself. This was due more to the Venetians being sea-carriers than salt-workers, although salt for the preservation of fish and other foodstuffs was of importance. It was in that same year that the first of the great festivals that became the *Sposalizio del mar*, the marriage to the sea, took place. Doge Orseolo ii, invested with the holy relics of St Hermagoras, the first bishop of Aquileia and disciple of St Mark, was proclaimed *Dux Dalmatiae*. He then sailed down the Adriatic to receive the fealty of the Dalmatian cities. Later the ceremony became more elaborate and included the casting of a propitiatory golden ring into the waters. From the beginning the sea had provided protection and sustenance, and subsequently it went on to provide more wealth than the first beleaguered inhabitants could ever have dreamed of.

As a city, Venice was unique in a number of ways. Unlike most of the cities of northern Italy that had survived until that time, it had not originally been a Roman foundation. It was not a revived old city but something quite new that had come into existence as the ancient world was falling apart. Also, unlike other cities that were protected by city walls, Venice had none. 'Its floor is the sea . . . and its walls are the flow of its waters' wrote Larner evocatively.[8] It was this peripheral and perilous location that guaranteed its freedom and from the very beginning helped to make it the most independent of city-states. It was thus quite different from those many cities that had survived the fall of the Roman Empire only then to be absorbed into the territories of its successors, the barbarian kingdoms. In 800 a new Roman Empire had been established with its centre north of the Alps and with the Frankish king Charles as its first emperor. By that time Venice had its own institutions of government and its independence was an established fact. In Schneider's opinion freedom was impossible on the mainland, while on the inhospitable islands and sandbanks of the northern

Adriatic it flourished as it had not done since before the Roman or Macedonian empires came into existence.[9]

While the city's site was a safe one, it might have seemed to be economically unpropitious. However, its location at the head of the Adriatic between west and east gave it an unrivalled opportunity for trade between the two. It had easy access to Constantinople, the principal western terminus of the trade routes from the east, while the Adriatic formed a maritime corridor leading to the Alps and the heart of western Europe. Located between the sea and the Alps, Venice was well able to conduct trade with the emerging Transalpine world via the Adriatic and the Brenner Pass. Although militarily strong, in material terms this world was relatively poor and backward and it was Venice that began to change this by supplying it with the products brought along the Silk Route. In this way Venice rose to become a city of great wealth and power, and attained the position of being the leading centre of the new commercial economy that was coming into being by the eleventh century.[10]

Most fundamentally, Venice was located in an intermediate position within that longitudinal strip of territory in which the boundary between the western and eastern empires continually oscillated. As the post-Roman world stabilized, its peripheral location changed from disputed frontier to connecting link. Its early trade was overwhelmingly with Byzantium, for which it acted as a kind of western base, and in which it established the first of its many trading bases or *fondachi*. 'In reality Venice belonged to the west only by her geographical location', maintained Pirenne, 'in the life that animated her and the spirit that inspired her, she was foreign to it'.[11] Many aspects of Venetian history and culture bear this out. St Mark was from Jerusalem via Alexandria, and Venice's most potent symbols, the winged lions of St Mark, are of eastern origin. According to Morris, the Piazzo San Marco is 'unmistakably an expatriated Byzantine forum' and its most famous architecture, such as its churches and the Doge's Palace, displays strong Byzantine influences.[12]

However, when it came to it, Venice made the choice to remain a part of the western world. In the Great Schism of 1054 Venice took the decision to stay within the Roman Catholic sphere rather than to take the Greek Orthodox road of the

Byzantine Empire. Venice then participated in the First Crusade in 1096, which heralded the beginning of trade with the Levant which from then on became its lifeblood and made Venice more independent of the Byzantine connection. It is significant that in 1177 Venice was chosen to be the place in which the great reconciliation between the Emperor Frederick Barbarossa and Pope Alexander III took place. It was acknowledged to be an independent state and furthermore was neutral ground. While to the Venetians, pope and emperor were both suspect and almost equally dangerous to the liberty of their Republic, they found it flattering to be, albeit briefly, the diplomatic centre of Europe. The meeting was hosted by Doge Sebastiano Ziani and was, in Norwich's view, one of the greatest days in Venetian history. The signing of the treaty between the two leaders of Christendom was accompanied by one of those displays of pageantry for which the city had already become famous. It inaugurated the entry of Venice into European politics as a 'power' in its own right. Subsequently the Venetian ambassadors culled information from the courts of Europe and the Venetian intelligence service gleaned invaluable knowledge that was then put at the disposal of the city's merchants. Venice was intimately involved with the Fourth Crusade of 1202, and as a result of the city's financial pulling power was able to engineer its diversion to Constantinople. The whole Crusade was financed by Venice, which supplied the ships and equipment and paid the soldiers who attacked and toppled the Byzantine Empire. Doge Enrico Dandolo made a ceremonial entry by sea into the port, and shortly after a Venetian quarter was established in the city. Subsequently the Venetian gold ducat replaced the Byzantine solidus as Europe's principal trading currency. Venice, *la Dominante*, now controlled the trade of the eastern Mediterranean and the Venetians established *fondachi* in all its principal ports.

Yet despite its naval, political and above all economic success, Venice never sought to become the new Rome. Territorial domination of that kind was not in the nature of this commercial state. From the outset its lifeblood was trade and the city remained above all a community of merchants. Success was always expressed more vigorously in ceremony and in artistic and architectural splendour than in territorial acquisition. Gordon East put the Venetian perspective clearly when he stressed that

> Venice had no intention . . . of involving itself in the difficulties of ruling large land areas. The republic was dominated essentially by maritime and commercial ambitions, and its superior knowledge of geography indicated clearly the relative value of different lands. Therefore it abandoned many of these territories in return for trade privileges within them, and retained in its own hands only those parts that would strengthen its commerce and could be effectively held by sea-power.[13]

Larner wrote that 'Merchandise flows through this noble city as water through fountains'[14] and the merchants fostered and cherished those freedoms on which their prosperity was seen to be based.

As part of this whole process, the powers of the Doge were gradually whittled down and his main role became eventually to preside over the great ceremonies of state. The real rulers of Venice were and remained that merchant class that had first established its power in the early centuries. From the outset these *nobili cittadini*, the 'merchant princes', kept a watchful eye on the Doge. In 1172 the *Maggior Consiglio* came into being, drawn entirely from the *nobili*, and this became the seat of all authority. Since the *Consiglio* was very large and met only infrequently, the *Pregadi* was set up, drawn from the membership of the *Consiglio*, in order to deal with the day to day business of the state. The *Collegio*, chaired by the Doge himself, was the executive that actually conducted the affairs of state. However, despite these various institutions, it was the *Minor Consiglio*, or *Signoria*, that was the real pinnacle of power in Venice. This had originally been set up for the purpose of keeping a watchful eye on the Doge. The influential Council of Ten was an extension of this and the Doge and the *Signoria* were always members of it. Established by the *Maggior Consiglio* in 1310 for the purpose of preserving the liberty and peace of the subjects of the Republic and to protect them from the abuses of personal power, the executive power of the state became more and more concentrated into its hands.[15] Like the consuls of the Roman Republic, the councillors held office for one year only. Many of those who held the office of Doge, such as Pietro Orseolo II, Sebastiano Ziani, Michele Steno, Tomaso Mocenigo and the triumphant Enrico Dandolo, were what Ruskin called 'hero princes' who contributed in no mean way to the power and prosperity of their city. Their activities always came under close scrutiny by the members of the *Minor Consiglio* who surrounded them. In 1355 Doge Marin Falier attempted to become *principe*, a route that had been followed by the Emperor Augustus in his bid for the attainment of absolute power. Falier was arrested, tried and executed in front of the Doge's Palace.

At the other end of the political spectrum, the mass of the people was accorded little say in the affairs of the state. A general convocation, the *arengo*, had existed in the earliest times but this fell into disuse and was abolished early in the fifteenth century. The specific interests of the various crafts and occupations came to be looked after by the *arti* and the *scuole* rather than by direct participation in government.

Venice was thus a true city-state to perhaps a greater extent than had been any city in the Italian peninsula since the days of Magna Graecia over a thousand years earlier. From the beginning it had asserted its independence from the territorial powers of west and east, and its maritime location, together with its mastery of the seas, enabled it to assert and maintain this independence over the centuries. Its external freedom was complemented by internal liberties. There was no Inquisition; there was freedom of conscience and expression; and the *Signoria* rarely applied the death sentence. In the sixteenth century the French traveller Jacques de Villamont described this when he expressed the opinion that

> there is nowhere in all Italy where one may live in greater liberty . . . first because the Signoria rarely condemns a man to death, secondly arms are not forbidden, third there is no inquisition in matters of faith, lastly everyone lives as he pleases in freedom of conscience.[16]

While Venice never became a tyranny, and representative government took a number of different forms during the long history of the Republic, the *nobili cittadini* invariably remained firmly in charge. Clarke expressed the opinion that

> Venice seemed to be balanced at a point halfway between monarchy and popular government; the balance was so sure and delicate that the Doge never became a tyrant and the Councils never became democratic . . . Venice, owing to its especially favourable political and economic conditions, was the archetype of oligarchic government.[17]

A basic difference between Venice and the ancient Greek *polis* was that it did not initially have a *chora* in the Hellenic sense of a rural hinterland. The early Republic was firmly anti-territorial and its very existence was based on distancing itself from the territories and territorialism of the mainland. However, by the thirteenth century this had changed and Venice had acquired its own small territorial base across the lagoon. An important reason for this was the defence both of the flourishing city itself and of the trade routes that led into the interior. As with other city-states it also provided a secure supply of the foodstuffs required by the people of the growing city. Yet Venice never embarked upon the acquisition of territory for its own sake. Venetia remained of relatively modest dimensions, usually far nearer the size of Attica than Italia. Although after 1400, during the period following the conquest of the eastern Mediterranean by the Ottoman Empire, Venice did become somewhat more territorial, particularly in respect to its trading empire in the Adriatic and the eastern Mediterranean, the city was never overwhelmed by its territory as had happened with Rome. The reality was that, in contrast to the triumphalism of much of the ceremonial connected with the *Serenissima*, the Venetian sphere was actually bound together in quite a loose confederal way. The cities of Verona, Vicenza and Padua were 'received' into the Republic by the Doge. They were required to make no formal submission and their heads of state, the rectors, continued to swear to uphold their own historic liberties and institutions.

10 *Serenissima*: Venice and her rulers in the sixteenth century.

Venice was also in the tradition of the city-state in its essential globalism, and the much acclaimed Venetian 'superior knowledge of geography' was less territorial than global. The main objective of Venetian geography was to paint the broad picture and in so doing to assess the relative values of different lands. In the age of the medieval *mappamundi*, the main purpose of which was to guide the faithful to the next world rather than to increase their knowledge of this one, it was Venetian traders who began the long process of rediscovering the true nature of world geography. In the thirteenth century, Marco Polo, together with his father Niccolo and his uncle Maffeo, all members of the Venetian merchant class, became the most famous initiators of a process of discovery that was to be continued over the centuries. The fifteenth-century world map by the Venetian monk Fra Mauro, while seemingly in the *mappamundi* tradition, actually had real geography injected into it and began the conversion of the world map from a religious icon into a representation of geographical reality.

Here we see Venice linking the ancient and the modern by precociously embarking on those developments that were to change the face of Europe. For many centuries the city retained its uniqueness and for nearly half a millennium it maintained its commercial pre-eminence. By the time this came to an end in the fifteenth century, the uniqueness was gone and Venice had become one city-state in a world of many. The Renaissance was above all about the rediscovery of the ancient world and one of the most important of these rediscoveries was the city-state itself. It was Venice which introduced the ancient *polis* to the new Europe that was then coming into being, and versions of the *polis*, in many different forms, were to become familiar features of the European scene during the coming centuries.

It was said that Venice was 'Byzantium's favourite daughter',[18] but the great Republic also produced its own daughters. The security of the main Venetian maritime trading route through the Adriatic was always one of the city's principal preoccupations. Ports and forts were built along its coasts and the Venetian sphere of influence spread along it and out into the eastern Mediterranean. By the fourteenth century much of the coast of Dalmatia and many of the Greek islands including the large island of Crete had become part of a Venetian commercial empire that dominated the eastern Mediterranean. Many of the settlements within this empire were to become city-states in their own right, and this was nowhere more so than along the Adriatic coast. Important port cities in this area included Zara, Spalato and Durazzo but the most important of them all was Ragusa. While for much of its history this city was part of the Venetian sphere of influence, it eventually moved into a position in which it was able to shake off Venetian control and assert its independence. In so doing it made its own special contribution to the revival of the city-state in the Mediterranean world.

Ragusa, now Dubrovnik, came into existence in much the same manner as Venice but some 200 years later. The official year of its foundation was 656 and, like Venice, it owed its origins to people fleeing from the barbarians. The first inhabitants came from the nearby Roman cities of Salona and Epidaurus (Cavtat) on the Dalmatian coast. They were seeking refuge from the Avars who had moved from the east and by then were in occupation of the middle Danube region. Built on a rocky stretch of coast, thanks to its remote and protected location it was able to maintain its independence during those dangerous early centuries. According to a papal bull of 1433, the city of Ragusa was 'situated on a hard rock, on the coast of the sea and therefore exposed to its ire and in a most sterile land'.[19] Early on it adopted a form of government that involved the citizen body and there is evidence of the existence of early forms of democracy.[20] Its patron saint was Stephen, the first Christian martyr, and the city is known to have become the site of the archbishopric of Dalmatia.

When it lost its early independence it was to the great city-state at the head of the Adriatic, rather than to the aggressive land powers that menaced its immediate hinterland. In the year 1000 it made official submission to Venice at that first of those great *Sposalizio del mar* intended to demonstrate the hegemony of the Most Serene Republic, and a Venetian count was subsequently installed as its head of state.[21] Venice accorded Ragusa a large measure of internal self-government within the overall Venetian sphere and the role of the count was to look after Venetian interests in the city. However, by the twelfth century we learn that the counts had become tyrannical and in 1152 the last of them was evicted by the Ragusans.[22]

At this time Venice was at the height of her power and was not inclined to relinquish her suzerainty that easily. The Fourth Crusade of 1202 resulted in the establishment of a Venetian commercial hegemony over much of the eastern Mediterranean and the Republic was quite unprepared to allow other centres of power to arise in the Adriatic. In 1204 Ragusa was forced once more to submit to Venice and a Venetian count and archbishop were installed. A limited form of self-government was again permitted within the overall aegis of Venice and only matters concerning trade and foreign relations were retained in the latter's hands.

It was during this second Venetian period that a system of government evolved in Ragusa that remained essentially the same after Venetian control finally came to an end in 1358. The basic institution was the *Consilium majus*, which was drawn from the nobility. As in Venice, this was a commercial aristocracy made up of the rich merchants of the city and from the outset the government was in their hands. However, there was also the *Laudo populi*, which was the assembly of the citizen body, the *cittadini*, and its assent was required to all laws made by the *Consilium majus*. The *Consilium minus*, chaired by the count, was in effect the executive body and its members were drawn from the *Consilium majus*. The *Rogati* (Senate), also made up of members of the nobility, was the body that actually made the laws and transacted business on behalf of the *Consilium majus*, which met only infrequently.

This constitution had much in common with that of Venice and was intended to ensure that the city never fell under the control of a tyrant. However, the large number of bodies involved in decision making made it difficult for decisions to be reached speedily. There was no body similar to the Venetian Council of Ten which could expedite the process and ensure that the government of the city was conducted efficiently. Over time the *Laudo populi* fell into disuse and Dubrovnik became an aristocratic republic along Venetian lines. Although laws continued to be confirmed 'Per Populum Rhacusinum' – much in the manner of Rome's 'Civis Populusque Romanus' – the reality was altogether different and the government of the city remained firmly in the hands of the rich merchants.

In 1358 Ragusa once more renounced Venetian suzerainty and assumed its independence. It was never again to come under the control of Venice. The count departed, and a new head of state, the rector, was appointed and from then on the head of state became an elected office. A treaty was signed with Hungary, the rising power in Dalmatia, which afforded the city Hungarian protection, but in all other ways the city remained a completely independent state. Interestingly, it took the side of Venice in the Chioggia War against Genoa in 1378 and after this soon established good trading relations with its former overlord and now sister republic. By the fifteenth century the Ottoman Turks had replaced the Hungarians in the Balkan hinterland and their vast empire dominated the whole of the eastern Mediterranean. The papal bull of 1433 granted Ragusa permission 'to navigate with its ships even unto the Holy Land and the ports of the Infidel for the purpose of conveying pilgrims thither, and of trade'.[23] A decade later Dubrovnik itself signed a treaty with the new masters of the eastern Mediterranean. In return for an annual tribute, the Sultan acknowledged the independence of the city-state and granted safe conduct and trading privileges within his domains. This independence of the city-state of Ragusa within the Ottoman sphere coincided with a period of economic prosperity that was to last into modern times.

The great prosperity of Ragusa came to rival that of Venice and it continued for long after the older city had begun its long decline. Like Venice, it was well protected by its inhospitable geography that had first made it a haven of refuge. If its 'hard rock' and 'sterile land' together with the 'ire' of the sea had made its site an unpromising one, its general location more than compensated for this. Dubrovnik is located almost directly on the Theodosian Line and thus is at the historic junction between western and eastern Europe. While at first this had been the boundary between the Holy Roman and the Byzantine empires, by the fifteenth century it had become the boundary between the Austrians, the heirs to the Holy Roman Empire, and the Ottomans, the heirs to Islam. Over the centuries the protagonists may have changed, but the Theodosian Line remained the most enduring of all European boundaries. During periods of conflict it was a place of strife but when there was peace it became a conduit of communication between west and east. The major land route from the Adriatic across the Balkans to Constantinople began at Ragusa and the city became as important for diplomatic activity as it was for trade. After the achievement of its independence from Venice, the city went on to thrive in particular from its trade with the Balkans. Most important was the trade in metals, particularly silver, lead and copper, which were lacking in Italy but which the Balkans possessed in abundance. The great success of Ragusa was especially linked to that spectacular growth in the Italian economy that increased the demand for metals for coinage. Much of the trade in metals went by sea to Venice, but of greater importance was the sea route around the south of Italy to Pisa and then up the Arno river to Florence. The papal dispensation to Ragusa to trade with the lands of the infidel seems to have been motivated above all by the importance of the trade in metals. Its importance both to the Papacy and to the Ottomans was such that, in a world becoming ever more territorial, it was able to both hold on to its independence and to its historic liberties.

Thus the revival of the city-state in the centuries that followed the fall of the Roman Empire in the west first took place around the shores of the Adriatic. This was not a sea that had been of particular importance in the ancient world, but in the conditions of the post-Roman world it afforded considerable protection from the barbarians and then an abundance of wealth from the trade with the east. Its success owed much to the emerging economies of Italy and northern Europe and the great demand for products that this generated.

For many centuries Venice and Ragusa were the two principal city-states in the region. Relatively free both from outside interference and internal tyranny, they both cherished their liberties and used them for the advancement of their material well being and cultural life. Representing the revival of the ancient Greek *polis*, they became beacons of civilization in an uncivilized world and displayed some of the finest characteristics of city-states.

One of the most basic characteristics of the Renaissance was the revival of urban life in Italy, and the Adriatic made a major contribution to the success of this. Its cities were the precursors of those of Italy and the fortunes of the two were bound closely together. It was in the former Gallia Cisalpina, which had borne the brunt of the first barbarian invasions, that urban life generally, and the city state in particular, first reappeared. However, the city-state could not be said to have 'revived' in this region in any sense because it had never actually existed in this Roman colonial territory beyond the Rubicon. In ancient times it had been the first location of those 'miniature Romes' which then became such characteristic features of the Roman provinces of Gallia Transalpina and Britannia. They were the Empire's substitute for the true city-states of antiquity and they gave the conquered peoples a taste of urban life but without its attendant freedoms. However, in the medieval epoch the cities of Gallia Cisalpina were to take Venice rather than Rome as their model, and the Renaissance then pointed them in the direction of the *polis* rather than the *imperium*.

SEVEN

Bishops, Dukes and Republics: The City-States of Renaissance Italy

Venice was essentially a product of the general breakdown of civilized life which followed the fall of the Roman Empire. While it arose almost literally out of the swamps, the adjacent regions of northern Italy had already been highly urbanized for half a millennium. The first inhabitants of Venice were refugees from those 'mini Romes' that had been established in Gallia Cisalpina and which then became the source of the urban civilization that was inherited by the new foundations on the Adriatic. They included Bononia (Bologna), Verona, Patavium (Padua), Vicetia (Vicenza), Genua (Genoa), Placentia (Piacenza), Florentia (Florence) and above all Mediolanum (Milan), inheritor of the mantle of Rome and last great capital of the Western Roman Empire. With the revival of city life within it, the Po basin became once again the physical and human link between the Mediterranean and northern Europe and was thus the key region in the formation of the post-Roman world.

Following the arrival of the Barbarians in the fifth century there was considerable destruction but the basic structures of civic life managed to maintain a tenuous existence. It was the Christian Church, which had become the Empire's official religion in the fourth century, that held together the remnants of the ancient civilization. As the Empire crumbled, the Church took over from the civil authorities and assumed the position of being a kind of surrogate government. By so doing, it took on a quasi-imperial role in which the diocese became heir to the Roman *comitatus* and as such ruled the surrounding countryside from the episcopal seat. Throughout northern Italy the towns, although often reduced to little more than villages in the midst of the ruins of once-great cities, continued to eke out a precarious existence. During the centuries that followed a gradual revival of urban life began to take place. By the tenth century Venice, by then a well-established city, had been joined by an increasing number of growing towns that were also seeking to re-establish their municipal status. These were beneficiaries of the same basic circumstances which had accounted for the success of Venice. They were located in that pivotal region in which trade and other contacts between south and north first resumed. Most especially the region was favourably located to take the products of the east, brought along the silk route to the barbarian north and west. As they prospered, these cities increasingly began to assume a more independent character and they then sought to advance from a municipal to a city-state form of government. As more powerful civic institutions began to emerge within them, the neo-imperial functions of the Church were gradually diminished. However, from the outset, the Church had been central to the return of an urban culture and this was reflected both in the splendour of the ecclesiastical architecture and politically in the continuing role of the Church in the government of the city.

The nature of the evolution of the political structures of the cities reflected their functions and the composition of their populations. Their prosperity was based both on trade and on the manufacture of the commodities that were traded. Out of this emerged a class system that reflected the distribution of wealth and status within the cities. While each city was in its own way different in its social and political structures, there were certain overall characteristics common to most of them and these became apparent quite early on.

At the top of urban society were the *maiores*, the nobles, who owned much of the land and property and possessed the most power in the city. Then there was the intermediate class, the *mediocres*, consisting mainly of the merchants, who were in charge of the most important elements in the economy of the city. Finally there were the *minores*, which consisted of the lower classes including craftsmen and workers. These were the *popolani*, the ordinary untitled and unpropertied class who invariable made up the bulk of the population of the cities.

While the merchant class and the *popolani* emerged in response to the specific functions of the towns, the nobility represented something rather different which was to prove to be of decisive importance. This was the continued existence of a landed aristocracy, the importance of which had grown in the uncertain conditions at the end of the Roman Empire. Now they sought influence and position within the growing towns that were rising up within their territorial domains. Like the Church, they reflected an earlier situation and also like the Church they were forced to accommodate themselves to the growing aspirations of the new commercial classes.

The basic aspirations of the cities were for increased freedom and independence from outside interference, and these came to be encapsulated in the *comune*. This was something that arose from within the city and its basic function was to represent its interests. It was not imposed upon the city by the external authority of either the Church or the territorial magnates who often found themselves in opposition to it. In rudimentary form such *comuni* were beginning to emerge in the Italian cities by the tenth century and early known examples were Milan, Genoa and Pisa. At the heart of the *comune* was the general assembly of the citizens known as the *arengo* or *parlementum*. From the beginning particular individuals were designated to act on behalf of the *comune* and these *boni homines* were chosen in a variety of ways. By the eleventh century consuls were being elected by the *comuni* to run the affairs of the city and to act on its behalf. Notable early examples of cities in which this took place were Pisa, Asti, Milan, Arezzo and Genoa. In all cases there were a number of consuls, often possessing specific functions, and they were given executive, financial, judicial and inquisitorial powers. The consuls were drawn from all classes of society and were chosen in a variety of ways. In most cases the *arengo* was at first involved, but later on such functions were likely to be delegated to a council or to an ad hoc committee. There are also records of the existence of a council house, the *domus civitatis*, mentioned in the records of Cremona in the tenth century, in which civic business was transacted.[1]

In assuming all these civic functions the *comune* was taking over what had until then been the role of the Church. Waley saw it as being 'the legatee of episcopal authority in the cities' and in view of this its reach extended out to the communities in the surrounding countryside.[2] Here the authority of the *comune* clashed with that of the Church in such matters as the powers of the ecclesiastical courts. The conflict between the two within the emerging city-region was to endure for some considerable time. Thus the early *comune* had to cope with the pre-existing episcopal and territorial power that enveloped it and in doing so it began to take on many of their characteristics. Most notably there was the incorporation of the surrounding territory and the consequent development of a territorial dimension as an integral part of the city-state. This was the *contado*, based on the Roman *comitatus*, into which the city expanded and which became its subject territory. At first the boundaries of this coincided with, or at least approximated to, that of the diocese, and thus the episcopal territorial unit came to be gradually re-secularized as the *contado* under the authority of the city. In so doing, observed Waley, 'it sought power and dominion in its own vicinity in the same way as any other lord'.[3] Formal 'submission' by villages, small towns and landowners within the *contado* then took place. However, the link between the diocese and the *contado* remained a close one and often it was the bishop who formally accepted the submission. The city thus came to exercise an ever greater control over the *contado*, which soon became an important part of the totality that comprised the city-state. From the *contado* came taxes, recruits for the army and food supplies. It also acted as a safe haven for traders and a buffer for the defence of the city. Special officials, called variously *capitani*, *visconti* or *rectori*, were appointed by the city authorities to run the affairs of the *contado*, and it was divided into smaller territorial units ruled by officials.

In this way a symbiotic relationship developed between town and country, and the city-state evolved into a territorial as well as an urban phenomenon. Immigration took place from town to country and the richer citizens came to possess properties in both. The result of this symbiosis was, in effect, the urbanization of the surrounding countryside. While in ancient Rome the result of the whole process had been the ruralization of the city, here the opposite took place. Large areas of the land came to be owned by those from the town and 'horticultural suburbs' stretched out from the city walls. The abolition of serfdom that was a feature of this process had mixed motives. It had the effect of both liberating a labour supply for the growing city and asserting the town's dominance over the countryside. A distinction was made between the *cittadini* and the *contadini*, those who lived in the city and those who lived in the country, and the superiority of the former was implicit in this. New towns were sometimes established in the *contado* which themselves then became important sub-centres of economic but not political activity. In this context, one contemporary traveller commented that

> The entire land is divided among the cities, scarcely any noble or great man can be found in all the surrounding territory who does not acknowledge the authority of his city . . . They are aided . . . by the absence of princes, who are accustomed to remain on the far side of the Alps.[4]

The form of government to which the city-states aspired was a republican one that was intended primarily to serve the interests of the city and its inhabitants rather than those of outsiders. However, the cities were by no means themselves single units but were highly divided by occupation, social status and wealth. This situation produced a variety of interest groups, the most important of which were the occupational ones catered for by the *arti* or guilds. These became essential components of the internal organization of all the city-states, and while they were basically economic, they inevitably entered also into the political field. Each particular trade had its guild which was intended to look after its own interests. The *arti maggiori* were the guilds of the most important trades such as wool, silk and dyeing, while the *arti minori* were the guilds of the lesser ones such as baking, cheese-making, tannery and the making of locks and keys. The *arti maggiori* were usually concerned with trade over longer distances and came to be linked to other activities such as finance and shipbuilding. As such they became powerful and influential in the affairs of the city. By the middle of the thirteenth century there were some 80 banks in Florence alone and the gold florin was soon accepted as the major currency throughout Europe. On the other hand, the *arti minori* were more concerned with smaller trading operations within the immediate vicinity of the city and were usually far less rich and powerful. Balancing the varied interests of the *arti* became an important function of government and the *arti* themselves became in many places part of the structure of government. They elected or nominated members to serve on other city bodies and their interests had to be taken into account when determining policies to be pursued by the state.

Government by the many, or even representatives of the many, could be a slow business, and from the twelfth century there was a movement towards the appointment of some kind of chief executive to run the affairs of the city. This was the *podestà* and the existence of this office is first recorded in Genoa in 1190.[5] By the following century most of the cities had a *podestà* or a similar office. A major requirement for the office was that the *podestà* had to come from outside the city, something intended to ensure that the *podesteria* stood above the factionalism and rivalry that was all too often characteristic of the internal politics of the cities. The actual role of the *podestà* varied among the city-states, but all had to swear to uphold the freedoms of the city and to protect its interests. For his period in office the *podestà* became a citizen of the particular state that he served and it was expected that his first loyalty would always be to it. At first the term that the *podestà* served was normally one year, but gradually this was extended and they served over longer periods. The activities of the *podestà* were watched carefully by the *comune*, and the *sindicatus* was the body charged with the investigation and evaluation of his activities after he had left office. With time it became increasingly necessary to appoint more officials to take charge of other aspects of the city's affairs. The most important such official was the *camerarius* who was in charge of the finances and therefore had a crucial role in the overall success of the city and its affairs.

The final major development in the period of the republican city-state was the establishment of the *Signoria*. What had began as an unofficial group of leading citizens monitoring the

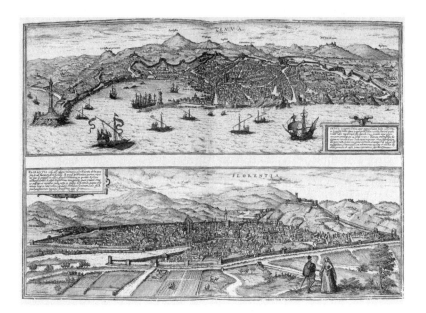

11 Genoa and Florence.

activities of the various bodies of the state tended itself to evolve into the central institution of the state. In practice its members usually came from the nobility and the wealthy merchant class. These gradually become coupled together as the *grandi* that comprised the old rural and the newer urban nobility. The *grandi* were at the opposite end of the economic and social spectrum from the *populo* and gradually a two-class system replaced the three classes of earlier times. The *Signoria* existed alongside the other institutions of the *comune* but came to prevail over them. Its role was to examine all the activities of the state, the legislation and the other bodies engaged in government. In particular it watched the *podestà* and brought to bear its views on the overall policies that were pursued. If they were to continue to maintain themselves as the real arbiters of power, the *Signoria* had to attempt to balance the interests of the various sections of the population, and in particular to take account of the demands of the ordinary people. Above all the main purpose of the *Signoria* was to maintain the power and influence of the *grandi* and this was often a delicate task to perform. The jostling for power that it entailed led eventually to the emergence of a 'strong man' and the complete transformation of the republican institutions that resulted from this.

The success of the city-state in establishing itself as the political norm throughout northern Italy from the eleventh century to the fifteenth was the result of both external and internal factors. The world into which these city-states emerged was dominated by the Holy Roman Empire, the successor state in the west to the former Roman Empire. This massive entity had been established in 800 when the Frankish king, Charles (Charlemagne), had been crowned Emperor in Rome by Pope Leo III. It was based upon a delicate balance of power between the Frankish and subsequently German kings, as inheritors of the imperial mantle, and the Pope as inheritor of the Chair of St Peter. The fact that it was the Pope who had crowned the first Emperor did not help to ease the relationship between the two. It resulted in a situation in which there was a lingering dispute over where the ultimate source of authority really lay. The doubt about this produced a certain void of legitimacy at the heart of the Empire. Perhaps Lord Bryce's famous comment that the institution was neither Holy nor Roman nor an Empire goes far to explaining the way in which the city-states arose and flourished within it as was rarely the case in any other empires before or since.[6]

Thus the power of the Emperor in Italy was and remained limited and uncertain, and this was caused by geographical as well as political factors. The centre of imperial power was beyond the Alps in Germany and the assertion of control over even the closest part of Italy was difficult. Italy was also the special province of the Pope, who rarely worked in tandem with the Emperor and who asserted a rival authority that was temporal as well as spiritual. The most important centre of papal authority was around Rome itself and over this region the Pope acted as a temporal prince. In effect the Pope was at the head of his own city-state. While Pope and Emperor each had his own geopolitical core of power, neither the reach of Pope nor of Emperor extended easily into northern Italy, which thus took on the position of being an indeterminate area between their two spheres. In these circumstances the religious and secular authorities played one another off in seeking the support of the region's rich and powerful cities. This often entailed making concessions to them which actually increased and even institutionalized their independence within the Empire. In the case of Venice, the full sovereignty of this city was implicitly recognized when it was chosen as neutral ground in which to effect a reconciliation of Pope and Emperor.

The long-running dispute between the Pope and the Emperor had come to the fore early on and centred on the question of the Investiture of the clergy. This right had fallen to the Emperor and had its roots in the civil functions of the Church as a surrogate government. The Church was seen as acting on behalf of the Emperor and was thus vested with the imperial authority by the Emperor himself. In 977 the Emperor Otto I made the bishops heads of the cities, and as a result of this they were invested with the ultimate civil as well as religious authority within them.[7] This was a situation that was not at all acceptable to the Papacy, and the dispute between Pope and Emperor was brought to a head during the reign of Pope Gregory VII in the eleventh century. The increased assertion of papal pre-eminence led to the Emperor Henry IV calling the Synod of Worms in which the German and north Italian bishops repudiated their allegiance to the Pope. The papal response was to excommunicate both the Emperor and the rebellious bishops. The ensuing turmoil acted in favour of the Pope and in January 1077 Henry IV was forced to present himself at Canossa to do penance before the Pope and to seek his forgiveness. The Emperor may have been humbled but the struggle had weakened the authority of them both. The only real winners from all this were the *comuni* of the northern Italian cities, which used the power vacuum that the dispute created to assert their independence of both Church and Emperor. For a time the imperial authority, in Freising's words, was confined to 'the far side of the Alps' and northern Italy was largely free from outside interference.

The most important attempt to reassert the imperial authority came in the following century with the two powerful Hohenstaufen Emperors Frederick I 'Barbarossa' and Frederick II 'Stupor mundi'. In 1154 Barbarossa demanded that all cities should recognize the imperial suzerainty. This demand was based on the *iura regalia* which comprised the historic rights of the Emperor founded on the 'translatio ad francos', the inheritance by the Frankish kings of the legal authority stemming from Rome. The legality of the *iura regalia* was then confirmed at the Diet of Roncaglia in 1158 by the jurists of the *studium* of Bologna, the first university institution in Europe. While there was much opposition to this, the cities had no option at first but to comply and, with the sole exception of Venice, they all did so. While the *iura regalia* in theory gave the Emperor considerable power over them, in practice successive Emperors had granted them a variety of rights and privileges that continued to have the force of imperial decree. Earlier Emperors had also come to accept their quasi-independent status and the *de facto* gains of the cities tended over time to win *de jure* recognition as Emperors sought allies in the cities. Thus a *modus vivendi* had over time been struck up between the Emperor and the cities from which both were in their own way gainers. The fear of radical interference with this situation by Barbarossa, the young and power-hungry occupant of the imperial throne, was the main cause of the coming together of many of the cities in the Lombard League in 1162 for mutual protection against him. This league initially included Verona, Vicenza, Padua, and Trivezo but was subsequently joined by Brescia, Bergamo, Mantua and Cremona. The League was supported by Venice, whose independent status was beyond question, and by the Pope who hoped thus to secure a diminution of the imperial authority south of the Alps. In 1176 the forces of the League met those of the Emperor at Legnano and in the subsequent battle the imperial army was defeated. In view of the reasons for this conflict, it is ironic that the neutral ground of Venice was then chosen for the reconciliation of Pope and Emperor. The Treaty of Constance in 1183 between the Emperor and the Lombard League recognized the full rights of the Italian cities. Although they remained notionally within the Empire, in practice the Emperor was left with only a titular supremacy over them.[8] In addition to this, the position of the bishops was weakened and the right of the cities to elect their own government and appoint their own officials was confirmed.

Barbarossa's grandson, the Emperor Frederick II, was more concerned with Italy than with Germany and he sought to impose his rule vigorously on the whole of the peninsula. Heir to the Norman rulers of Sicily, for much of his reign his court was in Palermo. In effect he moved the centre of the Empire across the Alps and dreamed of a revival of its ancient Roman predecessor. In this connection he worked on a plan to divide Italy into imperial provinces and thus to end for good those divisions that had plagued the peninsula for so long. Alarmed at this prospect, the Pope proposed an alternative plan to divide Italy into provinces that would be states of the Church. In these circumstances, the conflict of papal and imperial power became more intense than ever. The city-states of the north of the peninsula saw themselves as being menaced to a greater extent than ever by an Emperor who wished to change the ramshackle political structure within which their freedoms had arisen into one that would be organized and centralized and firmly placed under imperial control. The Pope also saw himself menaced by an Emperor whose aim was to move towards the establishment of a powerful and basically secular state and saw no option but to ally himself with the cities and to became the champion of their rights. The debate on the future of Italy extended into the cities themselves and a great divide opened up within them between those who advocated complete independence and those who were content with a measure of imperial overlordship. These rallied respectively to the causes of the Pope and the Emperor and thus began the long and bitter conflict between the Guelfs and the Ghibellines. Taking their names from the conflict within Germany between the Welf and Waiblingen factions – respectively the supporters of the Ottonians and Hohen-staufens – the terms appear to have been first used in Florence in 1242.[9] There the Guelfs were the Florentine patricians who held power and aimed to keep hold of it while the Ghibellines were those who opposed them and were quite prepared to use outside forces – in particular the Emperor – in order to further their designs.

The consolidation of these ideas in the middle of the fourteenth century came to divide state against state, class against class and even family against family. Initially, in general the

Guelfs supported the Pope and the freedom of the city-states, while the Ghibellines supported the Emperor and the belief that Italy and its city-states were better off within the overall imperial framework. While the Guelfs retained a powerful memory of what the Italians had suffered at the hands of the Germans – the *furor Teutonicus* – in time their objectives became less clear and, as with Florence from the beginning, they came to be submerged within dynastic rivalries and city conflicts. The conflict between Pope and Emperor took on the now familiar characteristics of the excommunication of the Emperor by the Pope and the deployment of imperial troops south of the Alps. Eventually in 1245 Frederick was defeated by a renewed Lombard League at the Battle of Parma and the Emperor was forced to concede. He confirmed the rights of the cities and their legal sovereignty within their own territories 'save only when the Emperor himself should be present'.[10]

Five years later Frederick was dead and his ambitions for a new imperial Italy died with him. In 1273 Rudolf of Habsburg was elected Emperor and he prudently pursued a policy of non-intervention in Italy. In 1307 the papacy was transferred to Avignon by the French and thus began that period of 'Babylonian captivity' that lasted throughout most of the fourteenth century. It also signified the rise of a new power on the European scene that was soon to present a powerful challenge to both the Emperor and the Pope and to bring further danger to the independence of the city-states. However, for the time being, there was little papal or imperial authority in Italy and the city-states were able for a time to enjoy their hard-won independence and to reinforce the rights that they considered legitimately to be theirs. In so doing they appropriated the *iura regalia* and behaved as fully sovereign states. Despite disagreements on the extent and nature of the imperial authority, the city-states had always sought the right to run their own affairs with a minimum of interference from outside.

In *Baudolino* Umberto Eco dealt with the complexities of the relationship between the Emperor and the cities in medieval Italy. He put this into the mouth of Bishop Otto of Freising, who was attempting to make his nephew, the Emperor

Frederick Barbarossa, understand 'the reasoning of the cities beyond the Alps' and warning him of the dire consequences of ignoring *Italia citeriore*.

> You are thinking of Milan, of Pavia and Genoa as if they were Ulm or Eu. The cities of Germany were all born at the command of a prince, and from the beginning they have recognized themselves in the prince. But for these cities it is different. They arose while the Germanic Emperors were engaged in other matters, and they have grown and taken advantage of the absence of their princes. When you speak to the inhabitants about the *podestà*, the governor that you would like to impose on them, they feel this *podestas insolentiam* is an intolerable yoke, and they have themselves governed by consuls whom they themselves elect. . . . They do not recognise the great vassals, lords of field and forest, because fields and forests belong to the cities.[11]

Barbarossa had little sympathy with such ideas of republicanism and popular freedom. 'So the world is upside down?' was his reply to Otto, 'These cities have appropriated all of my rights . . . What demon so clouded their minds?' It was not like that at all, replied the bishop. It is not a demon but the reflection of the new realities in the world. 'These cities are now the places through which all wealth passes. Merchants gather there from all over, and their walls are more beautiful and solid than those of many castles'.[12] It is my duty, he concluded,

> to help you understand their strength . . . If you insist on obtaining from those cities that which they don't want to give you, you will waste the rest of your life besieging them, defeating them, and seeing them rise again, more proud than before, in the space of a few months; and you will have to cross the Alps to subdue them once more, whereas your imperial destiny lies elsewhere.

This imperial destiny was to take Frederick to his death on the Third Crusade in 1190, and although he had earlier crowned his son Henry as 'Caesar' in Milan, this assertion of imperial authority in the middle of the *Italia citeriore* made little difference to their independent stance.

While the Emperor was always the greatest danger to the independence of the Italian city-states, dangers also came from nearer at hand. The more powerful among them invariably sought to increase their power further and this entailed increasing the size of the territories under their control. In doing this they invariably came into conflict with other cities which often had similar aspirations or at least wished to protect what they had. Thus conflict with neighbours was always a feature of the life of the Italian city-states and in many ways conflict became more the norm than cooperation, which was usually of limited duration and only for specific purposes. 'Neighbour' often became a synonym for 'enemy'.[13] Armies were always a familiar sight marching across northern Italy and usually they consisted of mercenaries hired by the cities to fight their various causes. Thus while great families arose that controlled the affairs of particular cities, other great families arose whose wealth derived from war. Sometimes these came from the old landed aristocracy but very often they were fortune-hunters from lower down the social ladder. One of the most infamous examples of this phenomenon were the Borgia. Rodrigo Borgia came from a minor Spanish landowning family and bribed himself to the papacy as Alexander VI. His illegitimate offspring Cesare and Lucrezia both became deeply involved in the power politics of city-state rivalry. As captain general of the papacy, Cesare was involved in incessant wars between the city-states of the north and he typified the circumstances which made it so difficult to create that city-state consensus that would have strengthened their collective position.

The death of Frederick II inaugurated the greatest age of the city-states of northern Italy. They prospered as never before and in them began the Renaissance, the great revival of learning, which was to have such profound effects on all aspects of European life in the following centuries. In many ways the Italian city-state was the vehicle for the Renaissance in much the same way as 2,000 years earlier the Greek *polis* had been the vehicle for the rise of that Hellenic civilization to which the Renaissance owed so much. 'Renaissance civilization is primarily an urban civilization', observed Clarke, 'its greatest contribution to art and literature came from the towns'.[14] The rebirth of urban life soon spread from Italy across western Europe and the role of the cities in all areas of activity increased. Besides being the centres of the emerging new commercial economy, they were also the centres of learning and the arts. Their political role, which until then had been largely confined to northern Italy and parts of Germany, then increased considerably. By the beginning of the fourteenth century the city-state appeared to be on the way to becoming the political norm once again as it had been in ancient times.

However, at the same time as this new urban freedom was consolidating itself after the prolonged struggle with the Hohenstaufens, the Italian city-states were in many ways becoming themselves less free. The republican institutions on which they had been based were giving place to forms of authoritarian government that came to be closely associated with the consolidation of the power of one particular family. The city-states were in effect becoming monarchies, and absolute monarchies at that. The main reasons for this development were the deep divisions within the cities, which made the achievement of consensus increasingly difficult. The persisting Guelf–Ghibelline conflict was at the root of this but there were many others. Most fundamental was the conflict within each of the cities between the patrician class, the *grandi*, and the ordinary folk, the *popolani*. In the case of Florence, the deepest division was between the 'Blacks' – the old nobility together with the bankers – and the 'Whites' who were the trade classes. Power may have come to rest with the *Signoria* but this monopoly of power by an institution that had insinuated itself into the political structures of the *comune* met with far from universal approval. In most city-states the hold of the *Signoria* on power was at best fragile and at worst it was swept away by the forces making for greater democracy. This generally produced not more but less democracy with the rise of the 'strong man' and the institutionalization of the power of particular families.

The factors lying behind the rise of dynastic government can be seen most clearly in Florence. In 1378, the year after the papacy returned from Avignon to Rome, came the uprising of the *ciompi*, the Florentine proletariat. This class had suffered greatly during the preceding decades as a result of a series of natural disasters culminating in the Black Death together with the damaging economic effects on Florence of the outbreak of the Hundred Years War.[15] There was thus great hardship among the poor of the city and its surrounding *contado* and this led to a mood of considerable dissatisfaction which came to be directed against the *grandi*. The situation in the city had been complicated by the long-standing conflict of Guelfs and Ghibellines and the divisions within the patrician class that resulted from this. The government of the city had come to be based on an uneasy alliance between the *arti maggiori* and the *arti minori*, but the latter had become increasingly uneasy at the policies that were being pursued in its name. While the *ciompi* movement was an alliance of the disaffected, it came to centre on the *arti minori* and was led by Salvestro de' Medici, himself a merchant, who was elected *gonfalier* of justice. The *ciompi* demanded greater democracy and the establishment of new *arti* for the specific purpose of looking after the interests of the workers. The strength of the movement was such that it was successful in toppling the *Signori* government and Salvestro then became involved in drawing up a new republican constitution. Clarke was of the opinion that this constitution 'might be taken as showing the high water mark of democratic government in the Middle Ages'.[16] New *arti* were then established specifically for the *ciompi*. Political power was distributed among all the *arti* of the city and together they elected an executive of nine priors. This constitution proved to be unworkable and eventually the working-class movement was put down forcibly. The wielders of economic power, the patrician classes, then resumed their hold over the political power of the city.

It was this solution to the social and economic turmoil that led to the consolidation of the power of the Medici family. By then this family had moved into banking and they used their growing wealth for political purposes. In 1434 Cosimo de' Medici became *podestà* and he then moved to make himself the permanent holder of that office. He did so, as had Salvestro before him, as the leader of the *ciompi* versus the patricians. On gaining power he pacified the situation and while apparently acceding to the demands of the *Ciompi* he actually maintained government by the patricians. This was the beginning of the dynasty that was to rule Florence for most of the next 200 years. The Florentine Republic became a 'veiled signory' and despotic rule was concealed behind an outward show of republican forms. The position of the Medici was consolidated further when Cosimo's son Piero was invested with the rank of duke of Florence by the Emperor in 1464. He was followed by the most remarkable of all the Medici, Lorenzo, who was duke of Florence from 1469 to 1492 and presided over the greatest period in the history of the city-state.

Besides its great commercial success and its becoming the financial centre of Italy, Florence was already the greatest centre of Renaissance civilization. Arnolfo di Cambio, Giotto, Boccaccio, Dante, Petrarch, Brunelleschi, Raphael, Leonardo da Vinci and Michelangelo lived and worked in the city. The city authorities were also involved and the arts came to be part of the whole city-state enterprise and benefited from corporate patronage. Michelangelo's *David*, commissioned by the city government, was perhaps the greatest symbolic representation of the city-state, small and vulnerable but opposing its intellectual gifts to the crude might of the forces that sought to destroy it. Another work of art commissioned in Florence, Donatello's *St George*, idealized republicanism and sought to represent the grandeur of the city-state of Florence.[17] The close links between artist and city were demonstrated by Domenico Veneziano's promise to the duke that 'my work will bring you great honour'.[18] Boccaccio was equally proud of his city and saw it as being by then the real centre of the world. He referred scornfully to Rome as the city that was once 'the head of the world' but that had now 'become its tail'.[19] The work of Leonardo da Vinci, encapsulating as it did the arts and the sciences, represented the Renaissance spirit of the unity of knowledge and of man as the measure of all things. In a way the genius from the village of Vinci on the Arno just to the south of Florence personified Florence itself with its immense diversity encapsulated within a single city.

While the independent city-state was clearly the vehicle for this great achievement, there was profound disagreement on the relationship of the cities to Italy and to the Empire as a whole. Boccaccio took the Guelf position, believing that the city-state represented civilization at its best. To him *cittadinesca-mente*, living as a citizen or in a civic manner, was the highest attainment and one that was most conducive to the greatest happiness of the individual.[20] On the other hand, Dante, while regarding Florence as being 'la bellissima e famosissima figlia di Roma', saw the city in artistic rather than in political terms. Politically, he took the Ghibelline position and regarded the Italian city-states as being petty and divisive. To Dante the answer to the problems of the peninsula was the creation of a single Italy and he advocated a *Rex pacificus* who would unify the country.[21] The later confrontation between city-states and nation-states thus had its roots in the thinking of two of the most important literary figures in Renaissance Italy.

A similar pattern of moving away from the republican institutions was also to be found in Milan. As early as 1035 a revolt had taken place there against the episcopal government. The bishops were forced out of power and Milan was declared to be a 'free commune of citizens'. This *comune* was run by representatives of the *arti* who were at first successful in balancing the interests of the various sections of society. The *comune* was particularly assiduous in increasing the size of the *contado*, and by the twelfth century a number of villages and towns had submitted to the overlordship of Milan. The territorial element in the government of the city was therefore particularly strong and the influence of the nobility was considerable. In the conflict between the cities and the Emperor, Milan was in the forefront in asserting the rights of the cities and was regarded by both the major Hohenstaufen Emperors as typifying the desire of the city-states to assert their independence. Barbarossa had proclaimed his son and heir as 'Caesar' in Milan, but this had not curtailed the independent spirit of its citizens. As a result the city was attacked on a number of occasions, resulting in considerable destruction and loss of life. It was in these conditions of vulnerability to external danger during the late thirteenth century that the Visconti family rose to power. The profound disagreements between the Guelfs and the Ghibellines made consensus government impossible and there was a move

12 Milan.

towards the creation of some form of dictatorship. In 1395 Gian Galeazzo Visconti (1379–1402) was invested by the Emperor as duke of Milan. His government and that of his successors was a kind of dictatorship by consent and the Visconti governed the city with a light touch. Gian Galeazzo embellished the city and built the great cathedral in the Gothic style of those north of the Alps. He also built the powerful castle to be both his stronghold and seat of government. He moved against the smaller towns such as Lodi and in so doing extended and consolidated the duchy. The Visconti retained their power until 1447, when as a result of popular dissatisfaction they were removed. A republic was declared, but this lasted barely three years and in 1450 a new duke of Milan was invested. He was Francesco Sforza, and he founded a dynasty that was able to maintain itself in power for the next half-century. Ludovico, the last of the powerful dukes, who reigned from 1476 to 1499, made Milan a leading city that for a time dominated Lombardy and strongly influenced the politics of the Italian peninsula at a time of great change. During his reign Milan was transformed into one of the largest and most splendid cities in Italy, and in this work Leonardo da Vinci, who moved there from Florence in 1482, was closely involved. In Milan Leonardo was in charge of a variety of projects ranging from town planning to military engineering, but in the middle of it all he found time to paint his masterpiece, *The Last Supper*, on the refectory wall of Santa Maria delle Grazie.[22] In many ways it was Leonardo who was most responsible for converting Milan from being a centre of military power into one of the great Renaissance cities. He claimed to Ludovico that his work in art, architecture and sculpture would 'endow with immortal glory and eternal honour the auspicious memory of your father and of the illustrious house of Sforza'.[23] Here as in Florence art was put at the service of the city-state and its embellishment was intended to be the visible sign of its success and of those who ruled over it.

Both the Visconti and the Sforza were able to maintain their power by treading softly through the minefield of Milanese politics. Like the Medici in Florence, theirs was a dictatorship by consent and they were able to maintain themselves in power only so long as they balanced the various sectional interests and kept a firm hold over the turbulent politics of the city-state.

Yet the spirit of republicanism remained and states that had submitted to autocratic rule by a single family nevertheless generally continued to pay lip service to their republican constitutions. When the dynasty failed to deliver, then there was usually a return to the republican principles. This was seen most dramatically in the case of Florence at the end of the fifteenth century. Lorenzo de' Medici presided over a glittering court and money was lavished on the arts and the embellishment of the city. By this time the power of the Medici family was such that it was involved widely in Italian affairs including the Papacy. Lorenzo's brother Giovanni later became Pope and reigned as Leo x. The lifestyle of the Medici and the *Grandi* of Florence had become a byword for luxury. In these circumstances the deep divisions within Florentine society intensified and there was growing discontent within the city. In 1491 the Dominican friar Girolamo Savonarola denounced Lorenzo and the licentiousness of the Florentine court. He also strongly criticized the Church itself for not having brought the crimes of the

Medici to book. Savonarola called for a return to true republican institutions, asserting that 'the republic consists of one body alone and this is the body of the whole people'.[24] A year later Lorenzo died and Savonarola, who had by this time gained considerable popular support, led an uprising against the Medici. The great dynasty was expelled from the city and republican institutions were brought back in triumph. The *Consiglio maggiore*, made up of representatives of all sections of society, became the major institution of the state. A process of redistribution of wealth was embarked upon and the old institutions were revived. Although Savonarola continued to criticize the Church for its inaction in the face of injustice, he effectively instituted a theocratic republic in which puritan values were proclaimed and all the signs of the previous ostentation, including many works of art, were destroyed. This 'bonfire of the vanities' began to turn the Florentines against Savonarola and when in 1497 he denounced the Borgia Pope Alexander vi for his evil deeds this was seen as going too far and his popular support began to ebb away. The Pope's response was to excommunicate the tempestuous friar, a move that had in the past ruined far more powerful figures than this theocratic ruler of a fledgling republic. In 1498 Savonarola was arrested, accused of heresy, found guilty and burned at the stake in the Piazza della Signoria where the bonfire of the city's works of art had taken place only a year earlier. Thus ended the brief attempt to restore republican rule and the Medici were, for a time at least, restored to power.

However, by this time the political situation in Europe was moving against the Italian city-states. In the turbulent times at the end of the fifteenth century, during which the Medici fell and an unrealistic attempt was made to resurrect the republic, a leading Florentine administrator embarked on an exhaustive examination of the ingredients for the making of a successful state. Niccolò Machiavelli, secretary of the Republic of Florence, used the fruits of his researches to produce what was basically a guidebook for the successful ruler. *The Prince*, published in 1513, advocated solutions to the problems then faced by his own and other states. While this famous work came to be seen subsequently as a textbook for unscrupulous politicians, and the word 'machiavellian' has entered the language as a synonym for devious and uncaring rule, Machiavelli was actually writing about his own city-state and was attempting to demonstrate how it could survive in a turbulent and fast changing world. 'The welfare of the civic order was his first and last thought', wrote one modern historian.[25] However, Florence did not regain its former greatness and the Italian city-states were picked off one by one by foreign rulers. Those who read Machiavelli's work down the centuries adapted its message to totally different political circumstances.

In 1494 the French king Charles VIII invaded Italy in pursuit of his claim to the Crown of Naples. Although unsuccessful in his immediate objective, he defeated a coalition of the Italian cities and the Emperor at Fornovo and for a time a number of the cities – including both Milan and Florence – were occupied by French troops. Thus as the sixteenth century dawned the circumstances that had been so favourable to the existence of the city-states drew to an end and Italy was about to become a battleground among the old and the new powers of Europe.

The city-states that rose in the north of Italy during medieval times were large and economically successful. This success gave them considerable power, which they then used to fight for their independence from Pope and Emperor alike. However, despite their success in achieving this, the larger ones in many ways came increasingly to behave in a manner all too similar to those powers that had sought to curtail their independence. Through territorial expansion they created large *contado*s into which the smaller towns and villages were absorbed. They thus themselves came to possess in microcosm many of the characteristics of the larger territorial states. Umberto Eco put this problem into the mouth of the Emperor Barbarossa when he enquired of Bishop Otto, 'if the condition of being a city is the ideal, why does each try to oppress its neighbouring city, as if it wanted to engulf that territory and transform it into a realm?'.[26] The fact was that most of the cities of *Italia cittadini* had gained a territorial dimension that over the centuries had come increasingly to dominate their thinking. This itself owed much to the way in which the government of the city-states had evolved.

Over time a close relationship had developed between the new nobility of trade and the old nobility of the land in the pursuit of wealth and power. Territoriality then became an important element in this. The consolidation of the power of the *Signoria* can in many ways be seen as being based upon this relationship. While during the period of the rise of the cities the surrounding country was increasingly urbanized, later on the opposite actually began to take place and the forces of the country began to move in on the cities. The Visconti of Milan were the most notable example of this and others included the Obizzo of Ferrara and the Monaldeschi of Orvieto. The Marquis of Montferrat's wider overlordship of the cities of southern Piedmont was a similar phenomenon. 'The commune and the Signoria . . . shade into each other and are hard to differentiate', wrote Waley, while at the same time 'many of the communes never really escaped the shadow of the lord's castle'.[27]

While all this was going on, the disagreements between Guelf and Ghibelline created a profound divide both within and among the city-states and prevented the formation of a real common front against their external enemies. This lack of a meeting of minds meant that the city-states became vulnerable to forces both from within and from without. From within, the divisions made government increasingly difficult and allowed dynastic tyranny to take over the republican institutions. From without, they became prey to the dangers posed not only by the Pope and the Emperor, but eventually by the rise of other powers. While alliances were formed, they were always intended to address specific problems and all proved to be relatively short lived. No long-lasting organization of the Italian cities ever came into being. The norm was that the city-states saw one another as being rivals rather than allies, and conflict rather than cooperation became increasingly the rule.

It was largely as a result of this situation that, as Europe changed and the medieval institutions of Christendom began to give place to those that characterize modern Europe, the Italian city-states failed to maintain that position of pre-eminence that had underpinned their leadership in virtually every field. They then became ever more vulnerable to the new forces that were being unleashed. Their already much diminished role by the beginning of the sixteenth century reflected their weakness in the face of the new power structures that were emerging. Failing to adapt to them, as Machiavelli had hoped they could, they were soon to become their victims.[28] In so doing they helped pave the way for a very different kind of Europe in which there was little place for city-states in the classical or any other sense.

EIGHT

Princes, Bishops and Republics: Cities and City-States in Russia

The human geography of that half of the Roman Empire that lay to the east of the Theodosian Line was totally different from that which lay to the west of it. The eastern Mediterranean had been the heartland of both the Hellenic and the Hellenistic civilizations and historically it had been a land of cities and city-states. The Eastern Roman Empire soon became more Greek than Roman, and by the early seventh century AD Rome had been replaced by the Greek Byzantium and the Greek language had taken over from Latin. This eastern successor state to the Roman Empire was dominated by one great city, Constantinople. This had been built by the Emperor Constantine in the fourth century as the new 'Christian' capital of his empire, and over the next few centuries what had been until then a small Greek settlement at the entrance to the Black Sea was transformed into by far the largest and most splendid city in the whole of medieval Europe.

The former Hellenic city-states that were located within the boundaries of the Byzantine Empire were completely overshadowed by the immense size and power of its capital, and they soon lost most of what was left of their former independent status. This highly centralized state was in many ways more truly the heir to Rome than was the Holy Roman Empire with its twin – and usually conflicting – centres of power, strong centrifugal tendencies and absence of a real capital city. Thus while in the west city-states proliferated, in the east they were almost entirely absent unless the whole edifice is considered to have been a gigantic city-state on an imperial scale.

However, within that part of the extended sphere of influence of Byzantium that lay to the north, city-states of various types became for a time almost as much the norm as they were in Renaissance Italy. The immense wealth and power of Byzantium was based overwhelmingly on its great commercial success and trade routes converged on the city from all directions. One of these followed the rivers of western Russia from the Baltic to the Black Sea, thus linking northern Europe with the Mediterranean. This route appears to have dated from sometime around the eighth century and evidences have come to light in the Baltic region of products and coinage from the Mediterranean and elsewhere.[1] The pioneers of this route were the eastern Vikings or Varangians who sailed in their longships from Scandinavia across the Baltic and then followed the rivers eastwards. In so doing they pioneered a number of river routes leading to the east and south. One of the most important of these was that which followed the Neva to Lake Ladoga and from there southwards along the Volkhov river to the Valdai Hills. Using a portage to connect it with the headwaters of the Dnieper, the route then followed this river to its mouth on the Black Sea. Known as 'the route from the Varangians to the Greeks' this became one of the most important commercial routeways in medieval Europe, carrying a large amount of the trade between the eastern Mediterranean and northern Europe. In this way the Varangians opened up the lands to the east of Scandinavia and unwittingly embarked upon the creation of the state that was to become Russia.[2]

By tradition Russia came into being in 862, which was the date of the foundation of the first Russian city, Novgorod, by the Varangian prince Rurik, the leader of the so-called men of Rus. It was located on the Volkhov river near to its junction with Lake Ilmen and at a point where other natural routeways from east and west converged. Originally known by the Viking name Holmgard, this settlement became an important staging point in the south–north trade and it was soon followed by the establishment of a number of others. The one that became the most important of these was Kiev on the river Dnieper, which was founded in 882 by another Varangian prince, Oleg. Others dating from this early period include Stara Ladoga, Smolensk, Tver and Pskov. It was out of this collection of settlements on the great rivers and lakes that the first Russia, known as Kievan

Rus, came into being. Kiev soon outstripped all the others and by the following century had become the leading city of the country. The Grand Prince of Kiev asserted his overlordship, a position that was at first accepted by most of the others. The principal axis of communication of this first Rus was the river routeway from the Baltic to the Black Sea and both Novgorod and Kiev, together with others such as Smolensk and Stara Ladoga, were located on or close to it.

The reasons for Kiev's pre-eminence were varied, but important amongst them was its relative proximity to Byzantium. Kiev was also located close to the junction of the forest and the steppe which in medieval times was of crucial importance as a physical and human boundary. The original Slav inhabitants had been forest dwellers and their whole existence was bound up with the forest and its products. The steppe was to them an alien geographical environment both as a result of its physical conditions and of the hostile nomadic tribes with which it was inhabited. In this respect Rus took on something of the character of the earlier Slav peoples. Despite the fact that the distance between Kiev and Constantinople was actually well over 1,000 kilometres, as a result of the hazards that were encountered on the journey Kiev became the last major port of call on the way south. As a consequence of this it developed into an important trading centre in its own right. A close relationship grew up between Kiev and Byzantium, and it was through Kiev that Byzantine civilization entered Russia. There its influence was deeper and more lasting than was generally the case in the more northerly settlements.

The assertion of overlordship by the Grand Prince of Kiev was an act that owed much to the Byzantine imperial tradition. In 989 Prince Vladimir I of Kiev became an Orthodox Christian and the rest of Rus was soon obliged to follow suit. Christianity was then instrumental in spreading Byzantine culture among the Slav population.[3] The Patriarch of Constantinople was recognized as being the head of the Russian Christian Church, a decision that was later on to have a profound effect on the development of the relations between the Russian Church and state. The close link between the two that was so characteristic of Byzantium was adopted by Kiev and the diarchy of basileus and patriarch was replicated in Kiev with the diarchy of Grand Prince and Metropolitan. The boyars, the great aristocrats, did have considerable influence and the popular assembly, the *Veche*, was called whenever important decisions had to be ratified. However, throughout its history Kiev remained autocratic and the state–Church diarchy always retained the final say. Both ecclesiastical and secular architecture was strongly influenced by the Byzantines, as was artistic decoration. Icon painting became of especial importance and a highly original school arose that was to be of considerable influence in the way the Christian religion was perceived. The Greek Bible was translated into Russian and a form of the Greek alphabet was adapted to the Russian language. In the twelfth century Grand Prince Vladimir Monomachus, who was the grandson of the Byzantine emperor Constantine Monomachus, was presented by the emperor with a crown to be used at his coronation. This was the so-called Cap of Monomach, which was believed to bestow legitimacy upon its wearer. From then on this became the official crown of the rulers of Russia. It is with reason that the city came to be known as 'Byzantium on Dnieper'.

While Kiev certainly shone out amongst the Russian cities, and while there was broad acceptance of a loose feudal allegiance to the Grand Prince, in reality the cities of Rus came to possess a high measure of independence. Each of them had its own prince, who initially possessed almost unlimited powers over the city. While over a time these princes became less powerful, the cities were vociferous in claiming rights and powers which they jealously guarded from the Grand Prince of Kiev.

The proto-Russia that had come into being by the twelfth century was thus in reality little more than a federation of city-states and in this respect at least it was very different from either Byzantium or the powerful centralized Russian state of later centuries. In order to determine the real position of the cities the reasons for this difference need to be examined. Certainly the Russian proto-state was of immense size, and by the tenth century the territory known as Kievan Rus was as large as the whole of western Europe put together. In the conditions of the time, holding together a centralized state of such dimensions was virtually impossible, and forms of devolution were built into its structure. Rus was also basically a commercial country and from the beginning this had underlain its existence. The towns located on the great routeways were commercial settlements and from the beginning the merchant classes exercised considerable influence over their government. As always, such influence was of a strictly functional character that concentrated on the interests of the city itself and opposed those grand designs which are always a feature of empires and imperialism. Perhaps most fundamentally, Kiev never became the accepted capital city of Rus in the way Constantinople undeniably was of the Byzantine Empire. After all Rus was a land of cities, most of which had been established at around the same time. Kiev did not possess any special historic or quasi-religious claim to a position of dominance over all the others. In this respect, although it also was the 'Christian' capital, it was quite different from either Rome or Constantinople. It was, after all, not even the first of them to have been established, a position that by tradition was accorded to Novgorod. There was no particular feeling among the cities of Rus for the special status of Kiev and this was to become all too apparent when the city came to face its greatest danger.

From the outset, of all the Russian cities Kiev had been the most vulnerable to attack by the fierce peoples of the steppe. The city's trade with Byzantium was protected by its great walls and by its fleet on the Dnieper and in the Black Sea. The steppe peoples such as the Polovts and the Pechenegs had made periodic incursions into the lands of the Rus, but over time they had come to live together, for most of the time at least, in relative peace. However, in the early thirteenth century the Mongols, the most aggressive of all the steppe peoples, arrived in the vicinity of Rus. Led by Genghis Khan, who had initiated the expansion of the Mongols across Asia, an advance party made the first contacts with the Russian cities. However, it was another two decades before they made their decisive onslaught on Rus. In 1237 a massive Mongol army arrived at Kiev and there was little time for the inhabitants to prepare an effective defence. In the ensuing onslaught Kiev was completely defeated and its people were either slaughtered or forced to flee. Travellers spoke of the devastation that had taken place and of the city being reduced to a pile of ruins.[4] The surviving inhabitants fled northwards into the forests, which afforded them some measure of protection. They were pursued by the Mongols who then went on to attack other Russian settlements, in particular those in the upper Volga-Oka region, invariably causing immense destruction and loss of life.

In this way the commercial system on which Rus was based came to a precipitate end and the land was reduced to being a Mongol fiefdom. The western Mongols, who were known as the Golden Horde, established their control and went on to be the dominant power in the country for the next 200 years. Kievan Rus was replaced by a Mongol Rus, and Sarai Batu on the lower Volga replaced Kiev as its capital and principal centre of power. The Volga took over from the Dnieper as the principal axis of communication and the routeway southwards to the Mediterranean was replaced by a routeway eastwards into Central Asia.

The collapse of Kievan Rus fits well into the historic pattern of relationships between sedentary and nomadic peoples and the implications of such relationships for city-states. As with the Phoenicians confronted by the Assyrians and the Ionian Greeks confronted by the Persians, the city-states of Rus on their own proved woefully inadequate to deal with the massive military onslaught by the Mongols. However, there were also other factors that made the collapse even more sudden and final than it otherwise might have been. Underlying its swiftness were the effects of the economic problems that were facing Byzantium, which had been in many ways the real mother city of Rus. A quarter of a century earlier, in 1204, the city had been attacked by the Crusaders and the Byzantine Empire had been replaced by the weak and unsuccessful Latin Empire under Crusader control. This was the outcome that had been intended by the Venetians who had subsidized the Fourth Crusade and who became the principal economic beneficiaries of its consequences. The pre-eminent position that had been held by Byzantium since the fall of Rome came to an end and economic power in Europe shifted decisively to the west. The damaging effects of this were soon felt in Kiev, which as a consequence found it increasingly difficult to sustain its leading role among the Russian cities.

There is also the question of the role of the city-states themselves in the disaster that befell Rus. Russian historians have
generally regarded the period of the Mongol occupation as
being the lowest point in the whole of Russian history before
the Second World War. Most of them have placed the main
responsibility for the catastrophe of the 'Mongol yoke' less with
the military power of the Mongols than with the city-states
system itself. This was a particularly favourite theme of Soviet
historians during the early twentieth century and was used as a
basic explanation of the catastrophic nature of early Russian history by Stalinist historians during and after the Second World
War. The Soviet historian S. V. Kiselev, in his preface to V. Yan's
book on Genghis Khan published in 1943 while the crucial bat-
tles for Russia's survival were being waged, appears to be in little
doubt that it was the disunity of Russia that made the country so
weak in the face of the Mongol aggression.[5] According to this
interpretation, each city was selfishly concerned with its own
interests and all were reluctant to send assistance to Kiev in its
hour of need. In fact, the plight of Kiev was initially something
that gave the others some cause for satisfaction since it freed
them from the city's claims to overlordship in Rus. However,
whatever the motive, the consequence was that when Kiev fell
the whole system fell with it and the other cities could be picked
off one by one. When Russia was divided as it was at that time,
wrote Kiselev, it became prey to foreign aggression. Had it been
united the outcome may well have been a very different one.
The Soviet answer to all this was that Russia had to be strong,
and strength required a powerful state firmly controlled from
the centre. Such indictments of the city-state system of Rus
were not just a Soviet interpretation of Russian history. As the
Mongol grip began to weaken in the fourteenth century, there
were already those among the surviving rulers of Russia who
concluded that disunity had been the principal cause of the
country's sufferings. As a consequence, they embarked upon the
creation of a Russian state that could not have been more different from Kievan Rus.

The recovery from the disaster actually began soon after the
collapse of Kievan Rus, and it was particularly associated with
two cities, Novgorod and Moscow. The geopolitical develop-

ments with which each was subsequently associated had very little in common and represented very different reactions to the city-state system. Both of these cities were well located in relation to the Russian river system and both lay deep in the forest and well away from the vulnerable southern boundary with the steppe lands. However, there the resemblance between the two comes to an end. Their aspirations proved to be incompatible and eventually they came into conflict.

Novgorod was by tradition the first Russian city and the birthplace of the Russian state. It was also the only city of any significance that avoided the Mongol conquest and remained completely free of any Mongol occupation. This is ironic, since the first intimations of the impending arrival of the Mongols are actually found in the Chronicle of Novgorod.[6] The city certainly owed its deliverance in large part to its being sufficiently far from the main centres of Mongol power to deter further Mongol advance. While Kiev was located a mere 100 kilometres from the edge of the steppe, Novgorod was 1,000 kilometres away from it and deep in the mixed and coniferous forest belt.[7] This was a considerable deterrent to nomadic horsemen who were used to fast movement across the great plains of central Asia. The Mongol advance westwards was halted by the death of the Great Khan Ogedai in 1234 and it was never to be resumed. The termination of a process of conquest is usually associated geographically with the onset of unfamiliar or uncongenial physical conditions, and the Mongols had halted well before they reached the shores of the Baltic Sea.

In a curious way, the fall of Kiev actually gave a new freedom to Novgorod. It had been within the overall sphere of Kievan Rus and, like all the rest of the Russian cities, had been ruled by a prince of the Rurikovichy dynasty. By tradition the eldest son of the Grand Prince of Kiev had become the prince of Novgorod and it was said in the Chronicles that 'The Grand Prince of Kiev put a Prince on the throne of Novgorod'.[8] Thus it was basically through the Rurikovichy that Kiev had been able to maintain footholds in Novgorod and elsewhere in Rus. However, gradually Novgorod had gained greater independence from Kiev and initially, at least, the Rurikovichy princes made an important contribution to this. Already in the early eleventh century an uprising had taken place in Novgorod against Kievan influence. As with other cities in Rus, a popular assembly, the *Veche*, had been set up and this asserted the increasingly independent character of Novgorod. Prince Yaroslav the Wise, who reigned from 1019 to 1054 and had become Prince of Novgorod shortly after the uprising and had agreed to uphold the liberties of Novgorod. In the *Pravda*, the laws for which Yaroslav became famous, the rights of the cities are expressly itemized and safeguarded. At that time the Grand Prince of Kiev still 'put a Prince on the throne of Novgorod', but by the end of the century this situation had changed. From 1075 the people of Novgorod 'invited' the prince to take the throne and it is clear that the princes were now there only so long as they satisfied the Novgorodians and obeyed their laws.[9] From then on the Chronicles of Novgorod contain such statements as 'the prince fled' or 'The people of Novgorod expelled the Prince' and – a favourite one – the Novgorodians showed the road to the Prince'.[10] The first time that a prince was actually driven out of the city was in 1078, when Gleb Svyatoslavich was removed. The Chronicles tell how 'The Novgorodians expelled him from the city' and the prince then fled 'beyond the portage' (the watershed between the Ilmen and the Dvina), where it seems he was killed by the local Komi-Zyryanian inhabitants. The nomination made by the Grand Prince of Kiev for his replacement was refused and the new prince, chosen by the Novgorodians themselves, was then 'invited' to serve an apprenticeship. From then on this was referred to as the 'rearing' of the prince and it was to recur frequently. However, only ten years later, in 1088, the son of the grand prince of Kiev, Vladimir Monomachus, was again accepted as the prince of Novgorod. Clearly it was the Rurikovichy dynasty, by then claiming its legitimacy by descent from the Byzantine emperors, rather than the paramount position of Kiev itself, that actually held the mystique for the people of Rus. However, this reversion was not a success. It provided an excuse for Vladimir to dabble in the affairs of Novgorod and the attempt made by the *Veche* to replace him with someone more acceptable to the citizens proved unsuccessful. In 1118 Vsevolod Mstislavich, the grandson of Vladimir, became prince and acted more as the agent of Vladimir than as one who had the interests of the city at heart. Vladimir summoned the Novgorod boyars to Kiev to swear fealty to the grand prince. There was a mass refusal to do this and in answer the Novgorodians embarked on the construction of new and far more powerful walls around the city. Dissatisfaction with Vsevolod grew and in 1136 he was finally condemned by the *Veche*. The prince was then arrested, imprisoned in the Bishop's Palace and expelled from the city. This was the 'Novgorod Revolution' and from then on the city was to all intents and purposes a free and independent republic.

At first the republic was dominated by the boyars, but they were soon forced to share their power with the merchant classes. The boyars still attempted to keep hold of the main levers of power, but by the early thirteenth century a wider sharing of power had been institutionalized. The city still had its prince, now chosen by the people themselves, but his power was very limited. The role of the prince became largely that of 'hired military commander' and he came into his own only when the city was in danger.[11] Thus by the time of the arrival of the Mongols in the Russian lands Novgorod had already become virtually a sovereign city-state. The claims to overlordship by the grand dukes, based on the pre-eminence of the Rurikovichy dynasty, continued, and Kiev remained a potential threat until its fall.

From the twelfth century the system of government of the Novgorod city-state was basically a republican one. The citizen body was represented by the *veche*, which was elected and had representation from all classes in society. The *knyaz* (prince) was elected by the *veche* and he remained only as long as he performed his office to the satisfaction of the citizens. Every new *knyaz* was obliged to sign a *ryad* (contract) obliging him to abide by the laws of the city. The *posadnik* was the highest officer of state after the *knyaz*. Originally the representative of the Grand Prince of Kiev, he came to fulfil a role similar to that of prime minister and was also elected by the *Veche*. The *tisyatski* in charge of trade and finance was also an elected office. The officials of the Novgorodian state remained in office so long as they discharged their functions efficiently and honourably. While a deposed *knyaz* was 'shown the road', deposed *posadniks* and

13 Novgorod, from a seventeenth-century icon and a drawing.

others often met a far worse fate. The report in the Chronicle of the riots of 1209 gives a vivid picture of this.

> The men of Novgorod held a *Veche* over *Posadnik* Dimitri and his brethren, because they had ordered the levying of silver on the people of Novgorod, for collecting money throughout the district [and] fines from the merchants, for enforcing the collection of taxes at fixed times, and everything bad . . . God knows how much any took secretly. And many grew rich from this . . . The same year they brought Dimitri dead . . . and buried him . . . The people of Novgorod wanted to throw him from the bridge, but the archbishop . . . forbade . . . And the men of Novgorod kissed the honourable cross.[12]

This kissing of the 'honourable cross' symbolized the power that the Church continued to wield in the Republic. While the Grand Princes of Kiev had lost virtually all their authority over Novgorod, the Russian Orthodox Church remained a force to be reckoned with and the *vladyka* (bishop) continued to be a figure of influence. Decisions were often stated as being made 'through God and St Sofia' and after one victory in battle it was reported that 'the Devil was crushed by God and St Sofia'.[13]

St Sofia had become a powerful symbol of the freedom and prosperity of the city. 'Where St Sophia is there is Novgorod' asserted the *knyaz* in 1215. As a result of the city's independence, the *vladyka* became the main link between Novgorod and Rus as a whole. He came under the authority of the Metropolitan of Kiev who was himself under the Patriarch of Constantinople. The structure of power in the Russian Church was thus far more in evidence than was the structure of power in Rus itself. By the end, for Novgorod and many of the other cities, Rus had become a nebulous concept and it was religion more than anything else that bound the Russian people together.[14]

The power structure of Novgorod itself was clearly reflected in its urban geography. The city was divided by the Volkhov and this river was also a human divide (see illus. 13). On the west bank was the old town with its great walled *Kreml* and the cathedral of St Sofia. This was the Sofiiskaya, which was dominated by the *knyaz* and the church and contained many of the urban residences of the boyars. On the east bank was the Torgovaya, the commercial quarter, which was occupied by the merchants, craftsmen and labourers. It also contained many churches in which these people worshipped. Some of these churches traditionally supported the commercial and industrial interests and often found themselves in opposition to the *vladyka* on the other side of the river. Here also sat the *veche* and other institutions established to safeguard the wider interests of the citizen body. Foreign merchants had their quarters in the Torgovaya and houses were built to accommodate them together with warehouses for their merchandise. Thus after its independence from Kievan influence, Novgorod remained divided between the prince, the Church and the aristocracy on one side and the wider body of citizens, who made their living from commerce and industry, on the other. Besides having a common interest in the well-being of the city, it was opposition to outside influence more than anything else that held the whole citizen body together and enabled Novgorod to continue as a successful functioning entity long after Kiev and Kievan Rus had ceased to exist.

Thus, while most of Russia lay at the feet of the conqueror, Novgorod retained its independence and, following the Mongol conquest of the rest of the country, it flourished as never before. This was because, while the significance of the old north–south routeway, which had been so vital to the rise and prosperity of Kievan Rus, had diminished considerably, the city's commercial links with northern Europe became stronger. The fall of Constantinople to the Crusaders in 1204 followed by the Mongol occupation of much of Asia precipitated the decline and eventual fall of the Byzantine Empire. In these circumstances, northern Europe, up to then very much in the shade of the Mediterranean, experienced a rapid commercial and economic upsurge. When the turbulence associated with their conquests had come to an end, the Mongols reopened the trade routes across Asia to Europe and this entailed the establishment of trade relations with Novgorod. In turn this led to the opening of a new commercial axis from the Gulf of Finland to the Volga and then down that river to the centre of Mongol power at Sarai Batu. The new routeway linked the Baltic with the Caspian Sea and its importance was indicative of the new northern orientation of trade. In the fourteenth century Nizhni-Novgorod was established in the middle of this routeway on the upper Volga and this was to play a significant role in the economic and political development of the new Russia. The epicentre of economic power had shifted northwards from the Mediterranean to the Baltic and the old routeway 'from the Varangians to the Greeks' was replaced by a new one 'from the Germans to the Mongols'. Novgorod, the northern heir to the economic power of Kiev, found a new role as part of this northern world.

Before the situation in the north stabilized and the new economic system came into being, Novgorod had yet one more danger to face and this time it came from the west. With the failure of the Crusaders to regain the Holy Land for Christendom, the decision was taken by the Pope to switch crusading activities to eastern Europe. This was initially motivated by the attempt to bring the pagan Slavs, and in particular the Lithuanians, into the Christian fold, but it was also in part motivated by the desire to advance Catholic Christendom at the expense of the Orthodox Church in the east. By the middle of the thirteenth century there was the added motivation of the Mongol conquests, deemed by the Church to be 'the scourge of God'. From then on crusading in eastern Europe had a leading role in the expansion of Christendom, and new crusading orders, notably the Knights of the Sword and the Teutonic Knights, were established for this purpose. The first Baltic Crusade took place as early as 1198 and it heralded the incorporation of the Baltic lands into the western political and economic, as well as religious, system. It also resulted in the foundation of the first cities in the region and these were to play an important role in its future development. In 1240 the Teutonic Knights advanced into that small corner of Russia that had not been occupied by the Mongols and in so doing menaced Novgorod. Faced with this new danger from the west, the Novgorodians elected Alexander, a member of the Rurikovichy dynasty, to be their *Knyaz*. In 1242 the Novgorodian army, led by Alexander and assisted by forces from neighbouring cities, notably Pskov, met the Teutonic Knights at the legendary Battle of the Ice on Lake Peipus. While there is controversy about the details of this battle there is little doubt as to its significance. The Knights were defeated and retreated westwards, leaving Novgorod and its neighbouring cities free. Alexander gained the suffix Nevski and became the first heroic figure of post-Kievan Russia.

Novgorod had become an independent city-state early on in Russian history and had nurtured institutions of city government in many ways similar to those of the city-states of the Mediterranean. Totally different from Byzantium, or from its protégé Kiev, Novgorod was sufficiently removed from them both to be able to proclaim and maintain its independent position. The institutions that were developed there had no precedent in the Byzantine tradition that was so strong in Kiev.

There the diarchy of Prince and Church had remained absolute and the *Veche* had little real authority. However, institutions of a similar type to those of Novgorod were also found in Pskov and certain of the other northern cities. It is thus its northern location that may be the real key to Novgorod's freedom from the constraints of the Byzantine political tradition. Despite the strong Byzantine orientation of Rus in general, from the outset northern influences are discernible in Novgorod. The original Viking heritage together with the close commercial contacts with their successors in the Baltic and Scandinavia made the routeways to the east conduits for far more than trade alone. The system of government that evolved in Novgorod had similarities to that found in other parts of northern Europe, a fact that reveals Novgorod as being in many ways as much a part of this northern world as of Rus. In fact, its absorption into Kievan Rus can be seen as having been in many ways a more artificial development than was its position in relation to the Baltic and the northern world. It was more than anything else the power of the Rurikovichy dynasty that held together so massive a grouping of cities and implanted the idea of Rus over vast territories which were so different in both geography and orientation. While from the outset the orientation of Kiev had been towards the south, that of Novgorod had been to a considerable extent to the north and west, and this was reflected in its political culture as well as its economic survival after Rus had gone.

By the thirteenth century Novgorod, besides being the sole major survivor among the Russian cities, was also the largest and most important of the cities of the emerging Baltic-Scandinavian economic region. Besides being the oldest of the Russian cities, it was also the precurser of the new city-states of this region. By this time it was already *Gospodin Veliki Novgorod*, the Lord Great Novgorod, that was the respected and powerful centre of a new Rus that had kept at bay invaders from both east and west and in so doing had kept Russia alive. With its daughter city of Nizhni-Novgorod on the Volga linking it to the Caspian Sea and Central Asia, and the new foundations on the Baltic linking it to Scandinavia and the west, it came to play a central role both in the revival of Rus and the emergence of the new northern commercial world.

However, by the middle of the thirteenth century there was very little left of Rus, and the Byzantine connection, formerly so overwhelming, had come to an end. As a result Novgorod was more integrated into the northern world than at any time since Rurik had founded Holmgard 400 years earlier. As the new Baltic trading system began to take shape, Novgorod was from the outset firmly implanted within it.

It was to be some time before the forces generated by that other Russian city, Moscow, which also rose to power in the wake of the Mongol conquests, became sufficiently strong to challenge the role of Novgorod and to bring about definitive change in both Russia and the rest of northern Europe. Before this happened the north had itself become a world of city-states and the relationships among them were to evolve in quite a different manner from those of the cities of the south.

NINE

The German *Hanse*

By the twelfth century throughout large parts of northern Europe the agrarian feudal society of the post-Roman world was already being replaced by a society in which trade and industry played an important role. One of the major changes consequent upon this was the increased importance of the cities. A new multiple city region was emerging north of the Alps that in many ways resembled that which already existed in northern Italy. This was part of a larger region that eventually came to extend from the shores of the Mediterranean to the North Sea and was becoming the economic core region of the new Europe. Like their cisalpine counterparts, the transalpine cities were emporia for the trade which flowed across the Mediterranean and entered northern Europe through the Rhone-Saône valley and the Alpine passes. The axis of this northern city world formed a great arc from the Alps to the North Sea and, as with the principal axis of the Russian cities, it also followed the major rivers. In many ways the Volkov-Dnieper route in the east was replicated in the west by the Rhine route connecting with the Brenner, St Gothard and the other Alpine passes to the Po valley and northern Italy.

The extended Rhine basin was thus becoming the economic core region of transalpine Europe. It was the economic, demographic and political centre of the Holy Roman Empire, and although the medieval emperors had no fixed capital city, the locus of their power lay in this region as it had done since the time of Charlemagne. During his reign the principal imperial residence had been at Aachen, located between the Meuse and the Rhine, and later on the great imperial gatherings were most often held in this region. Worms, Speyer, Mainz, Augsberg,

Nürnberg and Württemberg became particularly associated with imperial diets, councils and edicts.

Like the cities of northern Italy, many of these German cities were also old Roman foundations. Important among them were the border cities of the Roman Empire which had administrative, economic and defensive functions in the provinces in which they were located. They followed closely the line of the *Limes* that had been built between the Rhine and the Danube and which separated the so-called *Romanitas* from the *Barbaritas*.[1] Important among the cities located along the Rhine itself were Castra Vetera (Wessel), Colonia Agrippina (Cologne), Confluentes (Koblenz), Moguntiacum (Mainz) and Argentoratum (Strasbourg). To the west of the Rhine were Augusta Treverorum (Trier), Divodurum (Metz) and Aduatuca (Aachen). In addition to these old cities there were also the new foundations that had been established in post-Roman times. Most of these were located in the former barbarian lands to the east of the Rhine and had been founded as strongholds by the princes who ruled these turbulent borderlands. Such places included Münster, Frankfurt, Ulm, Nürnberg and Regensburg.

From early times certain rights and freedoms had been accorded to the cities of the Empire. These usually related to such matters as the construction of walls, the establishment of city institutions and the holding of trade fairs and markets. These rights had been bestowed by the Emperor as the ultimate source of authority. The cities were thus originally as much part of the feudal system as were the lands of the territorial vassals, and in general these German cities were and remained far more submissive to the Emperor than were those to the south of the Alps. The Emperor was also the king of Germany and there he had more immediate control than elsewhere in his extended domains. In the words of Bishop Otto, in Umberto Eco's *Baudolino*, 'The cities of Germany were all born at the command of a prince, and from the beginning they have recognised themselves in the prince'.[2] In Frederick Barbarossa's Germany the *iura regalia* was respected and the world was as it should be and not 'turned upside down' as it had been in those 'cities beyond the Alps'.[3] Of course, what the Emperor gave he could also take away and this he was quite prepared to do. He was frequently called upon to adjudicate in internal disputes and to ensure that the government of the cities was conducted in a proper manner. Whether he chose to do these things or not he always remained the ultimate authority and the *regalia* gave him the right of intervention whenever the need arose.

What began to bring about a fundamental change in this situation was the beginning of a development that was of immense consequences for the future of Germany and this was already well under way during the reign of Frederick Barbarossa. This was the beginning of the colonization by the Germans of the lands to the east. From then on this *Drang Nach Osten* became one of the principal elements in German history and it took place most vigorously during the period from the twelfth century to the fifteenth. Although it began as a religious movement, the reasons for it were varied and it was eventually to affect all sections of German society. Following the costly failure of the Third Crusade of 1189, during which Frederick Barbarossa had died, the decision was taken to switch the main thrust of crusading activity to eastern Europe. This had come to be considered as being altogether a more fruitful area both for crusading and in other more material ways. While as far as the Church was concerned the main purpose of the Crusades was to extend the boundaries of Christendom eastwards, another motive for it was to give the feudal aristocracy a cause to fight for so as to make them a less dangerous and disruptive force internally. They were given the prospect of gaining new lands and so of increasing their wealth and status within an extended Christendom. The first Baltic Crusade took place in 1198 and was led by Albert von Buxhoevden, a canon of Bremen Cathedral and the founder of the Knights of the Sword. Following the acquisition of new lands in the east there was an influx of colonists from the west. After this the territorial expansion of Germany to the east was accelerated, and the social and economic systems of medieval Germany were increasingly replicated in eastern Europe and the Baltic.

Besides the motives of religious conversion and territorial acquisition there was also a third motive, and this was the expansion of trade to the east through the Baltic. There had been, of course, a long tradition of trade in this direction since the opening up of the route from the Varangians to the Greeks which had such immense significance for the whole of northern Europe. However, the trading system which over the centuries had been based on this was adversely affected by the disruption caused by the Fourth Crusade and the Mongol conquests (see chapter Eight). Thus the necessity to stabilize a fluid and uncertain situation was another important reason for the German movement to the east. The *Drang nach Osten* was begun by the crusading knights, in particular the Teutonic Knights and the Knights of the Sword, and these were followed closely by the Church, which established bishoprics and incorporated the new lands into Christendom. Strongholds and bishoprics were the twin elements in the foundation of the cities which rapidly then became centres of trade and economic activity. These new cities, and the relationships that they came to have with the other elements in the eastern scene, opened up a whole new chapter in the story of the city-state.

Since the time of Charlemagne, the Elbe had been the historic eastern boundary of Germany and of Christendom. Beyond it by the tenth century a succession of small boundary states or marks had been established from the Baltic to the Danube that were intended to be buffers between Christendom and the Orthodox Christian or pagan Slavs. By the time of the Crusades, they included the Nordmark and the marks of Lusatia, Thuringia and Billungs. The beginning of the *Drang nach Osten* signalled a fundamental change in the purpose of these marks from defence to offence. Instead of being boundary states protecting Christendom from the dangers from the east, they were transformed into the principal bases for the eastwards advance.

The economic side of the new eastern orientation was initiated by the founding of Lübeck in 1158 on an island near the mouth of the small river Trave. This was the first *Kolonialstadt* east of the Elbe and until then Hamburg, on the estuary of the river, had been the most easterly of the north German trading cities. Located on the west of the Jutland peninsula, this city looked naturally out towards the North Sea rather than the Baltic. Nevertheless, it was from Hamburg that trade with the Baltic had been conducted using the overland route, the *umlandfahrt*, across the isthmus. Lübeck, on the other hand, which is a mere 60 kilometres from Hamburg, is located on the east of the neck of the Jutland peninsula and therefore had easy access to the Baltic. The city was founded by Henry the Lion, one of the great vassals of Frederick Barbarossa, who had been elevated to the dukedoms of Saxony and Bavaria. He entered vigorously into the eastern project, seeing it as being a way of increasing his own power. It was for this purpose that he founded Lübeck, which soon took over from Hamburg as the most important base for the Baltic trade. As German control extended eastwards into the lands between the Elbe and the Oder, the marks were reinforced and more cities were founded along the Baltic coast. Important among the early foundations were Wismar, Rostock and Stralsund. In the early 1180s a new base of operations for the eastern trade was established at Visby on the island of Gotland in the middle of the Baltic. Harbours and warehouses were constructed there and a large mercantile community came into being. The initial purpose of Visby had been to protect the merchants and merchandise using the Baltic and it became the major link in the growing trade between east and west. From the east came timber, furs, skins, flax, hemp, honey, wax and fish, while from the west came manufactured articles, wine, salt and metals.[4] It was the first great trading emporium run by western merchants as far east as this. The fact that it was so successful and became the centre of a flourishing trade gives some indication of how important this trade route had already become by the end of the twelfth century.

As more of the southern coast of the Baltic was incorporated into the growing German sphere, the crusading knights were moving further east. New Baltic crusades by sea opened up the lands of the eastern Baltic as far as the fringes of Russia. By the thirteenth century this region was firmly under the control of the Knights, who then advanced eastwards and confronted the Russians in the famous Battle of the Ice at Lake Peipus (see chapter Eight). In the Baltic area itself, bishoprics were established and a form of theocratic government came into being. The first city in the region was Riga, which was founded in 1201 by Albert von Buxhoevden, and this became the centre of the new archdiocese of the Baltic. In 1219 this was followed by Reval (Tallinn), which was founded by the Danes who came

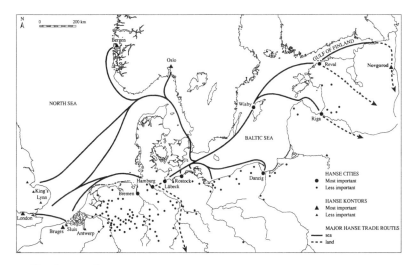

14 The German *Hanse*.

eastwards in the wake of the Knights. Stettin was founded in
1237, Danzig (Gdansk) in 1242, Königsberg in 1256. The fur-
thest east of them all, Dorpat (Tartu), was founded in 1262.

Initially the urban geography of these cities had been dominated by two principal buildings, the castle and the cathedral,
but soon a third, the *Rathaus*, the centre of city government, was
added to them. They soon became centres for the increasing
Baltic trade and new trade routes into the interior were pioneered. Riga was situated at the mouth of the Daugava (Dvina)
river along which a route extended eastwards to the Valdai Hills
watershed (see illus. 14). Reval was on the Gulf of Finland,
which had good water communications via Lake Ladoga to
Novgorod, and Dorpat was a short distance from Lake Peipus,
which connected it to Pskov and the Volkhov river. Other
important foundations on the eastern Baltic coast included
Memel, Windau, Pernau and Narva, and they were all soon
populated by immigrants from the west. The main sources of
these immigrants were usually the recruiting grounds for the
Knights themselves. The Order of the Teutonic Knights had
been founded in 1191 by the merchants of Bremen and Lübeck,
and both these cities and their trading activities were from the
outset closely associated with the eastwards advance. Craftsmen

moved to the east where there was great demand for their services in the building of the new towns and the requirements of their growing populations. While some of these immigrants came from the overpopulated countryside, most came from established towns such as Hamburg and Bremen. Since both these places were so closely associated with the eastern trade, close links between the new foundations and the towns from which their inhabitants came, or with which they had important commercial contacts, were soon established. Because of its origins, Riga was particularly closely linked with both Bremen and Hamburg, and the keys of Bremen and the towers of Hamburg appeared on its court of arms.[5]

The foundations to the east of the Elbe were all outside the traditional eastern borders of the Holy Roman Empire, and despite the fact that successive emperors made claims to the new territories, the extent of imperial authority over them was bound to be limited. That tight imperial control that the emperors could exert over the cities of the Rhineland could not easily be extended eastwards. There were a number of reasons for this, one of them being the pre-eminent role of the Teutonic Knights and the Knights of the Sword. Since these were religious orders, they operated under the authority of the Pope rather than the Emperor and took their instructions from him. The situation of the establishment of bishoprics was much the same and thus the original foundations were in this respect more papal than imperial. Furthermore, successive emperors found it difficult to exert their authority over these areas because of the huge distances involved. The great nobles who took part in the eastern movement, and who were loyal vassals of the Emperor in Germany, did not consider themselves as being automatically his vassals in respect of these newly conquered lands. Thus there was a far greater independence from imperial authority in the whole operation and this affected all aspects of it, including trade and the towns. The towns soon established their own governments, which arose out of a *modus vivendi* with the Knights and the territorial princes. It was not easy for either Pope or Emperor to challenge the arrangements that arose out of this. Since, as elsewhere, the two were not in unison in the exercise of their authority, the extent of the authority of Christendom was usually itself highly ambivalent.

With the absence of close imperial or papal involvement, and the need to establish order in the conquered lands, the relations of the new cities with one another became of crucial importance. If they and their activities were to be protected then they had to do it themselves. The foundation of Visby had been an early example of this, but it gradually evolved into an association that eventually became more comprehensive than anything that had existed up to that time.

The word *Hanse* is derived from an old High German word meaning troop or group.[6] It had frequently been used to describe associations or groups and came to be applied particularly to the grouping of the merchants who were principally concerned with the Baltic trade. It was the absence of overall authority in these lands, and of the protection that such authority would have afforded, that led the merchants to establish an organization of this sort. The relatively limited power of the territorial princes meant that there was little to prevent them from doing this. In particular the death of Henry the Lion, the founder of Lübeck, and the breakup of his duchies, was the trigger for making the cities of the Baltic more independent and prepared to enter into their own mutual arrangements. Besides affording a degree of protection, the basic aim was to bring order to the trading arrangements in the Baltic and to reach an agreement on the joint use of facilities. The first mention of the word *Hanse*, and the first indication of the existence of such an organization, is to be found in an English document dated 1267 in the reign of Henry III.[7] The organization's centre was in Visby and the main facilities that were jointly owned were located there. Besides a harbour and warehouses for the storage of merchandise, the *Hanse* also owned ships for the transport of the goods belonging to its members.[8] The merchants of Visby were known as *communes mercatores* and they had their own seal bearing the inscription *sigillum Theutonicorum Gotlandian frequentancium* ('seal of the Germans frequenting Gotland'). The essential thing about this first *Hanse* was that it was an association of merchants rather than of cities, but in the nature of the way in which things were developing, the cities themselves soon became involved.

The origins of the *Hanse* of towns, that union which has come to be known in English as the *Hanse*atic League, appear to go back earlier than those of the *Hanse* of merchants. In 1241 Hamburg and Lübeck established an alliance for their mutual protection and they agreed to the setting up of defence arrangements to be paid for jointly. In 1259 Lübeck, Rostock and Wismar established a league that involved both towns and merchants. The preamble to the treaty that set up this organization began as follows:

> We, the citizens of Lübeck, Rostock and Wismar . . . have in common council decreed . . . that all who rob merchants in churches, in cemeteries, on water or on land, shall be outlaws and punished by all cities and merchants. No matter where these robbers go with their booty, the city or land that receives them shall be held equally guilty . . . and shall be proscribed by all cities and merchants.[9]

It was thus in the eastern marchlands of the Empire, and in particularly in Holstein and the Mark of the Billungs, that the origins of the *Hanse* can be traced. It was another century before the organization was extended more widely, and when it did so it arose out of the amalgamation of the *Hanse* of merchants and the *Hanse* of cities.

It was in 1358 that the *Hanse* of merchants was transformed into the *Hanse* of cities. The league came into existence as a result of the war between the *Hanse* of merchants and Flanders, which forced the merchants and the cities to identify much more closely with one another. Lübeck took the lead in the transformation into a *Städtebund* and invited representatives of 'all cities belonging to the *Hanse* of the Germans' to come together to discuss their common problems.[10] The meeting took place in Lübeck and about fifty cities accepted this invitation, most of which subsequently joined the new *bund*. The largest and most important of the founder members were Hamburg, Bremen, Visby and Lübeck itself. Others that later became important and influential members included Rostock, Danzig, Riga and Reval. The epicentre of the new organization was to the east of the Elbe in Holstein and the Billungs Mark. It was thus on the boundary of the Empire and beyond it that the cities showed themselves to be most independent. The statutes of the *Städtebund* bound all member cities to protect and defend their mutual interests. It had treaty-making powers with other states and when necessary could act on behalf of all or any of the member cities. A court of arbitration was established to adjudicate in disputes between members of the organization and this court had the power to expel any member who was judged to be in contravention of its rules.

At its heart was the *Hansetag*, the parliament, to which representatives were sent from all the member cities. The meeting place of the *Hansetag* was again Lübeck and it was this city that remained responsible for the calling of the *Hansetag*. The permanent executive of the union, which was given responsibility for carrying out the decisions of the *Hansetag*, was also located in Lübeck. The first meeting of the *Hansetag* took place in 1359 and from then on there were regular sessions. Very soon an army and a navy had come into existence for the purpose of defending the common interests of the *Städtebund*. The *Hanse* had its own coinage, the *pfund*, which came to be widely used throughout northern Europe. In the countries to the west it was known as the *easterling* (sterling), which was accepted outside the area over which the union had authority and came to be considered as a strong currency throughout the north of Europe.[11] The *bund* paid for its activities by the levying of a tax on its members, the *pfundzoll*, and this became of particular importance for the maintenance of the navy. It also employed its own cartographers, who produced maps of the coasts along which the merchants sailed, and the famous *Hanse Seebuch* was a detailed chart of the coasts of Europe from Reval to Lisbon.

After 1358, the word *mercantores*, which had been used until then, was replaced by *civitates* and the overall designation *Städte von der dudeschen Hanse* came into general use. As its success became apparent, more cities joined and by the time of its greatest power in the fifteenth century all the more important cities north of a line from Cologne to Dorpat had become either full or associate members. They were organized into districts on a voluntary basis and representatives met periodically to discuss the implementation of joint policies and initiatives. In this way the *Hanse* had the effect of creating a new economic region in northern Europe that bestrode the historic boundary of the Empire and made this boundary, in economic terms at least, largely irrelevant. In many ways the *Hanse* became a model of independence for those cities that were not part of it or were only loosely associated with it. The cities and the organization that they had together created became for a time the single most dynamic force in northern Europe, and the city-state showed all the signs of becoming the next type of state in Europe. In the Baltic region in particular it was the basis for the creation of a geopolitical region that took over from the territorial states and for a time converted the Baltic into a *Hanse* lake.

In addition to the full members, there were many associate members in which *Hanse Kontors* or merchant quarters were located. Important among these *Kontors* were those in Bergen, Oslo, Bruges, Ypres, Ghent, Antwerp, London and Novgorod. The largest, such as the Deutscher Bruke in Bergen, the Steel Yard in London and Sanct Petershof in Novgorod, had an extra-territorial status and were surrounded by high walls and had their own soldiers for protection. All had their own living quarters and churches for the merchants.[12] The 'great axis' of the *Hanse*, according to Dollinger, lay on a line from Novgorod to London and at its epicentre was Lübeck.

The power of the *Städtebund* was soon put to the test in war with Denmark. This territorial state had risen in the thirteenth century and rapidly became the most formidable power in Scandinavia. Scania was seized from Sweden, giving Denmark control over both sides of the Øresund and consequently the all-important entrance to the Baltic. Dues were exacted on all foreign vessels, including those of members of the *Bund*. The Danes then moved into the Baltic and established themselves in a number of places in Estonia, including Reval, which they had founded and were able to keep out of the hands of the Knights. Visby, still very much the centre of *Hanse* trade, was attacked and its facilities destroyed in 1361. As a result of this Danish threat a conference of the *Hanse* cities was called and this met in Cologne. It was decided that a tax should be raised and a fleet was hastily gathered together. This fleet was then used for the attack on Denmark. The Danes proved to be no match for the forces of the League at sea. The *Hanse* was an alliance of cities whose livelihood depended on the sea and as such they were no strangers to maritime activity, naval as well as mercantile. Copenhagen was captured together with the great fortresses of Helsingør and Hälsingborg on either side of the Øresund. Denmark sued for peace and the Treaty of Stralsund in 1370 established the *Hanse* as the major power in the Baltic. The *Bund* was accorded a monopoly of Baltic trade for 70 years and the Danes were totally excluded from it. The right of unhindered passage for *Hanse* members through the Øresund was also secured. In order to ensure this, the forces of the *Hanse* occupied the fortresses on either side of the Øresund and the ports of Falsterbö, Malmö, Helsingør and Hälsingborg became foreign depots. The facilities at Visby were rebuilt, and Reval, which had been occupied by the Danes, rejoined the union. This early success put the *Hanse* into a strong position against the emerging territorial states of the region. Denmark had been humiliated and its power was held in check for a century. The control over the Baltic that was then established was to last until the revival of the territorial powers at the end of the fifteenth century.

The independence enjoyed by the Baltic and north German cities thus owed a great deal to the existence of the *Hanse* and to the support that it was able to give to its members when confronted by the ambitions of the territorial princes. Both the *Städtebund* and its members owed their considerable success to a number of factors. As has been observed, the organization's principal centres lay well outside the major spheres of influence of either Emperor or Pope. They were for the most part *Kolonialstädte* and as such they were largely free from those constraints that had forced the German cities into a more subservient position. Although Riga, the oldest of the foundations in the eastern Baltic, had been established by the Knights and the Church – and its powerful castle and dominating cathedral remain witness to this – their power was not backed up from the centre. This allowed for greater independence to be exercised from the outset. The arrival of the immigrants from the west then began that process of the internal redistribution of power that was to weaken both the Knights and the Church and eventually to transfer the government of the city from the ecclesiastical authorities to the merchants. In this way the basis of city government was widened and its independence from outside interference became greater. This gave the city the attributes of a state and consequently an increase in its discretion in its relationships with other states. This discretion was used to weaken the ties with both Rome and the Empire and to promote its membership of the grouping of merchant cities as the most important element in foreign policy. Another important factor was the weakness of the territorial states in the Baltic at this time. This weakness had been amply demonstrated by the defeat of Denmark, the most powerful state in Scandinavia. Russia, of course, had already been defeated by the Mongols, and by the middle of the thirteenth century most of it was tributary to the Golden Horde; only Novgorod, which had a *Hanse* counter, together with a few neighbouring cities, had been able to hold on to its independence. Sweden was yet to become a power to be reckoned with. The Baltic was thus wide open to the activities of the *Hanse* and, following the defeat and exclusion of Denmark, it alone possessed either the strength or the will to bring order to the emerging northern world.

The weakness of the Holy Roman Empire at this time has been already observed (see chapter Seven). The foundation of Lübeck by Henry the Lion had taken place during the reign of Frederick Barbarossa, who then stripped him of his dukedoms because this over-mighty vassal refused to take part in the Third Crusade, choosing instead to devote his energies to the *Drang nach Osten*. The fall of Henry and the death of Frederick produced a situation in which Lübeck and the other Baltic cities were able to assert considerable independence within a few decades of their foundation. Despite the emperor's invocation of the *iura regalia* in respect of those cities over which he was able to exert control, his actions had the effect of allowing those in the marches of his realm to embark upon a more independent course. Ironically, the liberties that these cities came to enjoy were to become even greater than those of the north Italian cities that Barbarossa had accused of flouting the *iura regalia*, and in so doing turning his world upside down. Barbarossa's grandson, Frederick II, saw Italy as being the true centre of his empire and took up residence south of the Alps. The fact that he was so notably unsuccessful in his plan for restructuring the unwieldy imperial edifice enabled the cities of the north to continue consolidating their freedom from an even more distant emperor.

While, as with city-states elsewhere, each was individual when it came to its internal government, a general pattern of government emerged in the cities of the League. The governing body of the city was the *Stadtrat* or council. This met in the *Rathaus*, the council chamber, which was usually one of the finest buildings in the city and on which much money was lavished. The city's working population was organized into craft guilds or similar associations, the purpose of which was to look after the common interest. The *Rat* was initially made up of members of the patrician class, the leading families in the city. They were organized into their own *Burgerstube*, aristocratic guilds, and it was overwhelmingly from their ranks that the governing class of the city was drawn. These people had usually gained their wealth in commerce and industry, and while they had initially been a part, although a highly privileged part, of the whole guild system, a result of their increasing monopoly of the city's wealth, they gradually distanced themselves from the rest. In this way they became a commercial nobility, the *Handelsadel*, which governed less in the interests of the city as a whole than of their own class. Thus the cities became divided into the patricians and the non-patricians, and social unrest was common. These internal struggles were democratic in tendency in that they aimed to replace the *Handelsadel* by the *Handwerksadel*, the rule of the patricians by the rule of representatives of the craft guilds. In some places the struggle was a violent one that led to fundamental change, while in others change took place more peacefully and its effects were less radical. In the latter case, representatives of the craft guilds were sometimes accepted as members of the *Rat*, although in many cases only as *ex officio* members. Nevertheless, the whole basis of city government was gradually enlarged. Such enlargement was never fully democratic in any real sense since the poor and the unskilled workers rarely had much say in matters. As with the cities over the Alps, mob violence was often a trigger for political change. When it came it involved the lower classes to only a limited extent, often entailing little more than the rearrangement of the personnel within the ruling oligarchy.

In Cologne the problem of the government of the city was addressed by the establishment of two separate councils, the *Enge Rat*, made up of patricians, and the *Weite Rat*, which was open to all and was elected annually on the basis of a wide franchise.[13] Yet the sharing of power proved to be too difficult a task, and after a period of authoritarian government, in which two *Obermeister* shared power after the manner of the consuls, the new constitution of 1396 vested political power in the hands of the guilds. They elected representatives to a single *Rat*, which became the real power in the city, and, in this way, Cologne came nearer to democratic government than any of the other major German cities. Throughout the whole of this period the city remained an important member of the *Hanse*, and by the early fifteenth century it had become the largest and most prosperous city in it. This considerable commercial success was based on its location at the junction of the north–south and the east–west trade routes, and in this way it was able to play a major part in both Mediterranean and northern trade. It had contacts both with northern Italy and with the Baltic, and its size and prosperity were indicative of the growing economic importance of the middle Rhinelands. Despite being so centrally located within the Holy Roman Empire, the high measure of independence demonstrated by the constitutional changes brought about entirely by internal forces was indicative of the loosening of the imperial ties after the Hohenstaufen period and the power that the larger cities had by then come to possess over their own affairs.

In those cities in which the *iura regalia* was strictly upheld, imperial decrees were required both to confirm the rights of the city and to legalize changes to its constitution. Even in those in which the imperial writ was less evident, some form of outside intervention often took place either to restore the status quo or to confirm the new arrangements. This was often performed by the territorial prince either on behalf of the Emperor or in his own right. In this way the patriarchate allied with the territorial nobility to safeguard the rights of the ruling class, whether this was represented by a territorial or a commercial aristocracy. Originally it was imperial decrees that had accorded the cities within the Empire what rights they possessed, and these were subsequently confirmed by specific decrees relating to such matters as city government, the holding of markets, the levying of duties, the construction of walls and even the right to bear arms. The legalization of the position of such cities into *civitates imperii* possessing a large measure of independence took place throughout the Empire. Outside the Empire, and particularly in the eastern marchlands, liberties were more often secured as a consequence of the weakness of imperial authority or even its complete absence.

While the *Hanse* was a force for the assertion of the independent status of its members and their freedom from papal and imperial authority, as far as the internal affairs of the cities were concerned it became a force for the maintenance of the status quo and particularly for bolstering the power of the ruling oligarchy. One of its statutes actually forbade member states from allowing members of the craft guilds to sit in the *Rat*. In 1374, when the patriarchate of Brunswick was forced to concede power to the guilds, the city was expelled, and by refusing to trade with it forced it to restore the patriarchate to power.[14] Only when the power of the *Hanse* began to wane were major cities such as Hamburg and Rostock able to ignore its decrees and change the basis of their government without interference. In spite of the imperfections of the city governments, the power of the patrician class and the dissatisfactions of the lower orders, there was rarely any recourse to authoritarian government or tyranny. This was because there was a certain balance of power in the cities of the *Hanse* that was so often lacking south of the Alps. Clarke maintained that in Germany and northern Europe 'the democratic tendency was strong enough to disturb, but not strong enough to counteract, [the] oligarchic tradition'.[15]

Lübeck, the heart of the *Hanse*, demonstrates more than any other city the evolving relationship between empire, league and city-state. As the first *Kolonialstadt*, Frederick Barbarossa had accorded it the limited privileges of *jura honestissima*, but following the fall of Henry the Lion in 1180, and the death of the Emperor shortly afterwards, the situation completely changed.

For a time there was weakness both in the Duchy of Holstein and in the Empire itself, and this gave the city the opportunity to assert its independence of its territorial masters. In 1227 Frederick II accorded Lübeck the status of imperial city – the only one to the east of the Elbe – and from then on its freedom and autonomy were guaranteed by imperial decree.[16] It then used its privileged position in order to assert its complete independence. It looked away from Germany and became deeply involved in Baltic affairs. It entered into close relations with neighbouring cities and the agreement with Hamburg in 1241 was the basis of the future *Hanse*. It was as a result of the initiative of the *Stadtrat* of Lübeck that the cities of the Baltic and North Sea went on to establish the *Hanse* during the following century. Although it was an association of equal cities, from the outset Lübeck put its imprint firmly on it. In the words of Braudel, 'Lübeck had been the standard-bearer of the *Hanse*atic League . . . Recognized by all as the capital of the merchant confederation . . . The city's arms – the imperial eagle – became in the fifteenth century – the arms of the League itself'.[17] It was the site of the executive of the League, and it was Lübeck that held the responsibility of calling the meetings of the *Hansetag*. At these meetings, a senior member of the Lübeck *Rat* 'hält das Wort', in other words acted as speaker or president. The *Rat* also acted as the collective executive of the *Hanse* and even issued decrees and proclamations on its behalf.[18] There was opposition to this leading role of Lübeck from other important cities, such as Cologne, but as a result of its political and economic importance it was able to retain its pre-eminence. The *Hanse* had first come into being around the Jutland isthmus and, despite the fact that it became a maritime power controlling the Baltic and much of the North Sea, its fulcrum remained the land route between Hamburg and Lübeck.

Lübeck was both the first and the largest of the Baltic *Kolonialstädte*, and by the middle of the thirteenth century it already had a population of some 30,000.[19] This was small by comparison with the Italian cities, but the Baltic was a newly colonized world and it did not possess the inherent wealth either of Italy or even of the more central regions of Germany. However, its power was attested to by the Italian traveller

Aeneas Silvius, who asserted in 1548 that 'Lubeck possesses such wealth and such power that Denmark, Sweden and Norway are accustomed to elect and depose kings at a sign from her'.[20] In 1375 the Emperor Charles IV paid a state visit during which he confirmed the city's rights and liberties. He also used the occasion in order to accord official imperial recognition to the *Hanse*. By then the League had become generally accepted as being a power in its own right and the pre-eminent position of Lübeck within it was acknowledged.

The cities of northern Europe, and in particular those that lay on or adjacent to the Baltic, were thus able to gain and maintain a large measure of independence and their position as true city-states is beyond question. The organization to which they belonged was not one that was imposed upon them, as was the case more widely in the German feudal system, but one that they had themselves created and to which they chose to belong. It was therefore consensual and, at state level at least, fairly democratic. However, they had a number of characteristics that made them in significant ways different from the city-states of Italy or those of the ancient world. The control by the territorial nobility and the Church was largely eliminated and city governments came to reflect basically the commercial interest. They possessed little or no territory beyond the city walls and consequently there was little of that symbiosis of town and country that was so much a characteristic of the Greek *polis* and the Italian *civitates*. The reasons for this difference are to be found in the geography of the area. The glacial moraines that dominate the geomorphology of the southern Baltic region produced far poorer soils than the rich sedimentary deposits in the valley of the Po, and the agriculture of the Baltic was consequently much less productive. Consequently, links with the surrounding countryside were less important, since more of the basic necessities of life had to be brought considerable distances. A wider trading organization was therefore more appropriate to their circumstances rather than the high degree of reliance on local supplies as was the case in Italy, and this was reflected in the very different geopolitical arrangements. The territorial nobility confirmed the rights of the cities and entered into economic arrangements with them. These cities were thus more purely commercial entities than were those of Italy, and when they entered into political arrangements these were designed above all to safeguard and protect their trade. They were less territorial than almost any city-states before them, but nevertheless together they created a power that was widely involved in both internal and external affairs and that for a time succeeded in excluding the territorial powers and dominating a large part of northern Europe.

On a map the *Hanse* appears not as a group of territories insulated from one another by frontiers but as a group of cities and ports bound together by trade routes on land and sea. Such a map is underlain by cooperation rather than confrontation among the geopolitical entities of which it is made up. Not one of these entities, not even Lübeck or Cologne, was strong enough on its own to look after its interests successfully, but together they made a formidable power which could do this with considerable success. The *Hanse* came into being at a time when the territorial powers, for a variety of reasons, were relatively weak, and it was this weakness more than anything else that allowed the city-states of the Baltic to become collectively a power in their own right. When territorial power again asserted itself, the city-states were to be confronted by a foe that they were not strong enough to combat. It was in the Mediterranean world that this process of change began and it was in the first great power of the modern world, Spain, that the confrontation between city-state and territorial state took place most violently.

TEN

The *Comunidades* of Castile

City-states, which had been so characteristic of the ancient world until the rise of Rome, revived in the conditions of medieval Europe. They flourished both in the Holy Roman Empire that was, nominally at least, the heir to Rome and in the new colonial lands to the east, within which they were able to assert an increasingly independent status. Over time the rights and privileges that they were granted by successive emperors evolved in many cases into full sovereignty. Even strong emperors such as Frederick Barbarossa, preoccupied as he was with the wider problems of Christendom, had limited time and resources to assert the Empire's legal authority, the *iura regalia*, over cities that desired above all to retain their liberties. His successor, Frederick II, attempted a radical restructuring of the internal government of the Empire, but by that time the divisions were too great to be repaired. The *civitates imperii* had become built in to the political structures of empire, and these and the other cities had become in many ways the most dynamic and forward-looking political entities within the Empire. They were outward rather than inward looking and resented being forced into the strait jacket of what was to them an increasingly irrelevant and outmoded structure.

The future organization of Europe had become a burning question for both Emperor and Pope and also for those territorial rulers who increasingly supplanted the imperial authority and asserted their paramouncy over their dukedoms, principalities and kingdoms. While Barbarossa had attempted to bind together the lands of historic Christendom more closely, overmighty vassals such as Henry the Lion had sought to build up their own power in the new Christendom that was coming into being east of the Elbe. 'Modern' Europe arose out of this increasingly tangled situation and it was most characterized by the institutionalization of political fragmentation. However, the aspiration to unity remained deeply embedded and a succession of powers sought in turn to achieve positions of dominance and to unite Europe around them. This succession of putative dominations was to characterize Europe for most of the next 500 years.[1] The implications of this power struggle for the world of the city-states were not good.

The first of these great powers which aspired to dominate modern Europe was Spain, a state that had come into existence only in 1492 following the union of the Crowns of Castile and Aragon. Under the joint rule of *Los Reyes Catolicos*, Isabella of Castile and Ferdinand of Aragon, the *Reconquista* came to an end, and Granada, the last Islamic state in the Iberian peninsula, was occupied and incorporated into the new Spain. Within a quarter of a century of its foundation the new state had moved into a position of being the most formidable military power in Europe with an aspiration to dominate the continent and to remould Christendom in its own image. In pursuit of this aspiration, *Los Reyes Catolicos* embarked upon the creation of a highly centralized state under despotic royal rule. This was especially so in Isabella's Castile, the heart of the new Spain, in which there was little room for anything that did not fit into the designated pattern of a Catholic kingdom leading the triumphant revival of a Catholic Europe. The divergence between the old and the new visions of Europe was most clearly seen during the reign of their grandson, the Emperor Charles V. On the death of his grandfather Ferdinand in 1516, Charles had ascended the Spanish throne as Charles I. At the same time he inherited the new Spanish possessions in Central and South America. Charles immediately set up his court in the Castilian capital city, Toledo, and from there he proposed to continue the centralizing policies of his predecessors.

As part of the strategy for reinvigorating Christendom, Spain's eyes had for some time been on Italy, the centre of the Christian world and the seat of the Papacy. It was also the location of the richest and most powerful cluster of city-states in Europe, in which the Renaissance had achieved its greatest flowering and which was collectively the dynamic centre of Europe's commercial economy. These city-states had for some time been the object of the attentions of the emerging territorial powers, for whom their possession was the greatest of prizes. In 1494 the French king Charles VIII invaded Italy in pursuit of dynastic claims and by so doing he was the first to shake the confidence of the city-states (see chapter Seven). However, it was Spain rather than France that actually became the inheritor of the wealth and power of Italy. In 1503 the Spaniards occupied Naples in pursuance of their own dynastic claims, and Naples, Sicily and Sardinia were incorporated into the Spanish domains. After securing control over the south of the peninsula, the Spaniards then moved north and in 1512 occupied Milan and other Lombard cities. From there they controlled the southern end of the so-called 'Spanish road' linking their possessions in the north of Europe with those in the south. The once proud city-states that had asserted their independence and defied successive emperors were now subjected to military occupation and absorption into the growing Spanish imperial sphere.

In 1519, following the death of his paternal grandfather, the Holy Roman Emperor Maximilian, Charles I of Spain was elected Holy Roman Emperor. As emperor and king of Spain and its overseas possessions, the new Emperor Charles v was now the most powerful ruler in Christendom. With personal possessions stretching from the Danube to the Atlantic and from the North Sea to the Mediterranean, he had a finger in every pie in Europe. He was in this way both a medieval and a modern figure, since the empire over which he ruled looked back to medieval Christendom and forward to the modern world of the great powers. The nature of his power, and the way in which he used it, owed something to them both. While he was the ruler of the Holy Roman Empire that had been founded by Charlemagne some 700 years earlier, he was also ruler of that Spanish Empire that had come into being with the Union of the Crowns and the discovery of America a mere quarter of a century before. Although from then on he spent little time in Spain, the country remained Charles's most important power base, and this power was underpinned by the wealth that increasingly poured in, in the form of gold and silver, from the newly acquired lands in America. The geopolitical centre of the Empire was and remained Castile and it was here that the first and perhaps most fundamental test of his authority as *Rex et Imperator* was to come.

Castile had been the largest and most important state to emerge out of the reconquest of the Iberian peninsula from the Arabs. It was located on the frontiers of Christendom, and its whole existence was engaged in the confrontation with Islam. The *Reconquista* had dominated its life and from the outset it had been ruled by a military aristocracy preoccupied with warfare and the acquisition of territory.[2] Huge estates, the *estancias*, owned by the *grandes*, the great aristocracy, covered most of the country. Effectively Castile was ruled by some 25 families and the rural economy was firmly based on pastoral farming, mainly for sheep, cattle and horses. The Church played an equally important role in this frontier state and the great cathedrals, together with the castles that had given the country its name, were the most outstanding features of its urban geography. The castles were the centres of aristocratic power while likewise the cathedrals were the centres of episcopal power. The cities then rose up around these two most visible signs of the country's power structure.

Many of these cities were on the sites of Roman foundations, notably Segovia, Salmantica (Salamanca) and Tolentum (Toledo), to which the capital had moved from Burgos in 1095. As they became the main centres of commerce and industry, they also became of great importance to the monarchs for the supply of the goods necessary for the pursuit of the endless war of reconquest. These included a variety of manufactures, most important among which was fine steel for swords and armour for which Toledo became especially famous. In order to get the merchants and industrialists of the towns to cooperate with them, the monarchs were forced to make concessions and this meant giving them certain rights. These *fueros* included the right to construct walls, to bear arms, to hold markets and to establish the institutions of city government. As a result of this, over time the spirit of independence of the Castilian cities gradually increased. The *Cortes*, the Castilian parliament, came to reflect in its composition the three major powers of the realm –

the *grandes*, the Church and the cities. Each of these had been able to demand concessions of various sorts, which the monarch, in order to retain their support, was forced to concede. Thus a balance of power was created in Castile that had to be carefully nurtured by the monarch and on which he came to depend. This was the situation that was inherited by *Los Reyes Catolicos* when they came to power in 1492. It was a situation that proved to be quite incompatible with their objectives and they soon embarked upon a process of change that was to create a centralized and despotic state in place of the loose feudal one.

By the early years of the sixteenth century the situation in Castile bore some resemblance to that in the north of Italy. There was a cluster of large and powerful cities, which were the main centres of trade and industry and possessed a considerable measure of independence. However, there the resemblance came to an end. In Italy the overall authority was distant and usually weak and divided, and this had allowed for the emergence of powerful and independent city-states, many of which by the standards of the time could be described as being sovereign. In Castile, on the other hand, the authorities were close and watchful and, although they had been prepared to make concessions for the sake of retaining support, were certainly not inclined to acquiesce in the disintegration of the state. In Castile there were no cities of the magnitude of Florence or Venice. By the fourteenth century Toledo, the capital and largest city, had a population of 40,000, while Valladolid, the next largest, had a population of 25,000 and Burgos, the earlier *Reconquista* capital, only 10,000.[3] Neither was the dominant position of the northern Italian cities over the whole urban and rural economy replicated in Castile. In Italy the urban population was considerably larger than the rural population, while in Castile this was far from being the case.[4] In Italy the cities were surrounded by regions of which they were themselves the centres. The cities of Castile were enveloped by the economic, demographic and political might of a surrounding countryside over which they had no authority. The *fueros* ceased at the city gates and beyond them the surrounding lands remained firmly in the hands of the *grandes*. Most importantly, Castile, formerly on the periphery of a loose medieval theocratic empire, was in the process being transformed into the core region of the most powerful of that new breed of European political units, the territorial (nation) state.

Although by the late fifteenth century the Castilian cities had come to possess considerable independence, this was still far more limited than that of the cities of either northern Italy or the Baltic. However, in the *Cortes*, together with the other estates of the realm, they were able to exert some influence over the policies of the state. In Castile there were eighteen cities which sent representatives to the *Cortes* and there they could argue the case for lower taxes, the increase of the *fueros* and in general less state interference in their affairs. In most cases their representatives were chosen by the *oficios*, the guilds of artisans. Each city had its own municipal council and its members were also usually elected by the *oficios*. The *ayuntamiento*, the municipal government, was then appointed by the council.

The conflict between the new centralizing Spanish monarchy and the Castilian cities began during the reign of *Los Reyes Catolicos* and came to a head during the reign of Charles v. As the new Spanish state began to assert its power, the *fueros* came to be increasingly challenged. Isabella and Ferdinand firmly believed that the cities should be full rather than semi-detached parts of their realm and as such should be brought more fully under their authority. From the outset, the monarchs took an increasing interest in the way in which the cities were governed and the implications that this had for the royal prerogatives. Such scrutiny of their internal affairs was resented by the cities, which had become used to a situation of increasing independence from royal controls in return for the support that they had given in the pursuance of the *Renconquista*. However, this period of Iberian history had now come to an end and the monarchs sought to establish more absolute control over their realm as the base for a new *Reconquista* that was to involve the whole of Europe.

For the cities the intrusion of the monarchs into their affairs was a most unwelcome development. Consultations took place among them and they reached an agreement that they should enter into an alliance for the protection of their common interests. This *Junta de Tordesillas* was set up in 1500 and its initial membership consisted of the eighteen cities that sent representatives to the *Cortes*. Most important among them, and the ones that drove the organization forward, were Toledo, Valladolid, Burgos, Segovia and Salamanca. The largest and most important cities in Spain during the Roman and the Arabic periods had been those of Andalucia, notably Cordoba and Seville, but none of these cities was a member of the *Junta* nor took part in the subsequent developments. In these most recently reconquered lands, the grip of the *Reyes* and the *grandes* was tighter and there was virtually no autonomy. Andalucia, which had known little freedom in the past, became the prototype for the government of the new centralized state and from the outset its cities were bound closely into it. Thus the reaction to monarchical absolutism did not take place where the urban feudal order was most oppressive, but in those regions in which the emerging urban society had already reached the highest level of autonomy.[5]

The basic aim of the *Junta* was to come to a common position in regard to the incursions of the monarchy and to defend themselves against it. The entity the rights of which they were defending was the *comun*, the body of tax-paying citizens, which was regarded as being not just a collection of those who happened to live in the cities, but as a distinct social grouping that collectively constituted the *comuna*. Not content with merely defending themselves, the *comuna* of Tordesillas went ahead to make demands for more freedoms. They also produced a programme for the achievement of a greater democratization of municipal power, including the election of municipal assemblies and of municipal officials. They moved to set up a full federation of the cities, which would have its own federal government together with a *Cortes* elected by the cities themselves. The underlying theme of all this was the desire of the cities to go it alone and to become independent of the monarchs and the *grandes* of Castile. In this they were consciously or unconsciously working towards becoming truly sovereign city-states and to creating a common organization after the manner of the *Hanse* in northern Europe.

The response of the monarchy was uncompromising. Its objective since the Union of the Crowns barely a decade earlier had been to diminish the *fueros* of the cities and they were not likely to acquiesce in the opposite taking place. They appointed *Corregidores*, royal governors, who were placed in each of the cities and were given considerable powers. They took over the main functions of the municipal councils and in doing so they were assisted by the royally appointed *magistrados*. The *Corregidores* chaired the meetings of the councils, the powers of which were increasingly restricted.[6] In this way in the early sixteenth century the grip of the monarchy over the cities became steadily tighter and the *fueros*, which had accumulated over a long period of time, were either abrogated or disregarded.

This all proved quite unacceptable to those city leaders who had sought to achieve a new relationship with the Spanish state. In 1519 the young king Charles ascended the imperial throne and as Holy Roman Emperor became immediately involved with the increasingly turbulent European scene. Two years earlier, in the German city of Wittenberg, Martin Luther had challenged the excesses and abuses of the Catholic Church, which was at this time presided over by the Medici Pope Leo x. In so doing Luther began the Reformation, which was to rock Christendom to its foundations. After his accession, Charles became preoccupied with religious affairs and from then on he spent little time in Spain. Taking advantage of his absence, in May 1520 the cities of Castile rose in rebellion. The *Junta de Tordesillas* was revived and demands were reiterated for more freedom and for the establishment of a federation of cities. The participating cities are known as the *comunidades*. Those involved in direct action were the *comuneros* and the revolutionary action itself was the *comunidad*. The *comuneros* were joined by others who opposed the power of the monarchy, including many members of the clergy and the *caballeros*, the lesser nobility. They had as great a dislike for the monarchy and for the *grandes* as did the *comuneros* themselves. In this way the revolt of the cities became the focus for a wider revolt against an absent and essentially foreign monarchy. The *Junta* proclaimed the establishment of a federation of free cities and an army was recruited for its defence. This was made up mainly of mercenaries together with members of the lesser nobility. The wealth of the cities enabled them to pay for this and to establish their own common organizations. The *Corregidores* were expelled, the *fueros* reinstated and municipal assemblies were elected. A democratic federation of *comunidades* came into being in the heart of Castile.

However, Charles was no Barbarossa and he had no intention of acquiescing in the disintegration of the centralized state that his grandparents had established. He was not long in returning to take charge of the situation and assembled an army that included members of the *grandes*. The *comunero* army was led by Juan Lopez de Padilla of Toledo. In April 1521 the two armies met at Villalar. At this battle the *comunero* army was completely routed and the *comunidades* were then exposed to the full might of the powerful Spanish army. One by one the cities were attacked and subdued. Those, such as Burgos, that had displayed an especially radical approach to the democratization of the institutions of government and in which the wealthy merchants had distanced themselves from the *comunidad*, leaving the revolt entirely in the hands of the *oficios*, were most harshly treated. Such cities were subjected to considerable pillage and destruction and their leaders were executed.[7] The last of the cities to continue the resistance was Toledo itself, but this finally fell in February 1522 and the revolt of the *comunidades* came to an end.

Following this the Crown moved to re-establish its authority more tightly than ever. The *Corregidores* were reinstated and their powers became absolute. The rights of the assemblies were whittled away and most remnants of devolved government were soon brought to an end. The government of the cities was put into the hands of those officials appointed by the monarch. As a result of this the cities were bound into the structures of the Spanish state more firmly than they had ever been before.

Following the end of the revolt, the Spanish monarchy, now freed from the threat of being subverted in its Castilian heartland, embarked upon the grand project of redesigning Christendom in its own image and – almost as an afterthought – becoming the first superpower of the modern world. The alternative project of the Castilian cities for political freedom, democracy and social equality came to an abrupt and bloody end. The wider implication of this was that the attempt to create a system in which political and economic ends could be achieved by cooperation rather than by coercion had been crushed by the overwhelming might of the territorial state. The principle of force had triumphed over that of voluntary union and in the wake of this the Spanish state moved definitively into an expansionist mode driven overwhelmingly by ideological considerations. Freedom was the greatest casualty and bigotry the greatest victor. In the words of Castells, 'The Spanish monarchy, relying on the Catholic Church and now supported by the nobility, felt strong enough to undertake the building of a world-wide empire, in a storm of bloody conquest, religious fanaticism and economic ineptitude.'[8]

The revolt of the *comunidades* was based on the idea that the *comun* was a reality that transcended the sum total of its parts. It arose out of the conviction that the townspeople of all classes had more in common with one another than that which divided them. Despite the confrontation between town and country that was inherent in it, many Spanish historians have viewed it as being less a class than an anti-class movement that was essentially democratic in its basic purposes. In this it was also both anti-feudal and anti-monarchical and proposed the establishment of 'a new form of city and a new form of state'.[9] This 'third way' between feudal balance and monarchical despotism was the essence of the city-state ethos. It sought to substitute power that arose from below for that which was imposed from above. In this the city had a central innovative role and the *comunidades* were engaged in attempting to transform this into 'a new cultural category and a new political reality'.[10] Castells concluded that while 'as a political revolution the *comunidades* failed . . . as a citizen movement they brought together for ever in the collective memory of the Spanish people the idea of freedom, the right of . . . self-government, and the hope for a better life'.[11]

While the Spanish monarchy had been able to crush effective opposition to its policies in its Castilian heartland, on the northern periphery of its European sphere of influence the situation was a very different one. In the Netherlands the desire for freedom was even more intense than in Castile and there the city-states played a crucial role in its satisfaction. The conflict between the city-state and the monarchical state was long and bloody, and the institutions that finally emerged owed something to them both.

ELEVEN

City, Province and Nation in the Netherlands

The violent confrontation between the Spanish monarchy and the Castilian cities, together with the Spanish occupation of Italy, brought to an end the second period in history during which the Mediterranean had been a world of city-states. By the middle of the sixteenth century, Venice, which was the oldest of them all, had become one of the few real survivors. Close to the historic junction between east and west, the city had survived the fall of Constantinople in 1453 and the occupation of the lands of the Byzantine Empire by the Ottoman Turks. While Venice had been one of the principal beneficiaries of the fall of Constantinople to the Crusaders in 1204, there was little to celebrate in the final end of the city that had first been Venice's admired model and then its bitter rival. Venice was able to negotiate a trade treaty with the new masters of the eastern Mediterranean, but its great days were by then in the past. Spain in the west and the Ottoman Empire in the east between them dominated the inland sea, which became once more the embattled frontier between Christendom and Islam.[1]

It was in these circumstances that the epicentre of the world of city-states moved north of the Alps and there it was to survive into modern times. This reflected both the shift in the balance of economic power in Europe from south to north and the difficulties experienced by Spain, the first modern European power, in her attempts to exert control over the north of the continent. Since the project for the reuniting and redesigning of Christendom had to include Germany as well as Italy, it was an essential requirement that Spanish power be extended north of the Alps. The change in the epicentre of economic power initially took the form of a movement in the balance of power northwards along the axis from Lombardy to the delta of the Rhine.

The Netherlands, an indeterminate area of swamps, multiple deltas, sandbars and low-lying plains, had come into the possession of the Spanish monarchy, and by the early sixteenth century Spain had become the dominant power along the whole of the axis. Historically a part of Lotharingia, the remains of the much disputed 'Middle Kingdom' between France and Germany, the Netherlands were subsequently partitioned between the French and the Empire, but only the county of Flanders fell to France. Although this was a small part of the whole area, it was the richest part and the one with the greatest potential for future economic development.[2] From the fourteenth century Flanders, together with most of the rest of the Netherlands, was incorporated into the expanding duchy of Burgundy. The indeterminate nature of the Netherlands within this large state is demonstrated by the fact that at first the area had not even been given a proper name but was known to the new masters quite simply as 'le pays de par deça' (the lands over there). In 1463, however, the so-called Burgundian Netherlands, made up of seventeen counties administered from Brussels, came into being. Following the death of Charles the Bold, the last duke, in 1477, the duchy disintegrated and most of the Burgundian Netherlands fell to the Habsburgs. In 1516 they were inherited by the new Spanish king, Charles I, son of Duke Philip of Burgundy and Joanna, the daughter of Ferdinand and Isabella. Out of this began that tempestuous relationship between Spain and the Netherlands that Charles's son Philip II called the 'damnosa hereditas'. This inheritance was to have the most dramatic effects both for Spain itself and for the city-states of northern Europe.

The Netherlands lie close to the principal junction of the major routeways of northern Europe. These run from north to south via the Rhine and its tributaries and from east to west around the coasts of the North Sea and the Baltic. Since the time of Charlemagne, the lower Rhineland had been one of Europe's most important centres of communication and also an important centre of its political and economic life. Colonia Agrippina and Aachen, both located on the southern fringes of the Netherlands, had been respectively the centres of the Roman and Carolingian administration, and Brussels subsequently had a similar political and administrative function in respect of the Burgundian possessions. The Netherlands was also the first centre of northern Europe's revived commerce and became its major link with the Mediterranean world. From there the products of the south were distributed to the countries of the north and products from the north were received in exchange. Northern Europe's first important manufacturing region was built on this commercial base.

The county of Flanders, the most important county in the Netherlands, had by the twelfth century moved into the position of being in effect the core region of the emerging north European commercial and industrial economy. The county is located on the southern edge of the Rhine delta, and the tributary river Scheldte is its principal line of communication into the interior. It was in this region that the first important commercial cities in northern Europe were established. The first of these was Brugge (Bruges), which already by the fourteenth century had become the largest and most important centre of commerce north of the Alps. The relationship of this city to northern Europe as a whole had become in many ways similar to that of Venice to the Mediterranean. It was like Venice in being located near the mouth of a great river on an unpromising coast of sandbars and marshes. Likewise, it had not been one of the ancient cities, most of which were located well in the interior, and this remote coast on the edge of their dominions had held few attractions for the Romans. There are in fact no references to Brugge before the eleventh century, and by then wine from Bordeaux, grain from northern France and wool from England were being exchanged there for the products of the Baltic.[3] The construction of the new harbour at Damme in the eleventh century was followed in the following century by an even larger one at Sluys. In 1252 a *Hanse* counter was established in Brugge and from then on the city became closely linked with the Baltic trade. Until that time, the trade of the Netherlands with the Italian cities had been by land over the Alps, but as navigation improved sea transport became more important and ships began to sail from the Mediterranean through the Straits of Gibraltar to northern Europe. In 1277 the first Genoese ship sailed into the harbour of Brugge and the first important maritime connection was established between northern Europe and the Mediterranean.[4] In 1309 the Brugge stock exchange (the bourse) was established and in 1314 the first Venetian ship arrived with a cargo of spices. A Venetian quarter was soon established and from then on 'Flanders galleys' sailed from Venice to Brugge twice a year. They brought spices, silk, sugar and pepper and returned with wool from England, cloth from Flanders and wines from France. At Brugge the trading world of Venice met that of the *Hanse*. Brugge dealt with trade from all over Europe and became, in Braudel's terminology, a *Weltmarkt*, a centre of the world economy that surpassed even Venice itself in importance.[5]

Brugge also became an industrial centre engaged most importantly in the fabrication of cloth. The most important centre of the cloth industry in Flanders, however, was Ghent, located inland on the river Scheldt. By the fifteenth century northern Europe's largest textile industry was located in Flanders using local flax, imported silk and, most importantly, English wool. Ypres to the west was another important centre for textile manufacturing, and by the fifteenth century the Brugge–Ghent–Ypres triangle had become northern Europe's most important economic core region. By then these cities were all *Hanse* counters and lay at the hub of a larger economic region that extended from England to the Baltic. They were linked by land and sea to Italy and the Mediterranean.

From early on the principal cities of the Netherlands had an important say in the running of their own affairs. There are records of conflicts with the lords and the bishops and this led to a situation in which the cities gained a growing sense of their own special identity. Most of the principal cities had grown up around castles, which were the seats of authority of the princes, dukes and counts. Initially the castellan had been given as much authority over the city as over the castle itself and the growing aspirations of the citizens became the principal cause of disputes between them. An early example of such a conflict was at Cambrai in the county of Hainault and here what is believed to be the oldest *comunitas* in the Netherlands was established in the eleventh century.[6] In the county of Flanders similar developments subsequently took place in Brugge, Ghent, Ypres, Saint-Omer, Lille and Douai. *Comunitates* were set up in all these cities and a legal framework was established within which the municipal institutions could function largely unhindered. The main institution of municipal government was the *Stadrat* and at the beginning this was given only very limited functions. It was usually made up of separate houses that represented the different guilds and particular groups, such as the great merchants. The nobility and the Church were also usually represented on the *Rat* and this frequently led to conflicts of interest. The elected members of the *Rat* were known as the *jures* and over time they became more important in civic government. The place in which their meetings took place was the community house or *Gildhalle*, which gradually replaced the castle as the most important centre of civic authority. From the outset, the guilds had been basic to the establishment of the *comunitates* and they remained the principal guarantors of the rights of the city. Members of the guilds also performed civic functions and took on the role of city magistrates.[7]

The counts of Flanders in particular had always taken considerable interest in the development and the prosperity of the towns and had been prepared to grant them the rights that they desired. These included exemption from military service and tolls, grants of land, the establishment of courts of justice and the limiting of episcopal authority. A major step forward in the independence of the Flemish cities took place in 1127 when a charter was granted to Saint-Omer. Recognition was accorded that the city was a distinct legal entity with full communal autonomy.[8] This precedent was soon followed elsewhere and similar charters were granted to the other major cities of the county. In this way their legal status as separate and distinct elements in the overall political structure was specified and guaranteed.

In a similar way in the adjacent counties of Brabant and Hainault, the towns were also usually supported by the counts against those who challenged their rights, notably the Church and the nobility. The counts saw the towns as being of great benefit to themselves and to their counties and they were quite prepared to give them the privileges that they sought. Relations between towns and counts appear to have been more often good than bad and cooperation rather than conflict between them became the norm. In any case the counts were usually otherwise engaged with territorial and dynastic matters and were more than happy to leave the towns free to create the wealth from which they were major beneficiaries. From the eleventh century this part of Europe was an important recruiting ground for the Crusades, which from then on took much of the attention of the counts. A notable example of this was Godfrey de Bouillon, count of Brabant, who was one of the leaders of the First Crusade and in 1099 became ruler of the Latin Kingdom of Jerusalem. Meanwhile Brabant was left to be governed by deputies and the authority of the count was diminished. Similarly, at the beginning of the thirteenth century Baldwin ix, count of Flanders and Hainault, became king of the Latin Kingdom of Constantinople. Many other members of the middle and lower nobility were likewise involved in crusading activities in the eastern Mediterranean and in these circumstances the delegation of power at local level became the norm. Cities were able to consolidate their *de facto* independence, although *de jure* they remained within the domains of the counts. This whole process culminated in 1354 when Count John iii granted a package of rights and privileges to the cities of Brabant. Most significantly, these included the right of the people to withdraw allegiance from tyrannical rulers. Known as the *Joyeuse Entrée*, this was a seminal event that made a great impact and is commemorated today in the Avenue de la Joyeuse Entrée in Brussels. This grant was the high point in the acquisition of liberties by the cities of the Netherlands and as a result of it they gained most of the freedoms enjoyed by sovereign city-states.

The German *Hanse* was also active throughout the Netherlands and *Hanse* counters were established in most of the main cities. The term *Hanse* was also widely used in the Netherlands itself to describe other associations of merchants. They elected *Hansgrafen* – counts of the *Hanse* – whose duty was to ensure the rights and privileges of the merchants. There were also other groupings of the cities, the most important of which was the 'Hansa of London'. The headquarters of this organization was actually in Brugge and its purpose was to control the wool trade with England.

As has been observed, while most of the Netherlands was within the Holy Roman Empire, the county of Flanders was in France and soon became subject to direct interference by the monarchs in a way that had become more rare in the Empire. While the Empire was a devolved structure in which the counts had considerable independence, by the twelfth century France was already becoming a more centralized state. The government asserted its power and the devolved structures inherited from the past became less acceptable to the French monarchs. By the end of the thirteenth century unrest was growing in the Flemish cities against this interference and an organization was set up to combat it. This was the *Clauwaerts*, the men of the claw, named after the claws of the Lion of Flanders. Opposed to it were the *Leliaerts*, the men of the Bourbon Lily, who favoured French rule. While the former were drawn from the guilds and the merchant classes, the latter included members of the aristocracy. In 1302 the French and Flemish forces met at the Battle of Courtrai (Kortryk) and there the French army was defeated by the *Clauwaerts*. Following this victory, the cities again asserted their freedoms from the French monarchy and further democratized their governments. In 1304 in Brugge the patriciate that had governed the city was overthrown and the craft guilds took over from them. Eventually a new constitution entrenched the power of the guilds in the city.[9] The Flemish cities went on to establish their own union. This was led by Jacob van Artevelde, the chief magistrate of Ghent, and its achievements included a union of the cities of Flanders and Brabant, which lay on opposite sides of the boundary between France and the Empire. It was also responsible for a further reduction in the power of the counts and increasing democratization within the city governments. The *Joyeuse Entrée* in Brabant was thus in many ways the culmination of a process that had been set in train after the Battle of Courtrai.[10] However, this never led to an organization comparable in power and influence to the German *Hanse*. Most of the major cities were in any case *Hanse* counters and they had wide and often competing trading interests. The rise of the House of Burgundy radically altered this situation and eventually led to a loose federal arrangement in which the cities retained their rights and the dukes benefited from their wealth.

The Netherlands, which had begun to take shape by the fourteenth century, was at the heart of northern Europe and, with the exception of Flanders, lay entirely within the Holy Roman Empire. Its vulnerable location gave it little protection from the full force of the imperial authority should the Emperor wish to assert the *iura regalia*. It was the situation of absentee or otherwise-occupied counts and emperors that had allowed the cities of the Netherlands to acquire and retain their freedoms. Even after the *Joyeuse Entrée*, the count's rights were never entirely abrogated but they became little more than nominal. As Clarke put it, 'harmony between towns and secular princes in the Netherlands' became the norm and 'emancipation [was] achieved without serious friction'. He commented that when 'in the fourteenth century peace was broken [this was] not by the princes but by civic factions'.[11]

The decline of the city-states of Europe that took place during the early sixteenth century was mainly the result of political disturbances and foreign invasions. The *civitates* in northern Italy, the *Hanse* in the Baltic and the *comunidades* in Castile all suffered from attacks and incursions by the rising territorial states. In England the consolidation of a powerful nation-state under the Tudor monarchy resulted in the concentration of political, religious and economic life into the hands of the state and a diminution in the role of non-national bodies within it. While in the fourteenth century the English economy had been bound closely to Flanders and the *Hanse*, and England had been part of the network of *Hanse* counters, by the sixteenth century the *Hanse* had become of little significance in the English economy. The English monarchs came to play a central role in the economy of the country and they did this by establishing mercantile companies to which they gave charters and exclusive rights over trading operations in particular countries or regions. The new nation-state was more exclusive in most areas of the country's life, and there was little place for a trans-state economic organization such as the *Hanse* any more than there was for a trans-state religious organization such as the Catholic Church. However, in Flanders this was not the case and by the beginning of the sixteenth century, in contrast to England, Spain and other parts of Europe, it had become more than ever a land of city-states. In 1516 this land of city-states was inherited by Charles I of Spain, who a few years later became the Holy Roman Emperor Charles V and destroyed the *comunidades* of Castile at the battle of Villalar.

Charles had been born in Ghent in 1500. He was brought up in that city and throughout his life retained great affection for it. On inheriting the Netherlands and the imperial throne, he restored the rights of those cities in which they had been eroded by the later Burgundian dukes. Thus from the outset, Charles's behaviour in regard to the cities of the Netherlands was very different from that which he displayed towards those of Castile. His early years had been spent in Flanders, which was still disputed between France and the Empire, and this background is reflected in his policies. These entailed a recognition of the unique position of the Netherlands within the Empire and an attempt to devise structures of government that would reflect this. Charles was faced with similar problems to those which had been faced by his predecessors regarding the government of the Empire. However, following the Reformation, these problems were magnified and the Empire was soon divided along religious and political lines. Despite his seemingly immense power, Charles was actually the ruler of an empire that was already in an advanced stage of disintegration.

At the time of his accession, the Netherlands was still not really a geopolitical unit at all and consisted of little more than part of the residue left over from the breakup of the duchy of Burgundy. In 1548 Charles unified those of his possessions in the north of the former duchy into 'The Circle of Burgundy'. This was given a common Supreme Court and an Estates General located in Brussels, to which the towns sent representatives. The government of this new political unit was a loose federal structure within which the cities were allowed to retain those charters which had accorded them rights and privileges in the past. The emperor reigned with a light touch and the Netherlands remained in reality a land of city-states unified into a sort of federation. In this way they achieved something that the *comunidades* had dreamed of but had never come near to attaining. What dramatically changed this promising situation for the worse was the religious divide that split Charles's empire. Spain and the Netherlands were on opposite sides of this divide and they saw the future of Europe from very different perspectives. Spain was the self-proclaimed heart of Catholic Europe, while the Netherlands was itself divided between a largely Catholic south and a largely Protestant north. This was to have the most dramatic consequences for the cities of the Netherlands and when it came the conflict began not in one of the great historic cities but in Antwerp, a relative newcomer among them.

Antwerp was not one of those historic cities of Flanders that had been in the forefront of the movement for independence. It was in the county of Brabant, but because of its small size and relative unimportance it had never been accorded the privileges conferred by the *Joyeuse Entrée* and had remained entirely dependent on decisions taken in Brussels. Its population in 1340 was only 17,000 compared to that of Brugge, which was 30,000, and Ghent, which was 56,000.[12] Its very existence was the result of the English decision to make it the centre of their European wool trade. Both English and German merchants favoured this small port, located some 90 kilometres east of Brugge. Situated on the lower Scheldt and close to the sea it was well located for the English trade. Most importantly, it was altogether far weaker and less able to impose those conditions and restrictions that were normal in the large port of Brugge. It did not have the powerful guilds that controlled the 'Hansa of London' and manipulated it in their own interests. Antwerp proved successful in attracting merchants, and by the fifteenth century besides wool its trade included wine, copper and silver. What began its transformation into the most important commercial city in the whole of the Netherlands, and then the whole of northern Europe, was the arrival of the first Portuguese ship bringing pepper in 1501. As the English had done with their wool, the Portuguese chose it in preference to Brugge for their spice trade. With the coming of the Spanish connection, Antwerp then became the main port for the trans-shipment of gold and silver from the New World, and this was in turn the cause of its rise as a great money market and financial centre. It also became the port for the export of goods from northern Europe destined for Spain and these included timber, textiles and cereals. By the middle of the sixteenth century it had become the most important economic centre in the whole of the Netherlands, ahead of the Flemish cities, and it had a central role in the economy of the Spanish Empire. As Braudel put it, it had become, like Brugge before it, a *Weltmarkt* at the centre of that new world economy that had been brought into existence by the Iberian powers.[13]

However, while it had become an economic phenomenon that transcended the Netherlands and even Europe itself, it still did not become a city-state in any sense of the word. Its rulers refused to grant it anything like the independence that had been attained by the older cities and this lack of political clout was one of the main reasons for its attraction to counts, kings and traders alike. Economically as well as politically, Antwerp rose to economic pre-eminence in a very different world from that in which the Flemish cities had prospered. It suited both the merchants and the princes to be able to exercise a tight grip over Antwerp's activities, and institutions of a civic type never took hold. This grip became even tighter, and by the second half of the sixteenth century all major decisions regarding Antwerp were firmly in the hands of the Spanish Viceroy of the Netherlands in Brussels.

While during the reign of Charles v this Spanish rule had usually been exercised with some caution, following Charles's abdication in 1556 in favour of his son Philip II all this changed. Philip was more Spanish than European and far more dogmatic in his religious beliefs than had been his father. He had little of that affection for the Netherlands that Charles had always shown, and within a few years indifference was turned into hatred and it became his 'damnosa hereditas'. He saw it more as a colonial possession of the Spanish monarchy than the grouping of free cities that his father had envisaged. It was Philip's intention to make the Netherlands a base for Spanish power in northern Europe from which the return to the Catholic fold could then be expedited. Under him, the Netherlands was rapidly transformed into a Spanish possession ruled by Spanish officials and garrisoned by the formidable Spanish army.

The cities of the Netherlands, used as they were to the freedoms granted by the Empire, and to playing an important role politically as well as economically, became increasingly unhappy at the harsh nature of this Spanish rule, and the opposition to it began in Antwerp in 1566. A petition was submitted to Philip through the Regent, Margaret of Parma, asking for religious toleration in the Netherlands. This petition was rejected out of hand, and when news of this peremptory rejection reached Antwerp there was great dismay, which soon turned into an outburst of unrest. The Protestant community of the city rose up and attacked the Catholic churches, and even the great cathedral itself was desecrated. Philip's response to these iconoclastic riots was to replace the mild Margaret of Parma as Regent with the harsh Duke of Alva and to embark on a policy of repression. It was this action that set the people of the Netherlands in fierce opposition to their Spanish masters. It also instigated a division of the country which in many ways mirrored that of Europe as a whole.

The south of the country, centring on the province of Brabant, was more easily controlled by the Spaniards, while the north, a land of rivers, lakes, mudflats and sandbars where the sea had to be held back by dykes and movement took place most easily by water, was far more difficult terrain. It was especially difficult for a land power that relied overwhelmingly on the effectiveness of its army. While the south of the Netherlands had remained basically Catholic, the remote and inaccessible north soon became a refuge for the Protestant cause.

The fiercest opposition to Spanish rule centred on the northern provinces of Holland, Zeeland and Utrecht, which were protected by their geography and had always been freer from outside controls than those of the south. Philip had appointed William of Orange, a member of a noble family which had lands in the Netherlands, to be the *Stadtholder* of these three provinces. This office had been created by the monarch in order to impose his will directly on the provinces, and in this capacity William was both the representative of the monarch and the *Hooge Overheid*, the supreme authority, in the province. Like others, notably Jacob van Artevelde in Ghent, William refused to do the monarch's bidding and instead became the leader of a rebellion. When this began in 1567, William resigned his office as *Stadtholder* and took up arms against the monarch. In so doing he put himself outside the law and became a fugitive operating in the north of the country. In the war that followed, the Spanish forces again and again failed to dislodge the rebels from the maritime provinces of Holland and Zeeland. They took to the sea and soon found that there they were most secure from the Spaniards. These 'Sea Beggars' then harried Spanish shipping and obtained aid from other Protestant countries. In 1572 the estates of the provinces of Holland and Zeeland reappointed William as their *Stadtholder*. Within five years the office had been transformed from servant of the monarch to elected popular leader. William was also made captain general of the army and grand admiral of the fleet. In 1575 the estates of the two provinces followed this up by revoking their allegiance to the Spanish monarchy and so inaugurating the split between the rebellious north and the more acquiescent south. This split culminated in 1579 with formation of the Union of Arras of the southern provinces and the Union of Utrecht of the northern provinces. The members of this latter were Holland, Zeeland, Utrecht, Friesland, Gelderland, Overyssel and Groningen. While the Union of Arras sought to reach a compromise agreement with Spain, the Union of Utrecht declared itself to be for complete independence. In 1581 the members of the Union of Utrecht collectively renounced allegiance to the Spanish monarchy and from then on these 'United Provinces' constituted *de facto* an independent state. The war dragged on, but the Spaniards, although firmly in control of the south, were able to make little headway against the north, which remained firmly and obstinately out of their control (see illus. 15).

The effect of the long and inconclusive war on the cities of the Netherlands was most dramatic. Those of Flanders were subjected to what Castells termed the 'bloody conquest, religious fanaticism and economic ineptitude' of the Spanish monarchy.[14] The same also happened to Antwerp, which was much more under direct Spanish control and had been of immeasurable economic importance to the Spanish monarch. The effects of the war on the Spanish economy were catastrophic and this cata-

15 The United Provinces: cities and provincial boundaries in the seventeenth century.

strophe spilled over into the commercial activities of Flanders and Brabant. In 1588, following the failure of the Armada to subjugate England, Philip decided to use economic sanctions against the Protestant countries. The port of Lisbon was closed to trade with northern Europe, and at the same time the river Scheldt was closed to all trading activity. This marked the end of Antwerp as a *Weltmarkt* and the commercial life of the Netherlands a whole ground to a halt. The United Provinces, dependent on the sea for their protection and supplies, urgently needed a port of their own that could take over from Antwerp and be the base for their maritime operations. This they found in Amsterdam, which soon became the new Antwerp.

During the great age of the cities of Flanders, Amsterdam had been a small fishing village on the tiny river Amstel flowing into the Zuider Zee. The counts of Holland, within which it was located, were as enthusiastic to see commerce thrive as were their counterparts in Flanders and Brabant. In 1275 Amsterdam was granted a charter by the count of Holland and from then on its commerce steadily increased. The growing city was almost literally built in the water, and piles had to be driven deep into the mud and sand that was the only foundation available. The river was dredged, dykes raised and a dam was constructed.[15] In 1306 Amsterdam was granted another charter confirming and adding to its rights and privileges, and this was followed later in the century by the building of the city walls and the first *Rathuis*. By this time its population had reached 8,000, more than a fishing village but still only a fraction of that of Ghent or Brugge at the time.[16] Following the troubles in Flanders and Brabant, the importance of Amsterdam to the trade of the northern provinces increased. In 1578, when William of Orange was elected *Stadtholder* of Holland by the provincial estates, an urban revolution took place in Amsterdam against the rule of the city magistrates. As a result of this they, together with the Catholic clergy of the city, were expelled and a new democratic system of city government was put in place.

The crucial year in the rise of Amsterdam was 1580 when the trade of Antwerp was brought to a sudden end by the Spanish closure of the Scheldt. This was followed by massive emigration from that city and refugees poured across the border into Holland. They came both to escape religious persecution and to seek employment, and the growing city of Amsterdam was their favoured destination. By the end of the century the city had in virtually all ways become the successor to Antwerp and the whole expertise of the southern city was transferred to the northern one. By then a third of the population was of foreign birth and a half of all the deposits in the Bank of Amsterdam was from Antwerp or other southern cities. 'Here Antwerp itself changed into Amsterdam' wrote one Antwerp merchant who had himself settled in the new northern capital.[17]

This transformation of the human geography of the Netherlands had indeed been a tale of two cities. As a result of

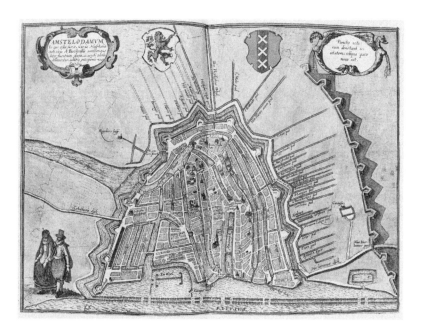

16 Amsterdam.

the massive immigration from Antwerp, by the early years of
the seventeenth century Amsterdam's population had tripled
from 30,000 to 100,000 and what had been until then a relatively small port became the major financial, industrial and
commercial metropolis of the Netherlands. In this it had taken
over lock, stock and barrel from Antwerp and soon became the
leading *Weltmarkt* in northern Europe.[18]

As to the implications that these developments had for the
existence and development of the city-state, it is necessary to
consider the extent to which Amsterdam, which had grown
within little more than a century from a fishing port to a leading
commercial city, actually fitted the model. Its 'mother city' of
Antwerp had not been in any sense a city-state at all, and was
more closely bound up with the counts, kings and emperors
than any other city in the whole of the Netherlands.
Nevertheless, the relationship of Amsterdam to the province of
Holland and the territorial authorities generally evolved into
something more like that of the older cities of Flanders and
Brabant. This kind of relationship was to become the basis for

the future government of the United Provinces and the general political evolution that then took place.

The province was the basic unit of the government of the emerging state which at first called itself the United Provinces. These provinces were based mainly on the old counties of the Netherlands, although only two of them, Holland and Zeeland, had actually been historic counties. The head of the province was the *Stadtholder*, an office created by Philip II and subsequently adopted by the free provinces themselves. The same person could, in theory at least, be appointed *Stadtholder* by a number of provinces and William of Orange held this office for both Holland and Zeeland. While the title implied town rather than country, the office was most specifically a territorial one and this fact demonstrates the close link that existed between town and country. The two were bound closely together, and the city was very much the heart of the province. The swamps, mudflats and sandbars of the Rhine delta had always been poor agricultural land and their pre-existing population had been very small. 'Half the country [of Holland] is under water' wrote the Spanish economist Ustariz, 'and scarcely a quarter of it is cultivated'.[19] However, by the end of the sixteenth century immigrants from Antwerp and the Flemish cities had settled in the northern towns, the populations of which rapidly increased and their grip over the countryside became steadily greater.

By the time the United Provinces became the Dutch Republic in 1648 the new state had become a land of cities, and this fact was nowhere more in evidence than in the province of Holland itself, in which the largest and most important cities were located. However, as a result of its huge population and economic power, Amsterdam dominated the province. While the supreme governing body of the United Provinces was the Estates General which met in The Hague, each province retained its own Estates. However, the reality was that the rich merchants of Amsterdam controlled the province, and since Holland supplied up to 60 per cent of the revenues of the federal treasury, in effect they also controlled the institutions of the state itself.

Thus in the late sixteenth century, while so many of the established city-states of Europe were already in decline, a new cluster of city-states made their appearance in the northern Netherlands. In the unpromising environment of the Rhine delta, which Ustariz called 'a land floating on water' and which had for this reason been largely avoided, a new group of cities almost literally rose out of the swamps. For them the two most significant attributes of the geography of the space that they colonized were that while it was safe from the incursions of land power it lent itself readily to the operations of sea power. It was able to turn these two attributes to its own advantage and to establish a maritime trading system which during the following century embraced the world. The Flemish cities which had fallen victim to the imperial power of Spain were in effect reconstituted in the swamps and sandbars of the Rhine delta. While Antwerp had not been granted any real freedom by either counts or monarchs, Amsterdam and the other cities of the United Provinces had proclaimed their own independence against the express wishes of the monarch, and no outside ruler was able to take it away from them. Thus from the outset they were sovereign cities in a more complete way than had been those of Flanders before the arrival of the Spaniards, or even Brabant after the *Joyeuse Entrée*. There were few cities anywhere in Europe in the late sixteenth century which possessed the kind of independence that these cities took for granted, and which they considered to be their inalienable right.

Together with political independence went religious and other freedoms. This was what the first arrivals from the southern Netherlands had looked for, and when, after the end of the war with Spain, these freedoms had become secure ever larger numbers of people were attracted there from all over Europe. In Landheer's words, these cities became 'a haven of refuge for all who sought freedom of worship, or safety from coercion'.[20] Flemings and Walloons, English separatists, Jews from Iberia, German Protestants all flocked to the cities of the Dutch Republic. Coins minted in Amsterdam were inscribed 'Haec Libertatis Ergo' (This is for Liberty), and although Calvinism was the most important religion, there was toleration for all religions, and attempts to create a religious state, after the manner of Geneva, came to nothing. As one Dutch writer put it, in Amsterdam 'all the peoples of the world can serve God according to their hearts and following the movement of their conscience and although the dominant religion is the reformed Church, everyone is free to live in the faith he confesses'.[21] This was all reflected in the planning and construction of the city. In Burke's view it was far from being 'the fruit of autocratic rule' like Paris, but rather 'the product of far-sighted citizen government in a city that has always been noted for its freedom – in trade, in religious toleration and in opening its gates to immigrants'.[22]

Yet while Amsterdam and the other cities were the places where these freedoms were most in evidence, it was the province rather than the city that was the basic unit of government in the United Provinces and subsequently the Dutch Republic. It is doubly paradoxical that the name of this unit of government came from the Latin *provincia* signifying a conquered territory, and that after the declaration of independence from the monarchy its leading official was given the title of *Stadtholder* that had originally been bestowed by the monarch. The fact was, however, that the cities were by far the most important parts of these provinces and that the principal function of the provinces was to supply, service and protect them. This was particularly the case in Holland, Zeeland and Utrecht.

In this respect there were close resemblances between this sixteenth-century Dutch Republic and the Hellenic world of 2,000 years earlier. In the symbiotic relationship of city and country the Dutch province possessed much of the character of the ancient Greek *polis*. In many ways the relationship of Amsterdam to Holland within the overall provincial structure was very similar to that of Athens to Attica. In this way in the seventeenth century Amsterdam can be seen as being essentially a city-state, of which the province was the rural part, and which itself lay within a cluster of other city-states. Each of the cities had its own council, which handled strictly urban affairs, but wider matters of policy were in the hands of the provincial Estates. In turn these then sent their representatives to the Estates General. Thus while the source of political power was officially located in the province, the economic and demographic power that underlay it was that of the city.

By the time of the proclamation of the Dutch Republic, the counts were long gone and had been replaced by *Stadtholders* appointed by the Estates. As *Hooge Overheid* these officials took on the role of the heads of state of the provinces. The most important of them all was the *Stadtholder* of Holland who, following the example set by William the Silent, frequently also held the same office in a number of other provinces. This particular *Stadtholder* was therefore the most important and became a kind of unofficial head of state for the whole of the Republic. The special position of this office had been made clear by the fact that for most of the time after the death of William the Silent in 1584 it remained in the hands of the House of Orange. In the early seventeenth century Maurice of Nassau was *Stadtholder* of five of the provinces and also held the positions of captain general and grand admiral. Within a short period of time, it had evolved into a quasi-monarchical institution with all the rights and obligations that this entailed. The princes of the House of Orange certainly saw themselves in this light and gradually came to act almost as monarchs in waiting.[23] As a result, the relationship between the *Stadtholder* and the Estates became a difficult one, and many of its members demanded a diminution in the power of the *Stadtholder* or even the abolition of the office. This confrontation centred on the *Stadtholder* and the *Landsadvocaat* of Holland, whose function was to uphold and ensure the rights of the province. It came to a head in 1618 when *Stadtholder* Maurice of Nassau took action against *Landsadvocaat* Oldenbarnaveld. The latter was arrested, tried on trumped up charges and then executed.

Despite the hostility and bitterness that this act of brutality produced, no further action was taken for the time being by the Estates General because of the momentous developments then taking place on the European scene and the effect that these were having on the United Provinces. This was the year of the beginning of the Thirty Years War, which plunged Europe into a final and bloody confrontation between Catholics and Protestants and from which the new 'Westphalian' territorial order came into being. The long war between Spain and the Netherlands was subsumed into this wider European conflict and the United Provinces once more faced grave dangers to their continued existence. However, Spain was now a declining power and a massive rearrangement was taking place in the balance of power in Europe. This had the effect of moving the centre of political power in the continent northwards. Here new territorial powers arose that challenged the older structures, including those of the Empire itself.

In 1648 the independence of the United Provinces was finally recognized in the Treaty of Westphalia. During this Eighty Years War the princes of Orange had been able to claim that the defence of their small and fragile Union necessitated not the abolition but the increase in the importance of the offices that they held. As a result of this their quasi-monarchical power steadily accrued and it was not until the end of the war that the confrontation between *Stadtholder* and province resumed. The *vroedschappen*, the 'regents' who oversaw the government of Amsterdam, were concerned that the large expenditure on the armed forces should be diminished as soon as possible. However, the *Stadtholder* had an interest in the maintenance of these forces since, in his capacity as Captain General and Grand Admiral, they were the basis of his power. In 1650 *Stadtholder* William II moved against Amsterdam with his army and attempted a *coup d'état*. The city authorities were alerted to the danger and the defences of the city proved sufficiently strong to keep William's forces out. Shortly afterward the young *Stadtholder* died unexpectedly and since his son was a minor the whole dispute ground to a halt. The Estates of Holland, led by the *vroedschappen* of Amsterdam, decided to take the initiative and began a process of drawing up new arrangements for the government of the country. In 1651 a Grand Assembly was called with representatives from all the provinces in order to approve a new constitution. It was then that the Dutch Republic was proclaimed and at the same time the office of *Stadtholder* was abolished. In the new constitution the powers of the Estates General were reduced and it was established that sovereignty lay with the Estates of each province. The *Landsadvocaat* became the leading figure and his responsibility was to the Estates that had appointed him and to which he was accountable for all his actions.

The Dutch Republic was a loose confederation, and the cities and provinces retained a high measure of independence within it. However, Westphalian Europe was the age of nation-states and absolutist monarchs and the state that was the heir to the United Provinces was soon forced to move in the same direction. Following the victory over Spain, France emerged as the new territorial danger and England as the great commercial rival. The result of this was the series of commercial wars with England and territorial wars with France that sapped the Republic's energy and weakened its capacity to play a leading role in world trade. In 1672, in the circumstances of danger in which the young state found itself, the office of *Stadtholder* of Holland was revived and conferred upon William II's son, William III. William also became Captain General of the armed forces of the Republic. At the same time, in a bizarre re-enactment of history, the *Landsadvocaat* de Witt was arrested, accused of treachery and executed. The Dutch Republic then moved into war mode and, in alliance with Britain, confronted the French bid to dominate the continent as the Spaniards had attempted to do during the previous century.

The nature of the Dutch Republic thus changed as a result of the external dangers that it faced and in conformity with the accepted norms of political behaviour. By the eighteenth century Europe had become a world of territorial states and externally, at least, the Republic appeared to conform to this pattern. However, the provinces remained the basic units of administration and the cities continued to enjoy their freedoms. The move to conform to the accepted political norm did not mean that the Republic conformed to it in every single way. Rather, in a world in which the city-state had become too vulnerable to external dangers to be any longer viable on its own, it was forced to adapt to the new realities.

The city-state ethos persisted in the Netherlands and what was in effect a grouping of city-states in the guise of a territorial (nation) state persisted into the twentieth century. Those freedoms lost in so many other places were retained, and the Dutch Republic remained a beacon light of freedom in a world dominated by authoritarian and centralized regimes.

Third Rome versus City Republics: Moscow, Novgorod and the Baltic

According to the records, Moscow was founded in 1147 by Prince Yuri Dolgoruky, a younger son of the Grand Prince Vladimir Monomakh of Kiev. It is situated on the Moskva river near to the earlier settlements of Vladimir and Suzdal. Like them, it was originally an *ostrog* or fortification near to the eastern boundary of the lands of Kievan Rus. Together with the other *ostrogs* in this region, it was both part of the project for extending Russian power to the east and north and of increasing the hold of the Rurikovichy dynasty by giving the younger sons principalities of their own. Its role was to assert Russian hegemony in these eastern lands and to maintain control over them with a view to the profitable exploitation of their natural resources.

When less than a century later Kievan Rus fell to the Mongol onslaught, Moscow, together with the other *ostrogs* of this region, was also attacked and pillaged. Most of Rus then became part of the great Mongol Empire that stretched from eastern Europe to China, and, with the division of the government of the Empire in the middle of the thirteenth century, it was allocated to the western Mongols, the Golden Horde, who ruled Russia from their capital Sarai Batu on the lower Volga. The princes of Moscow, together with most of the other princes of Rus, became vassals of the Khan and paid annual visits to Sarai for the purpose of paying homage and bearing tribute. The Mongol conquests brought about a massive shift to the north in the human geography of the Russian lands, and within less than a century of the Mongol conquest Moscow, until then a remote *ostrog* deep in the forest, had taken over from Kiev as the leading city in Rus.[1] It had done this by becoming the main centre of the new core region of Rus. This was the *mezdurechie*, the Russian mesopotamia between the Volga and the Oka rivers in which Moscow, Vladimir and Suzdal were located. It was in the mixed forest belt lying to the north of the steppe and this was one of its main strengths in becoming the centre around which the new Russia arose.[2] The Mongol horsemen, so confident in the steppes, were reluctant to penetrate into the forests except for punitive expeditions to secure tribute from the princes of Rus. This region was endowed with the brown forest soils character-istic of the mixed forest and which made for a productive agriculture. It was thus able to support a much higher popula-tion than were the coniferous forests to the north with their harsh climate and unproductive podsol soils. Perhaps most sig-nificantly of all as locational factors were the rivers that had from the beginning been basic to the communication system of Rus. The Moskva flowed into the Oka, which in turn flowed into the Volga, the largest river west of the Urals. The Volga flowed south-eastwards from its source in the Valdai Hills to its mouth in the Caspian Sea. It provided the main link via the Valdai portages to Novgorod and the other cities of the north and west and, in the other direction, to Sarai and on to the Mongol heartlands. It was thus located halfway between the freedom of the north and the servitude of the south, and it used both in its rise to power. Whilst developing trade relations with Novgorod and the Baltic, it paid tribute to the Mongols at Sarai but soon also began to trade with them. This resulted in the establishment of a new trade route following the Volga river from the Baltic to the Caspian and from there on eastwards. In the late fourteenth century Nizhni Novgorod was established at the junction of the Volga and the Oka rivers and this soon became a central point on the expanding trading system linking Europe with Asia.

It was in the context of its location in the *mezdurechie* that Moscow was able to increase its power and to gain ever more autonomy within the lands subjugated by the Golden Horde. In order to understand why it was Moscow rather than one of the other cities in the *mezdurechie* which rose to a position of such pre-eminence it is necessary to examine the policies pursued by the princes. In the first instance they became the tax gatherers for the Mongols, a role that began with Yuri Danilovich at the beginning of the fourteenth century. It is then particularly associated with Ivan Kalita, who reigned from 1325 to 1352 and who began to use the resources acquired to increase the wealth and power of the city. At the time it was Vladimir, to which the Metropolitan had fled after the Mongol conquests, that appeared to be the natural successor to Kiev. However, the princes of Moscow gained power through their growing influence with the Mongols and the financial resources that as tax gatherers they increasingly had at their disposal. In 1326 the metropolitan moved definitively to Moscow and, during the reign of Dimitri Donskoy (1359–89), the Prince of Moscow was able to assert his pre-eminence over the greater part of the *mezdurechie*. The size of the territory over which the Prince of Moscow ruled continued to increase steadily, and towards the end of his reign Dimitri felt strong enough to defy his Mongol overlords. In 1380 he defeated them at the Battle of Kulikovo on the lower Don. Although the Mongols returned and reasserted their hegemony, they were never again as strong as they had been and the Princes of Moscow became recognized as the successors to the Princes of Kiev. The Princes then extended their control southwards and northwards from the *mezdurechie* and, as the Mongols became weaker, they were forced back into the steppes.

By the end of the fourteenth century Moscow had wrested a high degree of autonomy from its Mongol overlords, and in 1480 it became completely independent of them. However, its new freedom did not lead it to attempt to recreate the structures of Russian government associated with its predecessor, Kievan Rus. There were to be no city-states in the new Muscovite world that was emerging in the forests of the *mezdurechie*. Located on the periphery of the lands of Kievan Rus, it had been founded as a stronghold by the Princes and this in its essentials is what it remained. There was in Moscow none of the diminution and eventual elimination of princely power that is an important characteristic of the city-state. The centre of power was the *Kreml* and the settlement grew in size around it. All the most important elements of authority, both secular and religious, were and remained within it. The close geographical proximity of cathedrals and palaces within the walls of the *Kreml* arose from the close State–Church relations that were so characteristic of the Orthodox Christian world and which were now perpetuated in Moscow.

Of course, in Novgorod and elsewhere in the Russian world the city had also originally centred on a *Kreml*. However, in Novgorod a new commercial quarter had grown up on the opposite bank of the Volkhov, which became a rival centre of power and which eventually challenged and replaced the old one. The rule of the *Sofiiskaya*, the old city centring on the great cathedral, was replaced by that of the *Torgovaya* across the river and centring on the *Veche* and the alternative churches. In Novgorod the role of the princes themselves came to be questioned and they were 'shown the road' when this was judged to be necessary. A new balance of power had been created in the government of the city that took into account the wider interests of the urban community as a whole. None of this took place in Moscow. Here the power of the prince remained absolute and the merchant quarter outside the walls was kept under observation and was well under princely control. It was never allowed to assert itself and did not come near to becoming an alternative centre of power. The Moscow *Kreml* with its formidable red walls, and from the sixteenth century dominated by the four cathedrals and the soaring Ivan the Great bell tower, symbolized the realities of power in the Muscovite state. This city was far from being in any sense a commune acting for the common good. It was and remained a base from which the princely power was consolidated and the new Russian imperialism was engendered.

The reasons for the profound differences between Novgorod and Moscow are to be found in the circumstances of the origins of the two cities. While Novgorod's origins go back to the great routeway from the Varangians to the Greeks, Moscow was established on a warlike periphery and the princes were and remained on a war footing.[3] With the arrival of the Mongols, the frontier became even more dangerous and the new core in the *mezhdurechie* became the boundary of the Russian lands in a cultural as well as a physical sense. The response of the princes to the dangers they faced was to increase their own military power and this involved increasing the size of the territory over which they ruled. Their aspirations were essentially territorial and thus the acquisition of territory, and the consolidation of their rule over it, was their central objective. This is seen clearly in the relationship between Moscow and the principality of Muscovy. This was far from being that of the city-state surrounded by a dependant territory like Athens in Attica or Venice in Venetia. Muscovy was not a city-state but an expanding territory, and Moscow was first and foremost the political and military base of its princes. In the sixteenth century it transformed itself from a principality into an empire, and eventually it sought to achieve control over the whole Eurasian geopolitical region. As has been seen elsewhere, in Rus the city-state and the territorial state were based upon quite different concepts of the nature and purpose of government and the incompatibility between the two was soon to become evident.

This situation was made more confrontational by those developments in the European world that had the effect of isolating Muscovy from the European mainstream and forcing it into the leadership role of a permanent 'other' Europe. Kievan Rus had been an integral part of the Byzantine world centring on Constantinople, and its whole culture, including its art, religion and politics, was derived from that of Byzantium. With the fall of Kievan Rus, the new Muscovite state that rose in the *mezdurechie* also looked to Byzantium and, like its predecessor, its government owed much to the Byzantine model. The new Russia which began to emerge in the fourteenth century was thus centralized, autocratic, Orthodox Christian and basically Byzantine in its artistic and architectural inspiration. However, while being within the Byzantine sphere, this Muscovite Russia was also within the Mongol sphere and the pull of these two great and antagonistic empires also served to keep Moscow in a state of uncertainty regarding its geopolitical relationship with Europe and the world. In 1453 Constantinople fell to the Ottoman Turks and Byzantium, which traced its origins back to the Eastern Roman Empire, ceased to exist. The legacy of the great civilization persisted in parts of the Balkans, but its greatest and most important heir was Russia.

Thus after 1453 Russia was left outside that European mainstream which derived its culture and religion from Rome and at the same time was cut off from the source which had been the basis of its own culture and religion. Russia was no longer part of the cultural sphere which had been presided over jointly by the basileus and the patriarch in Constantinople and was consequently obliged to adjust its world view to the new circumstances in which it found itself. Its response to the new situation was a dramatic one: it assumed the mantle of the defunct Byzantine Empire and took on the role of defender of Orthodox Christianity. In effect both the basileus and the patriarchate were transposed to Russia and Russian versions of them both were installed in Moscow. The Russian Church was declared to be autocephalus, with the metropolitan of Moscow at its head. At the same time Grand Prince Ivan III – the Great – took on the role of heir to the authority of the Byzantine emperor and thus indirectly to Rome itself. It was he who first used the title of 'Tsar', a Russian version of Caesar, and, transcending Muscovy, he asserted his position as ruler of 'Great Rus'. The legitimacy for his actions derived from the transfer of authority implicit in the legend of the Cap of Monomakh, which had been presented by Constantine IX Monomachus to the Grand Prince Vladimir Monomakh.

At the beginning of the sixteenth century this transformation from principality to empire culminated in the idea that Moscow was the 'Third Rome'. This was an idea that appears to have originated with Philotheus, a monk in the monastery of Pskov. In a letter to Vasily III, Philotheus wrote:

> I wish to add a few words on the present Orthodox Empire of our ruler; he is on earth the sole Emperor [Tsar] of the Christians, the leader of the Apostolic Church which stands no longer in Rome or in Constantinople, but in the blessed city of Moscow. She alone shines in the whole world brighter than the sun . . . All Christian Empires are fallen and in their stead stands alone the Empire of our ruler in accordance with the prophetical books. Two Romes have fallen, but the third stands, and a fourth there will not be.[4]

In 1547 Ivan III's grandson and successor, Ivan Grozny ('The Terrible'), was crowned Tsar 'of all Russia' with the Cap of Monomakh and the full regalia of Byzantine ceremonial. Muscovy had become Russia and Moscow had been transformed from a princely into an imperial city. Its destiny was to be the unification of 'all the Russias' under the twin rule of Tsar and Patriarch.

It was Ivan III who began the implementation of this Muscovite destiny, and as part of this he moved against Novgorod, the most important Russian city still independent of the Muscovites. 'Gospodin Veliki Novgorod' (Lord Novgorod the Great) had continued to flourish over all the years since the Mongol conquest and, freed from Kievan intervention, had been a more independent city-state than ever before. It derived its wealth from the Baltic trade and became an important *Hanse* counter. It was a cosmopolitan city in which merchants from all over Europe were to be found buying and selling goods. Many languages were spoken in its streets and written in its documents and a variety of religious traditions flourished in the city. Novgorod's greatest source of wealth was in the products from the northern forests, and its furs commanded high prices in the markets of the *Hanse*. The Tsar coveted both its trade and its independence and in pursuit of these in 1478 he moved against the city. Unwilling to enter into conflict with Ivan, the Novgorodtsi put up no resistance and reluctantly accepted the principle of Muscovite overlordship. The result was that Novgorod, and the lands within its sphere, were incorporated into the Muscovite Russian state, adding greatly to its size and wealth. While this all increased the power of the Tsar, it put an end to the sovereignty of the city-state of Novgorod. It also put an end to the possibility that the future for Russia could be one of city-states rather than of territorial domination. The break with the old Rus was now complete. Nevertheless, Ivan's peace terms were relatively generous. Novgorod was allowed to retain many of its economic and political privileges and its association with the *Hanse* was allowed to continue. The city remained a *Hanse* counter until 1494, when the merchants were finally expelled and their property was confiscated.

The change in the position of the city brought about by Ivan's actions had been a most fundamental one. Novgorod had become part of the growing empire of Muscovite Russia and was from then on inextricably bound up with Muscovy and its 'destiny' to dominate. In view of this it is ironic that it was Alexander Nevsky, prince of Novgorod and defender of Russia's remaining city-states against the Teutonic Knights, who was the founder of that renewed Rurikovichy dynasty that led Moscow to the achievement of its dominant position. It is also ironic that the idea of the 'Third Rome' was born in Novgorod's sister city of Pskov, which, like Novgorod itself, had guarded its independence over the centuries but which was at the same time as its larger neighbour absorbed into the Muscovite state.

Initially the 'Third Rome' had behaved in a not dissimilar manner from the first Rome in respect of this particular city-state and there was a measure of tolerance of its unique commercial and economic position. This all changed, however, under Ivan III's grandson, Ivan the Terrible. This tsar's version of the 'Third Rome' was far closer to the Rome of the *imperium* than to that of the *res publica*. The Russian state was to be centralized on Moscow and there was to be no tolerance of diversity or of the slightest hint of disloyalty. There was as little room for semi-independent cities in the Russia ruled by Ivan IV as there was for them in the Spain ruled by *Los Reyes Catolicos* and Philip II. After the rejection of petitions submitted by the Novgorodtsi to the Tsar asking for a restoration of their historic rights, Ivan decided to act. On the pretext that Novgorod had been conspiring with Russia's enemies, in 1570 he moved against the city. He used the dreaded *Oprichnina* – part secret police, part army and part quasi-religious order – in order to deal with the city that he had come to believe was the greatest threat to his rule. This time the destruction and carnage in Novgorod were appalling. The bulk of the population was killed and it is said that the Volkhov ran red with blood for weeks afterwards.[5] The same would have happened to Pskov had it not been for the extreme humility shown by the citizens, which appears to have mollified the tsar somewhat.[6] Both Pskov and Novgorod were now firmly incorporated into the Muscovite Russian state and royally appointed *nastavniks* (governors) were placed in them both. Ivan had eliminated his most powerful potential rival, and from then on there was room for only one dominating city in Russia.

While the geopolitical objective of Muscovite policy was to dominate, the strategy for the achievement of this included breaking out of the country's continental isolation and acquiring access to the sea. It was Ivan's aim to establish direct trade connections with Europe and so to link his realm directly with the European trading system.[7] In the 1550s a maritime trading connection had been opened up with England using the Arctic route from Archangelsk on the White Sea, but this proved hazardous and often icebound, and Ivan wished to re-establish more direct connections via the Baltic.[8] This was the economic motive that had underlain the brutal attack and subjugation of Novgorod. Following the destruction of the city, it was Ivan's intention to gain access to the sea and to establish ports on the Baltic. In the pursuance of this objective, Ivan advanced westwards into Estonia and Livonia. By then the Teutonic Order had relinquished its hold over this area and it was coveted particularly by the Poles and the Swedes. The Russian army besieged the *Hanse* cities of Reval and Riga and occupied the *Hanse* city of Dorpat. By 1577 most of Livonia and Estonia had fallen into Russian hands with the exception of their two most important *Hanse* cities, which continued to hold out against him. In response to Ivan's advance, the Swedes moved into Estonia and occupied Narva. This was an important port with a *Hanse* counter located at the point where the river Narva flows into the Baltic and having close commercial connections with Dorpat and Pskov. Despite persistent attempts, the Russians failed to wrest Narva from the Swedes, whose naval power made them the natural heirs to the *Hanse* in this area. The Swedes demonstrated their intentions in the eastern Baltic by embarking on the construction of a powerful fortress at Narva. Ivan's response to this was to build his own fortress facing it across the Narva river. This fortress was named Ivangorod, but despite the associations that this name brought with it, the Russians were not able to keep even this toehold on the Baltic against the increasing might of the Swedes. It was to be a century and a half before they again returned in force to the Baltic.

By the late sixteenth century the remaining *Hanse* cities in the Baltic were in a highly weakened state and were certainly not in

17 Confrontation in the Baltic: The castles of Narva and Ivangorod.

any position to confront those territorial powers that were showing an increasing interest in its commercial activities. In the
fourteenth century Denmark, the precursor of these powers, had
been defeated by the *Hanse*, which had gone on to build on this
achievement by converting the Baltic into what was in effect a
Hanse lake. However, two centuries later the territorial powers
were in the ascendant and it was Sweden rather than Russia
which then came to dominate the Baltic. Already by the end of
the sixteenth century the Baltic was well on the way to being a
Swedish lake, something that it became fully in the following
century. The strongholds confronting one another across the
Narva river clearly indicated that the new age was to be one of
confrontation and war among rival powers and that the unity of
the Baltic created by the *Hanse* city-states had come to an end.[9]

Riga, Reval, Dorpat, Pskov, Novgorod and many others had
been at their apogee powerful and prosperous city-states which
had drawn their strength from the fact that they were part of a
single economic area. At their best they had been able to cooperate in many spheres; they created unity where there had been
division and wealth where there had been poverty. They had also
been part of a wider commercial world, the routes of which

extended across northern Europe and linked the Baltic via Russia to the centre of Asia. While in the fifteenth century the close commercial links along the route joining Reval, Dorpat, Pskov and Novgorod had demonstrated the unity of the Baltic, by the following century the confrontation between the strongholds of Narva and Ivangorod demonstrated the division of the region and the growing rivalry of the territorial powers for its possession.

It was Peter the Great at the end of the seventeenth century who made the decision that the drive to the sea should be resumed and that Russia's destiny lay in the Baltic. At Schlusselburg – Peter's 'key' to the Baltic – built at the point where the river Neva leaves Lake Ladoga, the first Russian fleet was constructed. This fleet then sailed down the Neva and out into the Baltic to confront and defeat the Swedes. At the beginning of the eighteenth century a new name appeared in the area that demonstrated a fundamental change in the balance of power in the Baltic. This was Pieterbruk, which soon became St Petersburg, founded in 1703, as Russia's 'window on the west'. Within a decade it had become the country's new capital, its major naval base and most important port. The Treaty of Nystad in 1721, which concluded the Northern War, added Livonia, Estonia, Ingria and eastern Karelia to Russia. Like Novgorod and Pskov before them, the *Hanse* ports of Dorpat, Narva, Reval and Riga became part of the Russian Empire and the coast from the Gulf of Finland to the Gulf of Riga became an extended 'window on the west'. Kronstadt, on an island in the Gulf of Finland, became the site of a formidable naval base that replaced Schlusselberg as the key to Russia's new pre-eminence in the Baltic. The independent city-states that had flourished there were now subjected to the power of Russia. Just as in the sixteenth century Moscow had towered over the other Russian cities, in the eighteenth century St Petersburg, the new capital of the Russian Empire, towered over those of the Baltic.

By this time the *Hanse* had come to an end, but the memory of its power was kept alive by the continued importance of its cities. They had a destiny too, and it was one far removed in spirit from the autocracy that had begun in Moscow and continued from its new base on the Baltic.

THIRTEEN

The Fall and Rise of the
Hanse Cities

By the middle years of the seventeenth century the second great age of the city-state had to all intents and purposes come to an end. The *Hanse* still clung on, but it played little part in the events that culminated in the Thirty Years War, which shook Europe to its foundations. In the later 1620s the war in the Baltic culminated in the conflict of the armies led by the Austrian Catholic Albrecht von Wallenstein and the Protestant Gustavus II Adolphus of Sweden. Wallenstein assumed the title of admiral of the Baltic and in this capacity he attacked the *Hanse* cities, thus endangering the whole northern trading system. At the meeting of the *Hansetag* of 1629, Lübeck, Hamburg and Bremen were officially deputed to act in future on behalf of all the cities of the *Städtbünde*. In the following year a defensive alliance was signed in Lübeck by these three cities that pledged them to act in concert in defence of their common interests. The *Hanse* was a mere spectator of the Treaty of Westphalia in 1648, which transformed the political map of Europe. Just two decades later, in 1669, the last meeting of the *Hansetag* took place in Lübeck. Only nine members attended, these being Hamburg, Bremen, Danzig, Rostock, Brunswick, Hildesheim, Osnabrük, Cologne and Lübeck itself. The authorities of Wismar, in their official letter of refusal to attend, wrote that the *Hanse* 'was more a shadow than a reality, and there was no hope of restoring it to its former prosperity'.[1] There was much discussion at this meeting, but little was achieved and the delegates dispersed for the last time, reaffirming their continued confidence in Lübeck, Hamburg and Bremen to look after their interests in the future. Legally speaking, these three cities became the heirs and executors of the *Hanse* and they continued to deal as agents for its property, including the London Steelyard, until the middle of the nineteenth century. They also arranged for the continued diplomatic representation of the *Hanse* in neighbouring countries, notably in Brandenburg-Prussia, around which the new Germany was to coalesce.[2]

However, a scattering of other city-states continued to exist on into the eighteenth century, a number of them still of considerable importance within a Europe that since the Treaty of Westphalia had been dominated by half a dozen great powers. Venice, the oldest and most illustrious of all Europe's city-states, appeared at first glance to shine as brightly as ever. By then, however, its great wealth and glory lay in the past and, for north Europeans, what Ruskin termed 'the stones of Venice' were fast becoming little more than a tourist attraction. The magnificent churches, palaces, paintings and statues were by then the backdrops for the masques, balls and grand ceremonies that delighted visitors and made Venice an essential destination for those northern Europeans coming south on the Grand Tour in quest of their history and civilization.[3] Eighteenth-century Venice did not, however, impress all of these visitors. To Edward Gibbon, on his way south to Rome, it had afforded 'some hours of astonishment and some days of disgust'.[4] This was a very different reaction from that of earlier travellers, who had usually found the *Serenissima* to be incomparable in virtually every respect.

The other historic cities of Italy, although most of them no longer 'sovereign' in the sense in which Venice still undeniably was, also jealously guarded what remained of their independence and cherished that civilization which in its heyday had shone out across Europe. They also had become destinations for those who embarked on the Grand Tour. Gibbon conceived of his epic work, *The Decline and Fall of the Roman Empire* (1776–88), while standing in the ruins of the Forum in Rome. He lamented the end of the great city and the civilization that it had represented. Yet the truth was that it was Rome which had brought to an end the world of the ancient city-states, and their re-emergence had taken place only after the Empire's fall.

Soon after the publication of Gibbon's epic work the rise of another imperial power set the seal on the end of the second

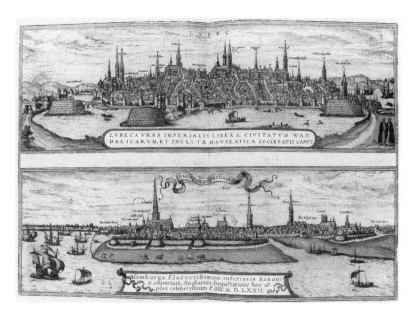

18 The flourishing of the *Hansestädte*: Lübeck and Hamburg in the sixteenth century.

great age of the European city-state. This power was France, which, as the eighteenth century approached its end, sought to transform Europe first in line with the basic tenets of the French Revolution and then using the classic methods of imperialism. While Revolutionary France had originally been based on the ideas of liberty, equality and fraternity, there was little liberty in the Napoleonic Empire that followed it, and this applied particularly to those vestiges of liberty that until then had been enjoyed by the remaining European city-states. As always, empire and city-state proved to be incompatible. In pursuit of the dream of a Europe united by and around France, in 1795 the army of Napoleon Bonaparte crossed the Alps into Italy. Like so many French generals and rulers before and after him, he came as both liberator and conqueror. In his case it was liberation from the evils of the *ancien régime* and conquest in the name of a France which he was about to transform into an empire. Most of the ancient cities of northern Italy were occupied by the French army and incorporated into the satellite kingdom of Italy under French domination. Pronouncing that

'I shall be an Attila to the State of Venice', Napoleon moved against the city-state, announcing that he had come to liberate the Venetians from the tyranny of the Doge and the oligarchy.[5] On 12 May 1797 the Grand Council met for the last time under the Doge and surrendered all its powers. Shortly afterwards the city was occupied by the French army, and the oldest and proudest of all the sovereign city-states came to an end. For a thousand years it had successfully retained its independence from both the Byzantine and the Holy Roman Empires. What had been born out of the ruins of one empire was brought to an end by the rise of another. It was this event, more than any other, that sounded the death knell for the city as sovereign state.

The French advanced eastwards across the Rhine seeking to modernize what they regarded as being the medieval political arrangements that they found there. Flanders was once more incorporated into France and together with the rest of the southern Netherlands was divided into the new *départements* which replaced the untidy local arrangement of the *ancien régime* with a new revolutionary political cartography. The Dutch Republic to the north, and in which the great cities were pre-eminent and in which their freedoms were guaranteed, also lost its independence. The city of Amsterdam, heir to Antwerp and Bruges, had emerged from the long war with Spain as, in effect, a sovereign city-state. The city lay within the province of Holland, a constituent province of the Dutch Republic, but the loose federal structures of the Republic, together with the economic power of the city, had made Amsterdam to all intents and purposes an independent state in its own right. This also came to an end in 1795 when Amsterdam and the other cities of the Netherlands were incorporated into the Batavian Republic and subsequently into the kingdom of Holland, which was part of the Napoleonic Empire. Finally, in 1806, following the Battle of Austerlitz in which Napoleon defeated the Austrians, the Holy Roman Empire was brought to an end. The long association of the Habsburg dynasty with the Empire was terminated and replaced by Napoleon's own dynasty. A Confederation of the Rhine was established under firm French control and this was divided into kingdoms and duchies ruled by members of

Napoleon's extended family and entourage. As part of this restructuring the free cities of the Empire were abolished and incorporated into the new territorial divisions.

The Confederation of the Rhine lasted for barely a decade and with the fall of Napoleon a further major change came about. In 1815, in the Final Act of the Congress of Vienna, the *Deutscher Bund* was established. This was a confederation of 38 states, among which were the three old *Hanse* cities of Lübeck, Hamburg and Bremen. Since 1669 these three had maintained their semi-official role as executors of the *Hanse*, and this special position was now recognized by international treaty. They were designated *Freistädte* and the constitution of the *Bund* guaranteed their sovereignty. Thus within a decade of the abolition of all the German city-states these three were once more back on the map. The survivors were the three cities that had been at the heart of the original *Hanse* and which had kept the idea of it alive over the centuries.

In 1834, at the instigation of Prussia, the *Zollverein* (Customs Union) came into being in the *Deutscher Bund*. Initially it had been limited to Prussia and a number of the states of south Germany, but gradually others sought to attain membership. These included the *Freistädte*, and Lübeck was the first of them to join in 1867. Hamburg and Bremen did not become full members until 1888, by which time a further major transformation had taken place on the German political scene. This was the foundation of the Second Reich in 1871 at the end of the Franco-Prussian War. It represented the culmination of the movement for the unity of Germany, which had its origins in the humiliations suffered at the hands of Napoleon. This Second Reich represented the *Kleindeutsch* (small German) solution to the problem of German disunity and entailed the exclusion of Austria, which had been the dominant power in Germany since the sixteenth century. Like the *Zollverein* before it, it came into being at the instigation of Prussia; the Prussian king became the German emperor; and Berlin became the capital of the new state. In its constitution the three old *Hanse* cities of Lübeck, Hamburg and Bremen became *Freistädte* of the Empire. As with the other constituent states, their constitutional position was that they were *staaten*, having their own governments and being autonomous in respect of their local affairs. While Lübeck was fully integrated into the new state from the beginning, Hamburg and Bremen actually used their autonomy in order to remain outside the *Zollverein* for nearly two decades after it had come into being.

The decades that followed were a time of great economic advance for the new Germany and the three free cities prospered within it. This was particularly the case with Hamburg and Bremen, which were located on the North Sea coast and so benefited greatly from the growth in their overseas trade. This success made them inclined to retain their economic independence as long as they could. Lübeck on the Baltic was less successful in this respect. The Baltic, the centre of the *Hanse* trading system in earlier times, had now become something of a backwater and the new Germany looked west to the opportunities afforded by the commerce of the world. Hamburg was its most important port, and with good communications inland via the Elbe and the Havel-Spree canal system it became the main link between Berlin and the North Sea. The completion of the construction of the Kiel Canal across the Jutland isthmus in 1895 gave the German Baltic ports direct access to the North Sea. The old *landfahrt* at the centre of the original *Hanse* was converted into a new *zeefahrt*, capable of taking very large vessels into the Baltic. However, despite this the Baltic did not recover its importance and the canal was used mainly for naval purposes.

Kaiser Wilhelm II, who reigned from 1888 to 1918, was especially interested in promoting German maritime activity, which he saw as being the way to achieve the world power that he craved. In his speeches he regularly recalled the *Hanse* as the model for the direction in which he wished Germany to go. In 1897, in an address in Kiel, which had only recently been linked to the North Sea by the canal, he drew attention to the fact that 'our commerce is not new; in old times the *Hanse* was one of the most powerful enterprises that the world has ever seen, and the German cities were able to build a fleet such as the sea's broad back had never carried in earlier days.' Wilhelm's verdict on the fall of the *Hanse* was that 'finally it came to naught because the one condition was lacking, namely that of an Emperor's protection'. In his famous 'Place in the Sun' speech, delivered in Hamburg in 1901, Wilhelm returned to the theme of the *Hanse*. He spoke of 'the vivifying and protecting power of the empire' over the modern *Hanse* and called for a revival of the Hanseatic spirit of enterprise. Addressing specifically the citizens of Hamburg, Bremen and Lübeck and complimenting them on their 'large outlook', he expressed the wish that it might be 'the function of my Hansa during many years of peace to protect and advance commerce and trade'.[6] By speaking of 'my Hansa' Wilhelm appeared to see his new empire as facilitating the rise of a kind of modern version of the *Hanse* of old.

The German 'window' on the ocean was the country's relatively short North Sea coast. Hamburg and Bremen were its main ports and thus, as in earlier times, they found themselves in the forefront of the German maritime thrust. They were joined by the new and enlarged ports of Emden and Wilhelmshaven, and for the increasingly large vessels they had respectively outports at Bremerhaven on the estuary of the Weser and Cuxhaven on the estuary of the Elbe. The *Hanse* spirit to which Wilhelm so often alluded had above all been built on the freedom of the cities, but this was something to which Wilhelm did not specifically refer in his speeches. Yet throughout the period of the Second Reich the three remaining *Hanse* cities were able to maintain their special status. They retained the full constitutional rights of *staaten* and in this federal empire the burgomasters of Hamburg and Bremen were, constitutionally at least, the equals of the kings of Bavaria or Saxony. In this respect, this empire was like its predecessors a very devolved state and when it fell it reverted to its component parts. These then became the components in the creation of its successor state.

The Second Reich came to an end in 1918 and after barely half a century the whole question of the political organization of Germany was once more an issue. There were uprisings in a number of the states, many of them, such as Bavaria, seeking to achieve greater independence or to attain radically different political arrangements with the central government. In 1919 a new German constitution was signed in Weimar. This created the Weimar Republic, which was a parliamentary democracy organized along federal lines. In it there were seventeen *Freistaaten* and these again included the three *Hanse* cities. The new constitution was politically a very advanced one for its time and highly democratic in its governmental structures. Each of the member states had its own parliament and was autonomous in its internal affairs. Thus in the Weimar constitution for the first time the idea of the autonomous city was incorporated into the political structure of a modern twentieth-century state.

The Treaty of Versailles, which ended the First World War, stripped Germany of much of the territory of the Second Reich. The greater part of the loss was in the east, where a great deal of territory was transferred to the resurrected state of Poland. As a result of this, East Prussia was separated from the main body of Germany by a 'Polish Corridor' which was intended to give Poland access to the sea, something that was regarded as being an essential requirement for any viable state. The Polish Corridor had a mixed population of Germans and Slavs, and this presented the problem of the delimitation of the frontiers and the rights of the various population groups. Part of the solution of this entailed the creation of a completely independent city-state. The old *Hanse* city of Danzig was located on the edge of the Polish Corridor at the mouth of the Vistula. With its mixed population of Germans, Poles and other Slavs it did not fit easily into either the new Germany or the new Poland. As a result of this, the newly established League of Nations decided to give Danzig the status of a free city, thus implicitly resurrecting the old *Hanse* idea. The League was all too well aware of the dangers to peace that nationalism had posed and its responsibility for the war, and it was interested in experimenting with alternative political arrangements. Thus while Hamburg, Bremen and Lübeck became *Freistaaten* within the new German republic, Danzig, which had been absorbed into Prussia in the seventeenth century, became a free city outside it. As the French geographer Goblet wrote, this gave reality to 'the dream of a modern Hanseatic town on the estuary of the Vistula'.[7] That 'Hanseatic spirit' – about which the Kaiser had waxed lyrical – ironically re-emerged out of the ruins of his empire.

During its twenty years of existence, Danzig proved to be a considerable economic and political success. It became the most dynamic of the ports of the southern Baltic and its free status attracted considerable commercial and industrial growth.[8] This can be seen in the trade figures below in which it is compared with Stettin, the old *Hanse* port on the Oder, which, like Danzig itself, had long been part of Prussia but had been accorded no special status whatsoever by the League.

TABLE I   The External Trade of Danzig and Stettin
Trade in millions of tons

	Danzig	Stettin
1923	1.7	6.0
1928	8.0	5.0
1931	8.1	3.8

Source: *Official Statistics of Danzig, 1935*

The burgomaster attributed the success of the free city to that freedom that arose from 'the Hanseatic character of modern Danzig'.[9] Goblet believed that it also came from its freedom from those 'national prejudices' that had increasingly beset the European states. He formed the opinion that 'Danzig is making more profit than it would make if it once more became a German port in German territory . . . Sound judges . . . believe that the maintenance of the status quo is the most satisfactory solution for everyone concerned.'[10]

The brief existence of the Weimar Republic came to an end in January 1933 with the assumption of power by the Nazis. They inherited the Weimar constitution but this did not last long under the 'Third Reich' that they proceeded to inaugurate. From June 1933 they began to promulgate decrees designed to change the whole structure of the government of Germany. These were known collectively as the *Gleichschaltung* (co-ordination), and while they were concerned with all aspects of life in Germany their impact on the internal government of the country was most dramatic. Abandoning the long history of devolution that had most recently been enshrined in the Weimar constitution, they embarked on the establishment of a highly centralized National Socialist state in which all decisions of any importance were made in Berlin. The *Freistaaten* were abolished and Germany was divided into eighteen *Gaue*.[11] The regional parliaments were abolished and all administration was put into the hands of the Nazi party apparatus. Each *Gau* was ruled by a *Gauleiter* appointed in Berlin and who was responsible to central rather than to local government. In this way the Third Reich created a Germany that was centralized in a way in which the country had never been before. The Hungarian historian Tihany regarded the Emperor Frederick II as being 'proto-Nazi' in his desire for greater control and centralization, but Frederick did not come near to the real Nazi, Adolf Hitler, in the creation of a centralized state.[12] This was something quite new in German history and was clearly incompatible with the continuing special status of the *Hanse* cities.

TABLE 2 Populations of Selected Cities of the Former
Hanse, 1800–1940

Populations in 1000s	1800	1900	1940
Hamburg	130	706	1,682
Bremen	40	163	342
Lübeck	45	120	153
Stettin	42	211	269
Danzig	53	134	266

Source: B. R. Mitchell, *European Historical Statistics, 1750–1970* (1975)

In line with the new arrangements, in 1937 the special status of Lübeck and Bremen was brought to an end. Lübeck was incorporated into the *Gau* of Mecklenburg and Bremen into that of Weser-Ems. The sole survivor among the *Freistaaten* was Hamburg. The retention of the special status of this city appears to have been due mainly to local factors affecting the lower Elbe region. These included the very large size that Hamburg had by then attained, its commercial and industrial importance, and the problems of local administration posed by its expansion along the lower Elbe.[13] In 1933 its population had reached over one million, while that of Bremen was 300,000 and Lübeck, until the nineteenth century the largest of the three, only 150,000. Greater Hamburg, which included the other towns around the lower Elbe, had a population of 1.5 million. There was also a strong sense of independence in this proud city which even the Nazis had not been able to eradicate. In January 1937 a decree was promulgated that created a new *Hansestadt Hamburg*. This was based on '*Gross Hamburg*', which included Altona, Harburg-Wilhelmsburg, Blankanese and Wandsbek, and thus acquired considerable territory from the *Gaue* of Schleswig-Holstein and Hanover. The new *Hansestadt* had a total population of 1.7 million and, after the *gau* of *Gross Berlin*, which had a population of 4.2 million, it was the largest urban administrative unit in the whole of the Third Reich (see Table 2).[14] It was also the sole survivor in which the name of the *Hanse*, and at least a token of its former independence, was retained throughout the ferocious centralization of the Nazi period. It is both ironic and tragic that in 1943 this last city to bear the name of *Hansestadt*, and in which the old traditions were still alive, was subjected to a massive bombardment by British and American aircraft. This resulted in a firestorm that caused the greatest destruction and loss of life of any bombing in Europe during the Second World War.[15]

By this time Hamburg had become the last remnant of the *Hanse* in existence. In 1939, when Poland was invaded by the Germans, the Free City of Danzig was reunited with the Third Reich and incorporated into the new *Gaue* carved out of those former territories of the Reich that had been detached in 1919. From then on Danzig ceased to exist as a separate political entity.

A curious conclusion to the whole *Hanse* enterprise then took place. In August 1939 the Nazi-Soviet Pact assigned the three Baltic Republics of Estonia, Latvia and Lithuania to the Soviet sphere. Their most important cities, notably Riga, Tallinn (Reval) and Tartu (Dorpat), were historically German and still had large numbers of Germans living in them. Despite the fact that they had been in Russia for most of the time since they were incorporated into the Russian Empire by Peter the Great, they had remained very German and over the centuries had retained the appearance of *Hanse* cities. Many of the old *Hanse* traditions were still kept alive within them and in many ways they had remained eastern outposts of Germanic Europe.

19 The ruins of a *Hansestadt*: Hamburg in 1945.

Even by the 1930s there was still much of the feel of the *Kolonialstädte* about these places and the geopoliticians of the Third Reich had been happy to incorporate them into the German *Sprachsboden* and *Kulturboden* that they delimited as part of the justification of the pursuit of more territory in the east.[16] The contribution of these cities and provinces to Russia over the centuries had been immense, and much of the development of the country had been particularly associated with those Germans who came from them. The Russians now coveted their return to the Soviet Union, but before this took place and, as part of the agreement with Germany, they demanded the expulsion of all the German inhabitants. Stalin's plan was for the complete Russification of these states in a way that had never taken place under the Russian Empire. As part of this plan, the Germans had to be expelled in order to make way for an influx of Russian immigrants. In accordance with this agreement, in September 1939 the German government ordered the Baltic Germans to leave their homes and to return to the Reich. This was the *Heim-ins-Reich Aktion* and it was the price that had to be paid for the agreement with the Soviets. A fleet of German ships sailed eastwards through the Baltic and made for Riga. All Germans from the three Baltic states were instructed to assemble there and to await transport to take them to the west. This they proceeded to do, and the armada sailed back to Germany bearing some 60,000 Baltic Germans. Most came from the old *Hansestädte* and most of them were professional people of various sorts.[17] This was the end of the *Hanse* enterprise in the east. It had effectively begun in 1201 when the Teutonic Knights sailed eastwards through the Baltic and Albert von Buxhoevden from Bremen had established the seat of his bishopric in Riga. It came to an end 838 years later when another flotilla of ships sailed westwards, this time to take their descendants back home to the Reich for good.

While the *Heim-ins-Reich Aktion* was the real end of the long German involvement in the eastern Baltic, the operation had a brief and terrible sequel. Two years later in June 1941 the Germans were again back in the Baltic region. The invasion of the Soviet Union, appropriately called Operation Barbarossa, included the occupation of the three Baltic states. The old *Hanse* cities of the region again fell into German hands as did the old *Hanse* counters at Pskov and Novgorod. Alfred Rosenberg, a Baltic German, born in Reval and educated at the University of Riga, became the ruler of the new Nazi province of *Ostland*. He and his racist cohorts dreamed of the permanent incorporation of his homeland into a new *Grossdeutschland* that would stretch from the Rhine to the Neva and result in permanent German dominion over the Slavs. This racialist perversion of the old *Hanse* enterprise lasted for barely three years and was brought to a cataclysmic end with the defeat of Germany in 1945.

The reimposition of harsh Soviet rule that followed the 'liberation' was arguably even less congenial to the re-emergence of anything resembling the *Hanse* spirit of enterprise and cooperation. Riga and Tallinn became respectively the capital cities of the Soviet republics of Latvia and Estonia, and by the 1980s their newer residential and industrial districts were barely distinguishable from dozens of similar urban sprawls throughout the Soviet Union. For the most part the old *Hanse* quarters were allowed to fall into decay, although the symbols of Russian mastery, such as the church of St Nicholas dominating the skyline of Tallinn, together with the reminders of the heroism of Alexander Nevski, were carefully restored. These cities had been fully converted into the western outposts of an Eurasian state ruled from Moscow. This can perhaps be regarded as being the renewal of the Muscovite onslaught on the Baltic *Hanse* that had been begun by Ivan the Terrible and was completed by Stalin.

In a strange way, the memory of the *Hansestädte* had been kept alive more in the commercial heart of the Third Reich than in the post-war Soviet Union. Ironically, the last 'capital' of the Third Reich was the old *Hanse* city of Flensburg situated at the head of a bay that looked out onto the Baltic. Here Admiral Doenitz, commander of the German Navy and Hitler's designated successor, formed the last government of the Third Reich after the dictator's death in Berlin on 29 April 1945. It is doubly ironic that the most terrifying regime in German history was finally brought to an end among the beautiful old buildings of this once thriving *Hanse* port city, located just to the north of Lübeck and founded just a few decades after the mother city of the Hanse. The last surviving city bearing at least the name *Hansestadt*, the devastated city of Hamburg, had been liberated from the Nazis in April 1945, and the German army finally surrendered at Lüneburg heath, just south of the city, on 8 May. The old *Hanse* cities, which represented so different a vision of Germany, thus came to play a strangely central role in the cataclysmic end of the Third Reich.

EPILOGUE: TOWARDS A NEW HANSE?

Just a decade after the trauma of defeat and occupation, a new German state came into being that was carved out of the zones of occupation of the British, French and Americans. This was the German *Bundesrepublik*, which, like the Weimar Republic before it, was a federal state. It consisted of twelve *Länder*, each of which had its own parliament and was responsible for its own internal affairs, including education, justice and the police. These *Länder* were the result of the complete redrawing of the internal political map of Germany, and both Hamburg and Bremen were included among them. In this way two of the old

Hanse cities again emerged as part of the new political arrangements.

In response to this the Soviets created the German Democratic Republic out of their occupation zone. This was a centralized Communist state on the model of the Soviet Union itself and there were no *Hanse* survivals. Lübeck, which had already lost its status as a free city in 1935, was incorporated into the province of Pomerania. The old East Prussia ceased to be German at all and was divided between Poland and the Soviet Union. Königsberg, formerly the capital of East Prussia, began a new life as Kaliningrad and became a detached part of the Soviet Union. This old *Hanse* city, which had been incorporated into Prussia in the eighteenth century, became a base for the projection of Soviet naval power deep into the Baltic. The free city of Danzig, which had lasted for only twenty years, was now incorporated into Poland and its name changed to Gdansk. It may perhaps be of some significance that the movement which was eventually to free Poland from Communism began in this city in 1980. It arose out of the Solidarity trade union led by Lech Walesa, which was strongest in the former *Hanse* ports of Gdansk and Szczecin (Stettin) and which spread from them to the rest of the country.

The collapse of the Soviet Union in 1990 again liberated the states of the eastern Baltic. They were once more free to conduct their own foreign policies in an unfettered way and this led them to revisit their old Baltic relationships. During the 1990s the Baltic states began to move towards economic, political and cultural arrangements with one another and for the first time in many centuries there were no great powers to prevent them from doing so. The Baltic began to re-emerge as a human region in a way in which it had not really been since the *Hanse* came to an end in the seventeenth century. By the beginning of the twenty-first century, ferry boats and hydrofoils were plying the Baltic and Helsinki, Tallinn, Riga, Klaipeda, Stockholm and many other cities have been linked together in a completely new way. Baltic cities have entered into economic agreements, town-twinning arrangements and cultural contacts. An example of the latter is the Baltic cultural festival, which takes place in different cities each year and brings together peoples who have close cultural and historical roots but were forcibly separated from one another for many centuries.

The magazine *Newsweek* called this growth in Baltic consciousness 'a new Hanseatic League'. In its view it represents, 'a post Cold War reincarnation of the mercantile monopoly that dominated the Baltic trade in the Middle Ages'.[18] As it did of old, the new dynamism focuses on the cities as the centres of economic, political and cultural life. Cities such as Tallinn now have as much to do with other Baltic cities, notably Helsinki, as they do with the rest of Estonia. Riga looks out onto the Baltic and less to its immediate hinterland, and even St Petersburg, the imperial city that put an end to the freedom of the Baltic, has endeavoured to forge links with its Baltic neighbours. It was to a large extent built and embellished by French, Italian, German and British architects and artists, and it looks out westwards to the Baltic.[19] In the great celebrations of the tercentenary of the city in 2003, emphasis was placed on St Petersburg's historic role as Russia's 'window' on the lands to the west. Unlike former times, today this role is seen as having more to do with the Europeanization of Russia than the Russianization of Europe.

Since the 1990s the idea of the *Hanse* has come back and a new organization has been established under the auspices of the United Nations to bring its cities together once more.[20] The members of the new grouping include Novgorod and Pskov in the east and Hamburg and Bremen in the west. While the former were forced brutally and bloodily to forsake their *Hanse* traditions by Ivan the Terrible, the latter, despite facing odds almost as great, were able to hold onto these same *Hanse* traditions through thick and thin. During the Second World War these cities were severely damaged and much of their *Hanse* heritage was destroyed. They have now risen again from the ashes and their ancient buildings have been lovingly restored. At the beginning of the twenty-first century the *Länder* of Hamburg and Bremen are once more proud to call themselves *Hansestadt* and the term is also now used by Lübeck, mother city of the Hanse, which, unlike its two larger neighbours, did not become a self-governing *Land*. At the other end of Europe, both Novgorod – now once more 'Velikhi' Novgorod – and Pskov look westwards to the Baltic and to

20, 21 Revival in Riga: The Stock Exchange and (opposite) the restored House of the Blackheads.

trans-frontier cooperation with neighbouring Tartu, Narva and Tallinn.

President Vladimir Putin of Russia, a native of St Petersburg, has spoken of the idea of a 'Baltic bridge' linking Hamburg to St Petersburg. In a post-nation-state world, such a concept signifies the return of wider regional cooperation after the manner of the *Hanse* of old. From one perspective, this can be seen as being the revival of an old kind of pre-state region. Alternatively, it can be seen as signifying the rise of a new kind of post-state region in which the cities rather than the nations become the states and move into the position of being the principal actors around its shores.[21] As cities look out more and more towards the geographical regions within which they are located, rather than inwards

towards those nation-states to which history has confined or even condemned them, this appears to become ever more a possibility.

In the eastern Baltic at least, the city of Narva was in many ways the place where the old world of the *Hanse* city-states was brought to an end and the new world of the great powers began. The two strongholds of Narva and Ivangorod, still facing one another menacingly across the river, are forcible reminders of this. Today in the Baltic another new world is coming into being of which the hydrofoil is certainly a more potent symbol than the castle. A trans-national entity is beginning to take shape which is embracing the economic, political and cultural aspects of the region. In this entity the cities are likely to play a more important role than at any time since the fourteenth century, when the *Hanse Städtebünde*, fresh from its victory over Denmark, moved to open up the Baltic and to ensure that, for a time at least, it would be organized on the basis of cooperation rather than confrontation.

FOURTEEN

The Globalization of the City-State

As has been seen, the city-state was a phenomenon that originated around the shores of the Mediterranean. From there it
spread eastwards in the wake of Alexander's armies through the
Middle East and Central Asia and on into northern India. As a
result the Hellenistic version of the *polis* made a brief and limited appearance in the mountains of Afghanistan and on the
plains of the Indus. Later the city-state spread northwards into
Europe, where it came to be most identified with the free cities
of the Holy Roman Empire. Throughout most of its history, the
city-state was thus an overwhelmingly European phenomenon,
the most important centres of its occurrence having been in the
eastern and central Mediterranean and the Baltic–North Sea
region.

By the end of the Second World War the last signs of this
once highly significant geopolitical phenomenon had all but
disappeared from the map of Europe and the ruins of the last
Hansestadt lay amidst the devastation of the last Reich. The
world that emerged from the Second World War was dominated by a small number of great empires. The European
empires of Britain, France, the Netherlands, Belgium and
Portugal extended across virtually the whole of Africa and
southern Asia. Of the five permanent members of the Security
Council of the new United Nations, two of them, Britain and
France, were avowedly imperial states, while another two, the
Soviet Union and China, although using the term 'republic' to
describe themselves, were in fact neo-imperial formations
dominated by a single nation, the Russians and the Han Chinese
respectively. Thus in 1945 there was more of Augustus'
imperium than of Cicero's *respublica* about them both and,

indeed, about the world generally, the greater part of which was controlled, directly or indirectly, by imperial or neo-imperial powers. Despite the ideals of freedom and self-determination enshrined in the Charter of the United Nations, the world was in reality one in which there was little real freedom and even less self-determination for most of its people.

Europe, where the city-state was virtually defunct, had since the nineteenth century been the main centre of the massive empires that swathed the globe. However, these empires emerged from the Second World War in a highly fragile state and a quarter of a century later most of them had fallen or had been transformed into loose post-imperial groupings, such as the British Commonwealth and the French Union. The principal inheritors of these empires were the territorial states which in the 1950s and '60s proliferated across Africa and southern Asia as earlier they had done in South America and eastern Europe. Although they were known as nations, few of them came anywhere close to being nations in any accepted sense of the term. However, after having fought for most of the century for their freedom from the imperial powers, this was the age of the triumph of the 'nation' and freedom was attained through the assertion of nationality and was based on the ideology of nationalism. Being a 'nation' in the 1950s and '60s was the ideal and this was what, officially at least, these new states were. This was despite the fact that most of them were made up of a mixture of ethnic, religious and cultural elements that had little in common and produced a situation in which the new states were confronted from the outset with immense problems of cohesion and identity.

There was, however, another group of inheritor states of the European empires which was a small but nevertheless significant one. It is ironic that just as the city-state became defunct in Europe, it emerged on the world scene for the first time as a global phenomenon. This transformation took place mainly in the territory of the former British Empire. The new 'nations' that were built on the ruins of Empire were mainly in areas that had been acquired by the British during the period of expansionist imperialism in the second half of the nineteenth century. The city-states which emerged at around the same time as these

territorial states had rather different origins. They had originally been trading points, 'factories', ports, naval bases, repair
yards and coaling stations which had been set up across the
world as bases for the establishment and retention of commercial and maritime power. When the Empire fell, many of them
had by that time become substantial communities which possessed sufficient individuality to resist automatic incorporation
into the nearest territorial state. The origins and development
of each of these was different, but collectively they represented
the return of the city-state on a global scale within a quarter of a
century of its demise in Europe. While 'city-state' is an appropriate collective term that covers them all, they were in reality
different in their particular characteristics and in their relationship to the territorial states which surrounded them. They
ranged from completely independent states having all the
attributes of sovereignty to states with a high measure of independence in the conduct of their affairs.

By the 1970s in the former British Empire two separate
clusters of city-states could be clearly identified. These were in
the Far East and in the Middle East. In the Far East this cluster
consisted mainly of two cities: Singapore and Hong Kong.
Both dated from the early nineteenth century and both had
been bases for the assertion of British economic and naval power
in the region. Singapore had been founded by Sir Stamford
Raffles, an official of the East India Company, in 1819.
Strategically located on an island in the Straits of Malacca
between the Malayan peninsula and Sumatra, it was intended to
be the link in the trade route by sea from India to China. As
such it became the principal eastern base for the operations of
the East India Company and became the key to the assertion
of British power in the Far East. Other settlements, notably
Malacca and Penang, were founded on the mainland and,
together with Singapore, they were grouped together as the
Straits Settlements, which became a Crown Colony in 1867.
This was expanded into the Confederation of Malay States,
which came into existence in 1896 and of which Singapore was a
constituent part. By that time it had become the most important
base for naval operations in the Pacific area. The increasing
fragility of this network of maritime power was revealed in the

22 Hong Kong Harbour.

Second World War with its capture by the Japanese, who attacked and subjugated it from the mainland of Malaya. With the return of the British in 1945, there was a turbulent period during which there was considerable resistance to the arrangement that the British proposed for the transfer of power to a representative government. In 1955 the colony was accorded a measure of self-government and in 1959 it was given complete control over its internal affairs. In 1963 the Federation of Malaysia came into being as an independent state. This was made up of North Borneo (Sabah), Sarawak, Singapore and Malaya itself. Singapore, however, did not fit well into the new Federation, and after prolonged discussions it finally seceded and became a sovereign state in 1965. Its constitution consisted of an unicameral parliament elected by universal adult suffrage, a cabinet responsible to parliament, and a directly elected president who was given considerable powers.

Hong Kong was established in 1842. Located like Singapore on an island, it is in the estuary of the Xun Jiang river, the main maritime entrance into southern China. By this time Britain had become deeply involved in trade with China, and sought a base of operations that was under British sovereignty. The

23 Hong Kong central business district.

Treaty of Nanking that ended the Opium War in 1842 opened the five 'treaty' ports of Canton, Amoy, Foochow, Ningpo and Shanghai to British traders and the island of Hong Kong was at the same time ceded to Britain. At the Treaty of Peking in 1860 the adjacent Kowloon peninsula was also ceded, and in 1897 the 'New Territories' were acquired on a 99-year lease granted by the Chinese. With Hong Kong as a base, the British were able to operate more easily and safely, and the trading operations of Hong Kong were widened from China to the whole of the Far East. As well as trade, the city became an important centre for manufacture and banking, the Hong Kong Stock Exchange becoming one of the most important in the Far East.

By the time of the Second World War, as with Singapore, the vulnerability of Hong Kong to a determined land power became clear. The island was occupied by the Japanese, who attempted to incorporate it into the new economic area over which they had gained control. On the return of the British in 1945, the Crown Colony of Hong Kong faced a China that was in turmoil as a result of the civil war between the Nationalists and the Communists. In 1949 this came to an end with the victory of the Communists and the People's Republic of China was established. The new regime asserted that the 'unequal' treaties regarding Hong Kong were no longer valid and that the colony was considered to be a part of China. The British retained Hong Kong throughout the difficult years that followed, but the colony was given more and more self-government. By 1995 all seats on the Legislative Council were democratically elected and the powers of the governor were much reduced. As the end of the lease on the 'New Territories' in 1997 approached, negotiations proceeded with the Chinese government and an agreement was finally reached to safeguard the colony's independence within China. In 1997 Hong Kong was transferred to China under arrangements that had been negotiated between Britain and the People's Republic. However, it retained its separate identity. Under the Basic Law, which had been agreed upon, the laws, government, and commercial and financial arrangements of Hong Kong were to be retained. Under the slogan 'one country, two systems', Hong Kong became a Special Administrative Region of China, its separate identity being guaranteed for a minimum of 50 years.

The second cluster of post-imperial city-states is in the Persian Gulf. From the middle of the nineteenth century, Britain had taken considerable interest in the coastal regions of the Arabian peninsula. This was particularly in connection with the security of the route to India and of trade with the Middle East. In 1839 Aden was annexed, and from then on this port of call and later coaling station was ruled from India. In 1861 the sheikhdom of Bahrain on an island in the Persian Gulf became a British protectorate. In the same year a number of other sheikhdoms in the Gulf entered into treaty arrangements with Britain. From then on these were known as the Trucial States and they included Abu Dhabi, Dubai and Sharjah. Their foreign relations, together with those of the sheikhdom of Oman, were put into British hands. With the opening of the Suez Canal in 1867 the Middle East became of vital importance in the safety of the new shorter route to India via the Mediterranean and the Red Sea. Port Said and Suez were built on either side of the canal in order to safeguard the vessels using it and Cairo became the centre of British power for the whole region. Finally, in 1899 the Emirate of Kuwait was made into a British protectorate. The amir remained on the throne, but

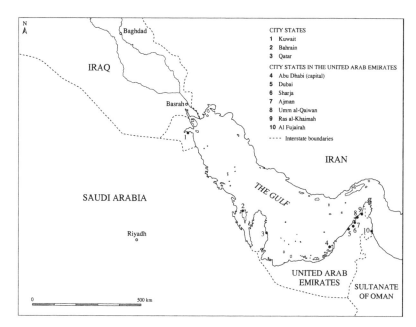

24 City-states in the Persian Gulf.

from then on all matters of importance, including foreign relations, were handled by the British.

Following the Second World War the British began to withdraw from the Middle East, and while the main successor states in this region, such as Iraq and Jordan, were territorial, there was also the legacy of the small states in the Gulf. These became independent as separate states from Saudi Arabia, which emerged in the post-war years as the major power in the southern Gulf region. Kuwait achieved its independence in 1961 and Bahrain and Qatar in 1971. All three had been sheikhdoms but on independence they became emirates with the amir as head of state and constitutions guaranteeing political and human rights. Although in all three assemblies were established by limited electorates, in reality at first the amirs had absolute power and over the years there was much friction between the authoritarian and the democratic forces within these states. In 1971 the Trucial States became independent as the United Arab Emirates. The capital of the Emirates is Abu Dhabi and the highest federal authority, the Supreme Council of Rulers, consists of the heads of state of each of the seven members. There is also a Federal Legislative Council that sits in the capital, and foreign affairs and inter-state economic arrangements are in the hands of the federal government also located there. Each of the members of the United Arab Emirates is technically a sovereign state and in practice is in charge of all its own internal affairs.

Overwhelmingly these post-imperial city-states were British, although some of the former possessions of other European powers moved in the direction of becoming city-states. They were accorded a considerable measure of self-government within the new territorial states in which they were located. They were mainly in India, where European ports and factories had been established along the coasts since the sixteenth century. Goa had become the main centre of Portuguese activity in the subcontinent and, together with a few other smaller ports, remained under Portuguese sovereignty after the British became the dominant power in the Indian subcontinent in the eighteenth century. Likewise the French had established settlements mainly on the eastern coast, and France was allowed to retain these after her defeat by Britain in the Seven Years War. By the first half of the twentieth century, Diu, Daman and Goa still remained Portuguese while Pondicherry, Yanaon, Karikal and Mahé remained French. When India became an independent state in 1947, the French and Portuguese possessions were ceded to it, only Goa remaining in the hands of the imperial power. In 1961 Goa was taken over by India and in 1987 was granted statehood within the Indian Federation. This gave it its own legislature, a Council of Ministers and a governor appointed by the Federal Government in Delhi. Although not given statehood, Pondicherry was given complete independence from the state of Tamil Nadu. Pondicherry, together with Karikal, Yanaon and Mahé, constitutes a Union Territory and within this the city of Pondicherry was granted its own state assembly.

One other non-British city-state is Macau, which is located on the other side of the Xun Jiang delta from Hong Kong. A Portuguese possession since 1557, it fulfilled a similar purpose in regard to Portuguese trade with China as did Hong Kong with British trade three centuries later. Far smaller and less high profile than Hong Kong, the negotiations for its relinquishment by the imperial power were neither so long nor so difficult. In 2000 it reverted to China and the arrangements for its relationship to the People's Republic were very similar to those of Hong Kong. It became a Special Administrative Region with its own

TABLE 3: Contemporary City-States

	Area Sq km	Population millions	Density per sq km	Birth Rate per 1,000	GNP $billion	GNP per capita
Kuwait	17,718	2.27	128	19.1	29.3	15,000
Qatar	11,437	0.60	52.2	19.4	15.1	20,300
Bahrain	712	0.51	914	20.2	10.1	13,900
UAE*	77,700	3.49	44.9	16.0	54.0	22,800
Singapore	660	4.2	6,310	11.3	109.8	26,500
Hong Kong	1,098	6.4	6,181	7.1	166.5	24,759
Macau	26	0.44	16,926	7.5		
Goa	3,702	1.34	363			
Pondicherry**	480	0.97	2,029			

* The United Arab Emirates which are made up of the seven sovereign states of Abu Dhabi, Dubai, Sharjah, Ajman, Ras al-Khaimah, Fujairah and Umm al-Qaiwan.
** Union Territory within the Indian Federation including Karaikal, Yanaon, Mahé together with Pondicherry itself. Sources: *National Statistics, 2003*

partly elected Legislative Council and chief executive and the rights of its citizens are guaranteed in its Basic Law.

Thus out of the decline and fall of the old empires, by the beginning of the twenty-first century there had been a small but significant global upsurge of city-states. Although some fifteen cities have been identified here as being city-states, they differ considerably in the extent to which they can be regarded fully as coming into this geopolitical category.

On the important question of sovereignty, these contemporary city-states vary from those, like Singapore, which are completely sovereign in every way, to Pondicherry, which, although there is an explicit recognition of its separate identity, is firmly bound into the Indian Federation. While the former was forced to wrest its independence from the territorial state to which it had been allocated, in the case of the latter there was a recognition by the territorial state that, because of historical factors, this city is unique. As a result it has not been amalgamated into the state of Tamil Nadu in which it is located and has been given the status of a Union Territory. Judged in this way,

TABLE 4: The Characteristics of the Contemporary City-State

	Sovereignty	Structure	Dominant City	Trade	Manufacture	Wealth	Region	Democracy
Kuwait	1	1		1		1	1	
Quatar	1	1	1	1		1	1	
Bahrain	1	1	1	1		1	1	
UAE*	1		1	1		1	1	
Singapore	1		1	1	1	1	1	1
Hong Kong			1	1	1	1	1	
Goa		1						1
Pondicherry			1					
Macau			1	1		1	1	
Totals	11	4	13	13	2	13	13	2

* The United Arab Emirates are made up of seven sovereign states.

only four of the fifteen city-states can be said to be completely sovereign (see Table 4).

In addition to this, only four of the city-states have anything like the *asty-chora* internal structure that is characteristic of the classical *polis*. In none of them does the *chora* really fulfil the same functions as it did in the *polis*. In the classical city-state the *asty* dominated the *polis* and this is also the case with thirteen of the fifteen contemporary city-states. Only in Kuwait and Goa is this not the case, and the capitals of both of these are fairly small places, having only a relatively small proportion of the total urban population of the state. Once more thirteen of the fifteen rely heavily on trade as the mainstay of their economy. While the Gulf states were all involved in trade from the outset, during the later twentieth century one commodity, oil, took over from all the others and became the most important element in their wealth. Today, air travel has converted such major junctions as Hong Kong and Dubai into huge trading emporia for travellers from all over the world where it is possibly to buy all manner of sophisticated manufactured goods. Only two of them, however, Hong Kong and Singapore, are also important centres of manufacture, mostly of consumer goods which are then exported. As to the overall levels of wealth, thirteen of them have per capita GNPs that are very high by world standards (see Table 3). The highest are Hong Kong and Singapore, while the United Arab Emirates and Qatar come very close. The lowest are Goa and Pondicherry, which, although their origins lay in trade, no longer have the same position as trading cities as do the others.

All these fifteen city-states are part of wider transnational groupings or organizations. The seven member states of the United Arab Emirates are in a federation, but they and the other Gulf states are also members of the Gulf Co-operation Council and the 'Gulf' is the wider geopolitical region of which they form an integral part. Singapore was a founder member of the Association of Southeast Asian Nations (ASEAN) of which all its immediate neighbours are also members. The purpose of this organization is to foster regional cooperation in the commercial, cultural and political spheres. While both Hong Kong and Macau are part of China, both of them are also involved in trading more widely. Their most important economic relationships are with China itself and with other Far Eastern countries, notably Japan, South Korea and Taiwan. All three of them are within the emerging Southeast Asian geopolitical region.

Finally, there is the question of democracy. In the context of the city-states themselves, this, of course, goes hand in hand with high levels of self-government, since it cannot really be said to exist fully in a state that is actually part of another state. Judged by the most stringent standards, only one of the fifteen city-states, Singapore, can be considered to be really a city-state democracy. As a member of the Indian Federation, Goa also has a considerable measure of self-government in its own local affairs. Elements of democratic participation in government exist in Hong Kong, Macau and Pondicherry, the last, like Goa, operating within the institutions of a functioning democracy.

Thus the principal characteristics that are to be found in the globalized city states of the twenty-first century are a high degree of sovereignty, the dominance of a single city, the overwhelming importance of trade, high levels of wealth *per capita* and membership of transnational economic and political groupings that are basically regional in character (see Table 4). Only in respect of democracy and internal structure does there appear to be a substantial deviation from the classical model of the city-state.

This all leads to the conclusion that these city-states represent more than just some kind of geopolitical residue left over from the fall of the empires in the late twentieth century. It suggests that they are a part of the wider phenomenon of globalization that began to take place in the aftermath of the fall of the empires and the need to establish functioning arrangements for the continuation of trade and economic cooperation. They are phenomena that in their economic and trading patterns, and in some cases at least, in their cultural diversity, transcend their immediate geographical environment. Rather they look out to the wider geopolitical region in which they are located and through this to the world itself. As such they may prove to be better adapted than the twentieth-century nation-states ever were to exist and to prosper in the increasingly globalized world of the twenty-first century.

Epilogue: The Ideal and the Reality

During the last 3,000 years the city-state has had a chequered history. Over this long period there have been times when the city-state has been one of the main components of the world political map and there have been other times when it has virtually disappeared from it. Most recently, this had taken place before the middle of the twentieth century, and while 50 years later at the dawn of the twenty-first century the political map is still mainly a representation of nation-states, the city-state has made a small but significant comeback.

Over the millennia the city-state has had many enthusiastic protagonists ranging from Aristotle, who was convinced that 'no higher form of social union was possible than that of the city-state', to the modern American sociologist Manuel Castells, who maintains that the free city is altogether 'a superior form of life and government'.[1]

Those who have espoused the city-state have done so because of the particular qualities that they have detected in it. One of the most important of these is its small size, as a result of which it has qualities that larger states do not possess. Unlike huge empires, which Aristotle considered to be 'artificial and unnatural', the city-state is very much on a human scale. Aristotle believed that it was necessary that the citizens of any state 'should know each other and know what kind of people they are'.[2] In order to enable this to take place, the city itself had to be small. 'The city', said Plato, 'can be allowed to go on growing so long as it preserves its unity: thus far no further . . . Only so will the city continue to be one city, and not a mere conglomeration of people'.[3] The desire to have 'more and more' is judged to be as disastrous in the life of the state as it can be in the life of an individual. Only by making the state better and not bigger can its citizens enjoy to the full the well-being that leads to real happiness. Rousseau took a similar view of the superiority of small states over large ones. He expressed the opinion that

> the social bond is enfeebled by extension; in general a small state is proportionally stronger than a great one . . . administration becomes more oppressive in proportion to its increasing distance . . . A body too large for its own constitution . . . perishes under the weight'.[4]

The increase in the size of the state, maintained Cassirer, cannot avert the ruin of the state but is more likely to hasten it.[5]

Small size also meant that the citizens were able to participate in government to an extent that was not possible in larger states. In fact, in a properly functioning city-state, wrote Aristotle, participation is not merely a right but a duty. The root meaning of citizen in both Greek and Latin is 'he who is summoned' and answers the summons for the purpose of defending the city and taking decisions in its best interests. The citizens of the city-state are thus far from being a passive body of people ruled over by some monarch; rather, they form a community that acts together for the common good. The whole *raison d'être* of the city-state is the well-being of its citizens and its highest expression is the *res publica*, the public good, and the institutions that bring this about.

This is all linked to that freedom that is perhaps the most central feature of the city-state. Freedom has always been seen as being one of the cornerstones of political life in the city-state. The old German saying that 'Die Stadtluft macht frei' is a statement of the belief that it was not in the empire but in the city that freedom was safeguarded. Pirenne expressed the opinion that burgher and freeman were synonymous terms, and Hobbes wrote that 'There is written on the turrets of the city of Lucca in great characters, to this day, the word Libertas'.[6] Seventeenth-century Amsterdam was 'a haven of refuge' in an intolerant world. It was a place where all could enjoy freedom of conscience and coins struck in Amsterdam had imprinted on them the words 'Haec Libertatis Ergo'. It was the 'frei luft' of city-states that invariably made them 'havens of refuge' from the tyranny outside their walls.

Thus size, participation, tolerance and freedom made up a totality that has commended the city-state through the ages to those who sought 'the good life' in the Aristotelian sense. Within its small compass humanity was able to express itself most fully in the arts, architecture, science and philosophy. Plato spoke of 'the symmetry and beauty of the whole' and Aristotle of *eudaimonia*, the sense of well-being leading to happiness. In Renaissance Italy the idea of the *città ideale* referred to its harmony as an architectural, artistic, intellectual and political whole.

While a great deal of this eulogy to the city-state does have a ring of truth, in many cases the reality has been a quite different one. What the protagonists of the city-state were speaking about was often a *città ideale* that was more an ideal to be aspired to rather than a reality that actually existed. In the real city-states, while there was democracy there was also tyranny and while there were wealth and beauty there were also poverty and ugliness. Plato and Aristotle were talking more about the ideal than the reality of the city-states that actually existed in Classical Greece. These philosophers, like others at later times, were attempting to guide the city-state in what they considered to be the right direction. However, in what Dickinson referred to as 'the best days in the best states', the city-state did come near to making the ideal a reality and to creating that 'rudimentary version of Paradise' that J.-L. Borges considered Athens to have been.[7]

The essential thing was not that the city-state was in all ways a perfect phenomenon compared to other political forms but that within it the ideal of a better life was more consistently present. In it the state existed for the benefit of its people rather than the people for the state. The city-state was never an ideological abstraction like the nation-state, which by the twentieth century had come in many cases to be in existence for itself alone. Far from giving its people a better life, it made them endure privations and sufferings in pursuit of its greater glory.

In contrast to this, the city-state has historically been fundamentally non-ideological. Its underlying purpose has been that of making a better life for its citizens. Despite all their faults, said Lord Bryce, in his epic work on the Holy Roman Empire, 'nevertheless our sympathy must go with the cities, in whose victory we recognise the triumph of freedom and civilisation'. Bryce recognized the essential 'nobility' of the city-state from the time when 'republican Athens rose above the slavish Asiatic and the brutal Macedonian'.[8] In ancient times the city was the place of protection from the barbarian hordes that threatened to engulf it, while in modern times it became the centre of freedom from the tyranny and ideological obsessions of the surrounding territorial states.

As a phenomenon in the political world, the role of the city-state has thus been very different from that of the nation-state. While the latter has sought its well-being within itself, and in many cases through the enlargement of itself, the former has usually looked outwards to a wider world of which it has invariably seen itself as being a part. While the nation-state has thus represented the segmentation of the world into watertight political compartments, the city-state has represented the opening up of the world and the formation of groupings within it. As a result both of its size and its vulnerability it has been ill-equipped to exist on its own, and in its own interests it has gravitated towards participation in wider regional groupings. This has had repercussions both for the city and for the wider region itself. For the city it is a situation conducive to repeated contacts among peoples of divergent cultures and this has made the city-state into a community of diversity. For the wider region it has meant that the city-state is the ideal component since it contains in microcosm much or all of that which is to be found in the macrocosm. The city-state has thus usually fitted more comfortably into wider groupings than has the nation-state. Most of these wider groupings have been cultural and economic, but, on occasions, they have also been transformed into something political.

Castells expressed the opinion that the project of the *comuneros* 'was the affirmation of the free city as a superior form of life and government'. While he went on to admit that 'as a political revolution, the *comunidades* of Castilla failed', he still asserted that 'as a citizen movement they brought together for ever in the collective memory of the Spanish people the idea of freedom, the right of municipal self-government, and the hope for a better life'.⁹ The hope of a better life has also lived on in the collective memory in many other cities and at many different times. It was to be found in the cities of Greece after the Macedonian conquest; in those of the Hellenistic world forcibly incorporated into the Roman Empire; in those of Renaissance Italy occupied by the Spaniards; in Venice fallen victim to Napoleon – the self-proclaimed new Attila – after a thousand years; and in the cities of the *Hanse* incorporated against their will and often with considerable violence into new imperial states.

Historically, city-states have been at their strongest and most powerful when the territorial states have been at their weakest. The greatest flourishing of the city-state has taken place at such times. This was so in the maritime fringes of the ancient world into which the Middle Eastern empires failed to penetrate; in medieval and Renaissance Italy where the Holy Roman Emperors could not easily impose their *iura regalia*; and in the Baltic during early modern times before the great powers had become strong enough to take over. At such times there were relatively brief windows of opportunity for city-states to demonstrate how effective they could be both for the benefit of their citizens and as actors on the world scene.

It is just as the windows have again begun to close that the perception of the virtues of the city-state has often been at its strongest. This is clearly seen in two works written in the early years of the sixteenth century just as the first great powers of the modern world were establishing their positions of dominance. These works were written by two remarkable statesmen who rose to the highest positions in their respective states. The first of these was Niccolò Machiavelli, the secretary to the Republic of Florence, whose work, *The Prince*, appeared in 1513. It was basically a belated attempt to rescue his city-state by demonstrating how it could be made to adapt to the changing world around it. The attempt proved quite futile, and Machiavelli's ideas were subsequently used by the enemies of the city-state to entrench their own positions and to accelerate the removal of all opposition to their schemes. The other was Thomas More, who subsequently became Lord Chancellor of England, and who in 1516, three years after *The Prince*, published a work entitled *Utopia*. This work was a vision of an ideal society in which all the ills and wrongdoings in the Europe of the early sixteenth century were swept away. The fact that Utopia was an island helped to insulate it from the realities of the world and to maintain its almost innocent idealism. Its government was a federation of city-states ruled by an elected monarch. These city-states were urban republics, each one sovereign and governed on rational lines for the common good. Thomas More wrote much of Utopia while on a mission to the Netherlands and it has been pointed out that this ideal society bears many resemblances to the Netherlands of that time.[10] More, a close acquaintance of Erasmus and other sixteenth-century humanists, was presenting a vision of a post-medieval Europe and it is significant that it was one based on city-states rather than on nation-states. Machiavelli and More represented respectively the realist and the idealist approach to the future of Europe and they held completely opposed views both on politics and on the nature of humanity that underlay it.[11] Yet they were at one in seeing the future as being one in which city-states continued to play a significant role.

By the time the Emperor Charles v, the inheritor and preserver of the system of which More so much approved, had handed over to his son, Philip ii, who was soon to destroy it, Machiavelli and More were dead. Both had fallen from grace and as a result of their beliefs Machiavelli had been sent into exile and More executed. Florence, like the Netherlands, was in the hands of Spain, and England was taking the lead in the successful establishment of the new nation-states that were to become the norm in modern Europe and the world.

While empires and nation-states in many different forms have been historically more the norm than any other types of state, the city-state has survived and has constituted an historical alternative to them. As such it has been part of an alternative geopolitical process that has encapsulated both the ideal of freedom and the hope for a better life. The alternative geopolitical process has been most in evidence when empires have been weak and unable to prevent city-states from asserting their independence.[12] The process has included the establishment of groupings of city-states that have themselves become actors on the interstate (international) scene and have produced forms of organization that have been powerful enough to challenge nations and empires alike. Thus the utopian federation of city-states has remained throughout history as a possibility that on rare occasions has been transformed into a tenuous reality.

Freedom, democracy and a better life have been at the root of the city as an ideal. This is encapsulated in the *città ideale*, which includes both the material and the spiritual, and in which the diverse aspects of life, material and non-material come together in harmony. In *Democratic Ideals and Reality*, a work that analyses the international scene in the aftermath of the First World War, Halford Mackinder contrasted 'ideals' and 'realities' and the problems involved in reconciling the two.[13] In the sense understood by Mackinder, the city-state has within itself elements of both Machiavelli's realism and More's idealism. The reality is what the city-state has accomplished throughout history and the ideal is what it still has the potential to become. In 'the best days in the best states' the ideal and the reality have approached together so closely that one can possibly talk of the *città ideale* has having at times actually existed. Certainly such times have remained throughout the ages in the collective memory and have encapsulated the hopes of humanity for a better society and a better world.

References

ONE · NATION, EMPIRE AND CITY: A GEOPOLITICAL
TYPOLOGY OF STATES

1 M. Horsman and A. Marshall, *After the Nation-State* (London, 1994),
pp. 3–22.
2 G. Parker, *Western Geopolitical Thought in the Twentieth Century* (London,
1985), p. 94.
3 Y. M. Goblet, *Political Geography and the World Map* (London, 1956),
pp. 19–20.
4 M. Glassner, *Systematic Political Geography* (New York, 1994), pp. 78–93.
5 G. Parker, *Geopolitics: Past, Present and Future* (London, 1998), pp. 32–3.
6 G. Parker, *The Geopolitics of Domination* (London, 1988), chap. 6.
7 J. Needham, *Within the Four Seas* (London, 1969), pp. 54–5.

TWO · THE BIRTH OF THE CITY-STATE

1 L. Mumford, *The Culture of Cities* (New York, 1938).
2 L. Mumford, *The City in History* (London, 1975), pp. 11–12.
3 The Bible, II Samuel 8.
4 The Bible, I Kings 5: 9.
5 Mumford, *The City in History*, pp. 121–2.
6 E. Ludwig, *The Mediterranean* (London, 1943), p. 59.
7 F. Braudel, *The Mediterranean in the Ancient World* (London, 2001),
pp. 21–5.
8 *Ibid.*, pp. 208–9.
9 E. Semple, *The Geography of the Mediterranean Region: Its Relation to
Ancient History* (London, 1932), pp. 579–609.
10 A. Lloyd, *Destroy Carthage!* (London, 1977), pp. 21–3.
11 Lloyd, *Destroy Carthage!*, pp. 91–3.
12 Braudel, *The Mediterranean*, pp. 216–7.

THREE · THE ANCIENT GREEK POLIS

1 T. Callander, *The Athenian Empire and the British* (London, 1961), p. 18.
2 A. J. Evans, ed., *The Penguin Herodotus* (London, 1941),Vol. VII, p. 55.
3 Thucydides, vol. I, p. 104, trans. B. Jowett, in W. W. Fowler, *The City-*

State of the Greeks and the Romans (London, 1952), p. 48.
4 Aristotle, *The Politics*, trans. T. A. Sinclair (London, 1977), pp. 120–21.
5 *Ibid.*, pp. 122–3.
6 W. A. Heurtley *et al.*, *A Short History of Greece* (Cambridge, 1965), p. 21.
7 A. Zimmern, *The Greek Commonwealth* (London, 1961), p. 205.
8 G. L. Dickinson, *The Greek View of Life* (London, 1941), p. 104.
9 Aristotle, *The Politics*, pp. 106–7.
10 E. Semple, *The Geography of the Mediterranean Region* (London, 1932), p. 390.
11 Dickinson, *The Greek View of Life*, p. 69.
12 *Ibid.*, p. 134.

FOUR · THE HELLENISTIC FOUNDATIONS

1 J.F.C. Fuller, *The Generalship of Alexander the Great* (London, 1998), p. 35.
2 A. B. Bosworth, *Conquest and Empire: The Reign of Alexander the Great* (Cambridge, 1993), p. 21.
3 Fuller, *Generalship of Alexander the Great*, p. 83.
4 D. I. Sly, *Philo's Alexandria* (London and New York, 1996), p. 41.
5 E. Ludwig, *The Mediterranean* (London, 1943), p. 115.
6 A.H.M. Jones, *The Greek City from Alexander to Justinian* (London, 1979), p. 3.
7 W. Schneider, *Babylon is Everywhere: The City as Man's Fate* (London, 1963), p. 125.
8 C. Freeman, *The Greek Achievement* (London, 1999), p. 355.
9 A. Hourani, *A History of the Arab Peoples* (London, 2002), pp. 128–46.

FIVE · NO MEAN CITY: ROME FROM URBS TO IMPERIUM

1 W. Keller, *The Etruscans* (London, 1975), p. 93.
2 *Ibid.*, p.45.
3 G. Parker, *The Geopolitics of Domination* (London, 1988), chap. 4.
4 Cato, 'De re rustica I', in W. W. Fowler, *The City-State of the Greeks and the Romans* (London, 1952), p. 237.
5 Aristotle, *The Politics*, trans. T. A. Sinclair (London, 1977), pp. 59–61.
6 A. Lloyd, *Destroy Carthage!* (London, 1977), pp. 98–9.
7 A. Siegfried, *Germs and Ideas* (Edinburgh and London, 1965), pp. 95–7.
8 E. Gibbon, *The History of the Decline and Fall of the Roman Empire* (London, 1995), Vol. II, p. 619.
9 Horace, *Epistles*, trans. H. R. Fairclough (London 1970), book 2.9.
10 D. Earl, *The Moral and Political Tradition of Rome* (London, 1966), pp. 123–4.
11 W. W. Fowler, *The City-State of the Greeks and the Romans* (London, 1952), p. 326.
12 *Ibid.*, p. 318.
13 *Ibid.*, p. 322.
14 Gibbon, *Decline and Fall*, II, p. 509.

15 W. Schneider, *Babylon is Everywhere* (London, 1963), p. 153.
16 Gibbon, *Decline and Fall*, III, p. 1081.
17 *Ibid.*, III, p.1062.

SIX · SERENISSIMA: VENICE AND THE CITY-STATES OF
THE ADRIATIC

1 J. Morris, *The Venetian Empire* (London, 1990), p. 3.
2 H. Pirenne, *Medieval Cities* (Princeton, NJ, 1969), pp. 82–3.
3 J. J. Norwich, *A History of Venice* (London, 1983), p. 5.
4 W. Schneider, *Babylon is Everywhere* (London, 1963), p. 203.
5 J. Ruskin, *The Stones of Venice* (London, 1906), Vol. II, p. 6.
6 N. Pounds, *An Historical Geography of Europe* (Cambridge, 1993), p. 91.
7 E. Ludwig, *The Mediterranean* (London, 1943), p. 266.
8 J. Larner, *Marco Polo and the Discovery of the World* (New Haven, CT, 2001), p. 36.
9 Schneider, *Babylon is Everywhere*, p. 262.
10 F. Braudel, *Civilization and Capitalism, 15th–18th Century*, III: *The Perspective of the World* (London, 1984), pp. 119–20.
11 Pirenne, *Medieval Cities*, p. 112.
12 Morris, *Venetian Empire*, p.14.
13 W. G. East, *An Historical Geography of Europe* (London, 1948), p. 307.
14 Larner, *Marco Polo*, p. 37.
15 Norwich, *History of Venice*, p. 282.
16 Braudel, *Civilization and Capitalism*, p. 30.
17 M. V. Clarke, *The Medieval City-State* (Cambridge, 1966), pp. 56–7.
18 Morris, *Venetian Empire*, p. 12.
19 F. W. Carter, *Dubrovnik (Ragusa): A Classic City-State* (London and New York, 1972), p. 214.
20 *Ibid.*, p. 40.
21 Norwich, *History of Venice*, pp. 54–5.
22 Carter, *Dubrovnik*, p. 62.
23 *Ibid.*, p. 214.

SEVEN · BISHOPS, DUKES AND REPUBLICS: THE CITY-
STATES OF RENAISSANCE ITALY

1 D. Waley, *The Italian City-Republics* (London, 1988), p. 9.
2 *Ibid.*, p. 55.
3 *Ibid.*, p. 69.
4 *Ibid.*, p. 34.
5 *Ibid.*, pp. 40–45.
6 J. Bryce, *The Holy Roman Empire* (London, 1897).
7 H. Pirenne, *Medieval Cities* (Princeton, NJ, 1969), pp. 168–73.
8 Bryce, *Holy Roman Empire*, p. 178.
9 *Ibid.*, p. 306.
10 *Ibid.*, p. 212.
11 U. Eco, *Baudolino* (London, 2002), pp. 44–5.

12 *Ibid.*, p. 46.

13 Waley, *Italian City Republics*, p. 89.

14 M. V. Clarke, *The Medieval City-State* (Cambridge, 1966), pp. 34–5.

15 B. Tuchman, *A Distant Mirror: The Calamitous Fourteenth Century* (London, 1995), p. 366.

16 Clarke, *The Medieval City-State*, p. 77.

17 L. Martinez, *Power and Imagination: City States in Renaissance Italy* (London, 1980), p. 254.

18 *Ibid.*, p. 243.

19 W. Schneider, *Babylon is Everywhere* (London, 1963), p. 202.

20 Boccaccio, *The Decameron*, trans. G. H. McWilliam (London, 1972), pp. 2, 3.

21 W.H.V. Reade, 'Dante's Vision of History', Annual Italian Lecture, *Reade* (London, 14 June 1939).

22 M. White, *Leonardo, the First Scientist* (London, 2000), pp. 148–50.

23 P. and L. Murray, *A Dictionary of Art and Artists* (London, 1966), p. 178.

24 Clarke, *The Medieval City-State*, p. 143.

25 J. Burckhardt, *The Civilization of Renaissance Italy* (Harmondsworth. 1990), p. 72.

26 Eco, *Baudolino*, p. 47.

27 Waley, *Italian City Republics*, p. 172.

28 J. Burkhardt, 'The Civilization of the Renaissance in Italy', in D. Selbourne, ed., *The Principle of Duty* (London, 1994), p. 102.

EIGHT · PRINCES, BISHOPS AND REPUBLICS: CITIES AND CITY-STATES IN RUSSIA

1 R. Hodges and D. Whitehouse, *Mohammed, Charlemagne and the Origins of Europe* (London, 1983), p. 102.

2 L.K.D. Kristoff, 'The Russian Image of Russia' in C. A. Fisher, ed., *Essays in Political Geography*, (London, 1968), pp. 349–51.

3 W. H. Parker, *An Historical Geography of Russia* (London, 1968), pp. 52–3.

4 *Ibid.*, pp. 66–7.

5 S. V. Kiselev, Introduction to V. Yan, *Jenghiz-Khan* (London, 1942).

6 D. Morgan *The Mongols* (Oxford, 1990), p. 23.

7 Parker, *Historical Geography of Russia*, pp. 42–5.

8 B. Rybakov, *Kievan Rus* (Moscow, 1984), p. 312.

9 *Ibid.*, p. 314.

10 J. Michell, N. Forbes and R. Beasley, trans., *The Chronicle of Novgorod* (London, 1914).

11 R. Beasley *et al.*, *Russia from the Varangians to the Bolsheviks* (Oxford, 1918), pp. 38–9.

12 *Ibid.*, p. 41.

13 *Ibid.*, p. 42.

14 N. Berdyaev, *The Russian Idea* (London, 1947), pp. 2–4.

NINE · THE GERMAN HANSE

1 R. Dion, *Les Frontières de la France* (Paris, 1947), pp. 59–64.

2 U. Eco, *Baudolino* (London, 2002), p. 44.
3 *Ibid.*, p. 55.
4 F. Braudel, *The Perspective of the World* (London, 1984), p. 102.
5 M. Eksteins, *Walking since Daybreak* (London, 1999), pp. 10–12.
6 *Duden Lexicon* (Berlin, 1963), entry on the *Hanse*, p. 249.
7 Braudel, *Perspective of the World*, pp. 104–5.
8 M. V. Clarke, *The Medieval City-State* (Cambridge, 1966), p. 180.
9 *Ibid.*, p. 181.
10 D. Sinclair, *The Pound* (London, 2000), pp. 78–81.
11 Braudel, *Perspective of the World*. pp. 103–4.
12 Clarke, *The Medieval City-State*, p. 95.
13 *Ibid.*, p. 92.
14 *Ibid.*, p. 98.
15 P. Dollinger, *The German Hansa* (London, 1970), pp. 22–3.
16 Braudel, *Perspective of the World*. p. 102.
17 Clarke, *The Medieval City-State*, p. 185.
18 J. C. Russell, *Medieval Regions and their Cities* (Newton Abbot, 1972), p. 107.
19 H.A.L. Fisher, *A History of Europe* (London, 1945), p. 257.
20 *Ibid.*, p. 257.

TEN · THE COMUNIDADES OF CASTILE

1 G. Parker, *The Geopolitics of Domination* (London, 1988), pp. 19–28.
2 *Ibid.*
3 J. C. Russell, *Medieval Regions and their Cities* (Newton Abbot, 1972), pp. 186–90.
4 *Ibid.*
5 M. Castells, *The City and the Grassroots : A Cross-Cultural Theory of Urban Social Movements* (London, 1983), p. 7.
6 *Ibid.*, p. 9.
7 *Ibid.*, p. 7.
8 *Ibid.*, p. 5.
9 *Ibid.*, p. 4.
10 *Ibid.*, p. 8.
11 *Ibid.*, p. 15.

ELEVEN · CITY, PROVINCE AND NATION IN THE NETHERLANDS

1 G. Parker, *The Geopolitics of Domination* (London, 1988), pp. 12–17.
2 D. Pinder, *The Netherlands* (London, 1976), pp. 1–4.
3 F. Braudel, *Civilization and Capitalism, 15th–18th Century*, III: *The Perspective of the World* (London, 1984), pp. 98–101.
4 *Ibid.*, p. 99.
5 *Ibid.*, p. 101.
6 H. Pirenne, *Medieval Cities* (Princeton, NJ, 1969), p. 177.
7 *Ibid.*, p. 188.
8 *Ibid.*, p. 190.

9 *Ibid.*, p. 191.
10 J. Eyck, *The Benelux Countries* (London 1963), p. 20.
11 M. V. Clarke, *The Medieval City-State* (Cambridge, 1966), p. 4.
12 J. C. Russell, *Medieval Regions and their Cities* (Newton Abbot, 1972), p. 117.
13 F. Braudel, *Civilization and Capitalism*, p. 143.
14 M. Castells, *The City and the Grassroots* (London, 1983), p. 5.
15 G. L. Burke, *Towns in the Making* (London, 1971), p. 46.
16 Russell, *Medieval Regions*, p. 117.
17 Braudel, *Civilization and Capitalism*, p. 175.
18 *Ibid.*, p. 187.
19 *Ibid.*, p. 177.
20 A. Landheer, *The Dutch Republic* (London, 1938), p. 42.
21 'La Guide d'Amsterdam' [1701], pp. 1–2 in Braudel, *Civilization and Capitalism*, p. 185.
22 Burke, *Towns in the Making*, p. 153.
23 G. J. Renier, *The Dutch Nation* (London, 1944), pp. 58–60.

TWELVE · THIRD ROME VERSUS CITY REPUBLICS: MOSCOW, NOVGOROD AND THE BALTIC

1 W. H. Parker, *An Historical Geography of Russia* (London, 1968), p. 70.
2 V. Cornish, *The Great Capitals: An Historical Geography* (London, 1923), pp. 175–81.
3 G. Parker, *The Geopolitics of Domination* (London, 1988), pp. 76–80.
4 N. Zernov, *The Russians and their Church* (London, 1945), p. 71.
5 I. Grey, *Ivan the Terrible* (London, 1966), pp. 178–80.
6 *Ibid.*, p. 181.
7 *Ibid.*, pp. 126–7.
8 A. M. Pankratova, ed., *A History of the USSR* (Moscow, 1947), part I, pp. 58–9.
9 P. Dollinger, *The German Hansa* (London, 1970), pp. 362–3.

THIRTEEN · THE FALL AND RISE OF THE HANSE CITIES

1 P. Dollinger, *The German Hansa* (London, 1970), p. 368.
2 *Ibid.*, p. 369.
3 J. J. Norwich, *A History of Venice* (London, 1982), pp. 584–6.
4 E. Gibbon, *Memoirs of my Life* (London, 1984), p. 142.
5 Norwich, *History of Venice*, p. 619.
6 C. Gauss, *The German Emperor as Shown in his Public Utterances* (London, 1915), pp. 182–3.
7 Y. M. Goblet, *The Twilight of Treaties* (London, 1936), p. 65.
8 I. Bowman, *The New World* (London, 1928), pp. 416–18.
9 Goblet, *Twilight of Treaties*, p. 61.
10 *Ibid.*, p. 66.
11 R. E. Dickinson, *The Regions of Germany* (London, 1945), pp. 19–21.
12 L. C. Tihany, *A History of Middle Europe* (New Jersey, 1976), p. 55.
13 Dickinson, *Regions of Germany*, pp. 92–9.

14 R. Lutgens, 'Hansestadt Hamburg', *Geographische Zeitschrift*, XLIII (1937), pp. 42–58.
15 V. Gollancz, *In Darkest Germany* (London, 1947), pp. 91–3, figs 117–24.
16 R. E. Dickinson, *The German Lebensraum* (London, 1944), pp 93–109.
17 M. Eksteins, *Walking Since Daybreak* (London, 1999), pp. 114–15.
18 S. McGuire, 'A New Hanseatic League', *Newsweek*, CXL/9 (3 March 2002), pp. 12–16.
19 L. Hughes, *Peter the Great* (New Haven and London, 1998), pp. 203–47.
20 G. Westholm, *Hanseatic Routes, Sites and Monuments* (Brussels: L'Institut Européen des Itinéraires Culturels, 1998).
21 G. Parker, 'Baltic Europe and the Idea of Alternative Geopolitics', in *Baltic Europe on the Eve of the Third Millennium*, ed. J. Wendt, (Gdansk, 2001), pp. 39–44.

EPILOGUE · THE IDEAL AND THE REALITY

1   M. Castells, *The City and the Grassroots* (London 1983), p. 8.
2   Aristotle, *The Politics*, trans. T. A. Sinclair (Harmondsworth, 1962), VII, iv.
3   Plato, *Republic*, trans. P. Shorey (London, 1946), IV, iii.
4   J. J. Rousseau, *The Social Contract*, trans. C. Frankel (New York, 1946), book II, chap. 9.
5   E. Cassirer, *The Myth of the State* (New Haven, CT, and London, 1967), p. 271.
6   T. Hobbes, *Leviathan* (London, 1914), XXI.
7   F. Braudel, *The Mediterranean in the Ancient World* (London, 2001), p. 273.
8   J. Bryce, *The Holy Roman Empire* (London, 1897), pp. 176–7.
9   Castells, *The City and the Grassroots*, p. 15.
10 J. McConica, *Thomas More* (London, 1977), pp. 33–4.
11 I. Berlin, *Against the Current: Essays in the History of Ideas* (Oxford, 1981), p. 122.
12 G. Parker, *Geopolitics Past, Present and Future* (London, 1998), pp. 160–66.
13 H. Mackinder, *Democratic Ideals and Reality* (London, 1919).

Acknowledgements

I wish to record my thanks to those who have given me their support and advice during the writing of this book. I wish particularly to thank Dr Burkhard Wolf of Berlin, who gave me valuable assistance with the chapters on the German *Hanse*, and Professor Michael Goulder of the University of Birmingham for his advice on the Greek and Roman city-states. Professor Paul Claval of the University of Paris first encouraged me to think of the city in a geopolitical context and it was as a result of this that my ideas on the subject took shape. I owe a particular debt of gratitude to my friend the late Philip Elliott of the University of Birmingham for his wisdom and encouragement in the many talks we had on this subject. I have also had many interesting discussions on the issues raised in this book with my adult students in the School of Continuing Studies, University of Birmingham, and these have helped to put the subject into a wider context.

I also express my thanks to Birmingham Library for granting permission to use maps from their Cadbury Collection and to Cambridge University Press and the Orion Publishing Group for permission to use illustrative material of which they hold the copyright. All the maps that have been specially prepared for this book were drawn by Harry Buglass of the University of Birmingham.

Peter Dent of Reaktion Books has been a considerate and helpful editor, and his comments and advice have made a valuable contribution to the book.

Most of all I wish to record my indebtedness to my wife, Brenda. From the outset she has been an active participant and partner, and her wide knowledge and critical eye have made her advice and willingly given assistance an invaluable part of the whole enterprise. She also compiled the index to the book.

Photographic Acknowledgements

The author and publishers wish to express their thanks to the below sources of illustrative material and/or permission to reproduce it:

From G. Braun and F. Hogenberg, *Civitates orbis terrarum* (Cologne, 1578–1618), photos reproduced by permission of Birmingham Library and Information Services: 10, 11, 12, 16, 18; maps drawn by Harry Buglass (University of Birmingham): 1, 4, 7, 14, 15, 24; reproduced by permission of Cambridge University Press: 6; reproduced from *Everyman's Atlas of Ancient and Classical Geography* (London, 1907): 2, 3, 8, 9; from V. Gollancz, *In Darkest Germany* (London: Gollancz, 1947), reproduced by permission of The Orion Publishing Group: 19; photos by Geoffrey Parker: 5, 17, 20, 21, 22, 23.

Index

Italic numerals refer to illustrations